Semantics

AF223243

Linguistische Berichte
Sonderheft 10

Edited by
Fritz Hamm and
Thomas Ede Zimmermann

BUSKE

Im Digitaldruck »on demand« hergestelltes, inhaltlich mit der 1. Auflage von 2002 identisches Exemplar. Wir bitten um Verständnis für unvermeidliche Abweichungen in der Ausstattung, die der Einzelfertigung geschuldet sind.

Weitere Informationen unter: www.buske.de/bod.

Bibliografische Information der Deutschen Nationalbibliothek

Die Deutsche Nationalbibliothek verzeichnet diese Publikation in der Deutschen Nationalbibliografie; detaillierte bibliografische Daten sind im Internet über ‹http://portal.dnb.de› abrufbar.

ISBN 978-3-87548-253-9

eBook ISBN 978-3-87548-950-7

LB-Sonderheft ISSN 0935-9249

Contents

Introduction

Fritz Hamm / Thomas Ede Zimmermann

The present special issue of *Linguistische Berichte* contains nine papers about recent developments in the field of semantics. While it certainly does not represent a full survey of the state of the art, we do hope to have selected central topics of present day semantic research, which together give an impression of some of today's typical semantic questions, results, and style of argumentation. Moreover we hope that this volume achieves to reveal some the diversity of methods of modern research in semantics.

The diversity of present day semantic methodology is illustrated by comparing Reinhard Blutner's contribution *Lexical Semantics* with Marcus Kracht's paper *Dynamic Semantics*. The difference in approach is not surprising given that classical model-theoretic semantics has little to offer for an adequate analysis of lexical meaning, whereas the more cognitively oriented approaches so prominent in the field of lexical semantics lack an account of anaphora and quantification, phenomena that gave rise to various dynamic modifications of traditional truth-conditional semantics. As a companion to Kracht's paper, our own contribution *Quantifiers and Anaphora is* concerned with more classical approaches to the semantics of quantification. We hope that the two papers together demonstrate that anaphora and quantification are not just two unrelated fields of semantic research but share common problems and insights. Ariel Cohen's article is devoted to the pervasive phenomenon of *Genericity* in natural languages. He argues for a probabilistic interpretation of the generic quantifier.

While the three last-mentioned contributions primarily deal with the interpretation of noun phrases, two other surveys focus on the contribution of the verb to the sentence meaning. Rainer Bäuerle reports on recent developments in the logical semantics of *Tense*, and Regine Eckardt shows that a broad range of empirical phenomena suggest that verbs not merely express properties of ordinary individuals but relate them to sectors of the world, as described in *Event Semantics*.

In his contribution *The Logic of Internal and External Observations*, Uwe Mönnich demonstrates that the gap between lexical and logical semantics need not be seen as a methodological schism. His model-theoretic formulation of abstract cognitive principles not only helps to explain the specific structure of certain perception verb complements under a cross-linguistic perspective, but also builds a bridge between the above-mentioned approaches in semantics.

One of the areas in semantics that has seen a huge progress since the early days of Montague Grammar is the relation between truth conditions and information structure, as most prominently illustrated in focus semantics. Some of

Linguistische Berichte Sonderheft 10 · © Helmut Buske Verlag 2002 · ISSN 0935-9249

this may be gleaned from Herman Hendriks's *Links without Locations,* which examines the rôle played by intonation for a lot of semantic phenomena including presupposition, adverbs, and anaphora resolution. His *Non-Monotonic Anaphora Hypothesis* opens the possibility to view intonation as a phenomenon that leads to a unification of theoretical approaches in diverse fields of semantics.

Ever since Frege, solutions to descriptive problems in semantics were only recognized as such if they observed the general principle that the meaning of an expression can be derived by combining the meanings of its parts. Sean Fulop and Edward Keenan's contribution *Compositionality: A Global Perspective* compares various subtle ways of interpreting this methodological principle and their empirical consequences.

Since Richard Montague's pioneering work in the late sixties and early seventies, semantics has developed an extremely broad range of empirical and theoretical topics, methods, and frameworks. The task of covering all these developments in a single book is an impossible one. As a consequence, this volume does not contain papers about many important topics such as plurals and mass terms, or the syntax-semantics interface. For much more comprehensive volumes about recent developments in semantics we refer the interested reader to Wunderlich & von Stechow (1991), Lappin (1996) or van Benthem & ter Meulen (1997).

The contributions are arranged in alphabetical order.

References

Lappin, S., ed. (1996): *The Handbook of Contemporary Semantic Theory.* Blackwell, Oxford.
van Benthem, J. & ter Meulen, A., eds. (1997): *Handbook of Logic and Language.* Elsevier, Amsterdam.
Wunderlich, D. & von Stechow, A., eds. (1991): *Semantics. An International Handbook of Contemporary Research.* de Gruyter, Berlin.

Issues in the Semantics of Tense

Rainer Bäuerle[1]

1 The tradition: tenses as operators

During the last decade, a number of ambitious state-of-the-art handbooks were published in the area of logic and semantics, and they all contain a concise survey of the semantics of tense and temporal expressions, written by different authors: Kuhn (1989), Fabricius-Hansen (1991), and Steedman (1997). This embarrassment of riches allows me to keep historical considerations to a necessary minimum in my own sketch of recent developments and to concentrate instead on topics which have either surfaced only recently or else have formerly escaped attention for some reason or other. The historical account given below does therefore not strive for philological accuracy and completeness. I want to take stock of what we have learned so far, of the problems and ideas. Necessarily, I quote authors who entertained these ideas, but in quoting them I make no claim that they offer the first or most mature or whatever solution of the problem. And thus I am also sure that some very important contributions will not be mentioned – I apologize.

If we let the history of temporal semantics, somewhat arbitrarily, begin in the late 1940s, there were two competing models right away. There was, on the one hand, Hans Reichenbach's (1947) relatively sophisticated tripartite system of speech time, reference time and event time, which nevertheless remained rather sketchy and kept researchers busy since then trying to spell out the nature of the opaque new parameter of reference time. On the other hand, temporal logic began to develop and offered an explanation of tenses as logical operators. And the basic pattern, formulated already in Duncan-Jones (1949), though far too simplistic, can still be found, in some form or another, in most introductory semantics text-books: "Brutus killed Caesar" is true iff "for some t, Brutus kills Caesar at t, and t is before now". A comparison and critique of these two lines of tradition as tools for an analysis of tense can be found in Øhrstrøm/Hasle (1995). For this initial stage, we may, somewhat crudely, say that temporal logic developed a rigorous semantics for tense operators which resembled natural language tenses only accidentally, whereas Reichenbach had a feeling for language, but no semantics.

On the way to a more realistic semantics for natural language tenses in the logical tradition, such widely differing concepts as e.g. "Betrachtzeit" (Bäuerle 1979), "temporal perspective point" (Kamp & Reyle 1993), and "topic time"

[1] I have to thank Brigitte Handwerker and Ede Zimmermann for reading earlier drafts. They kept me from making even more mistakes.

(Klein 1994) have been introduced as a third parameter besides speech time and event time. And from this we may conclude not only that the two traditions have merged, but also that things may be even more complicated than foreseen by Reichenbach, which in consequence might mean that there is no unique semantic reconstruction of his schemas (a fact which already follows when we replace the points in Reichenbach's analysis by intervals, because this move allows for more temporal relations). But the increasing sophistication in the semantics of tense has not only let Reichenbach look rather vague, it has also changed the original version of the operator approach to such an extent that, as we shall outline here, it is time for a final transformation. But first we should take stock of what we have learned in the process.

In its original form, a temporal operator was an index shifter which shifted the evaluation time index:

$$[\text{PAST } \alpha]^t = 1 \text{ iff } \exists t'(t' < t \text{ and } [\alpha]^{t'} = 1)$$

This made the truth of a sentence depend on the truth of another, more basic sentence. As the "most basic" sentence invariably was a present tense sentence, there simply was no present tense operator, and there was absolutely no account of non-finite phrases. Furthermore, as pointed out by Galton (1984), the formula does not even work properly for languages such as English, for a simple past tense

I went to school

may have to be rendered as a present progressive

I am going to school

rather than a simple present

I go to school

which has to be interpreted habitually. We shall come back to this defect, but first we turn to another shortcoming, which at the time was of more interest to semanticists: as Partee (1973) pointed out, there is a negation problem. For

I did not turn off the stove

cannot mean that at some time in the past it is true that I do not turn off the stove, i. e.

PAST (NEG (I turn off the stove)),

for that would be almost trivial – there are surely very many past times which do not feature a turning off of the stove by myself. Nor can it mean that there was no past time at which it was true that I turn off the stove – this being almost trivially wrong:

NEG (PAST (I turn off the stove)).

The first conclusion drawn here was that tenses should not invariably be interpreted as indefinite tenses. A simple means of achieving a "definite" interpretation was to restrict the choice of shifted times by another parameter of interpretation, the reference interval I of e.g. Guenthner (1979):

$$[\text{PAST } \alpha]^{t/I} = 1 \text{ iff } \exists t'(t' < t \text{ and } t' \in I \text{ and } [\alpha]^{t'/I} = 1)$$

This seems to lead us out of Partee's predicament, but unfortunately into the wrong direction. For we can now represent a sentence like

>Yesterday John did not play tennis

as

>Yesterday (NEG (PAST (John plays tennis))),

meaning, obviously, that with respect to the reference interval "yesterday", it is not the case that there is a t' before now, within yesterday and such that "John plays tennis" is true at t'. What we cannot have is

>Yesterday(PAST(NEG(John plays tennis))),

for that would again give us the meaning that at some time in yesterday, John did not play tennis – which may be true even if he played at other times during yesterday. This solution thus requires negation to have wide scope over tense – which is probably too much when we consider German examples like

>Ich werde mich gut betragen und nicht in der Nase bohren
>(I shall me well behave and not in the nose pick)

where future tense seems to range over a conjunction of negated and unnegated verb phrases. The locus of the problem is the quantificational part of the tense definition – and an explication in terms of existential quantification gets into even more trouble when we add explicit adverbs of quantification to our sentences. How are we to explain

>Yesterday John always played tennis

>Yesterday John played tennis twice.

The inescapable consequence, drawn in Bäuerle (1979), is that tenses simply are not quantificational, that all quantification is done by adverbs of quantification, and that this requires a covert existential adverb in cases where no other adverb is overtly present. But if tenses are not quantificational, they can no longer fulfil their above role of shifters of the evaluation time index, which we diagnosed as linguistically problematic from the outset. And the idea of shifting the evaluation time comes hand in glove with a theoretical problem anyway: by shifting the evaluation time index to a new value, we lose track of the old value and have thus no means of interpreting deictic/indexical expressions which occur later in the sentence. Gabbay's (1976) famous example

>A child was born that will be king

illustrates the problem: neither tense in this sentence is evaluated from an index provided by the other, both are to be evaluated at the deictic "now". Tense, in other words, is a deictic phenomenon and cannot be evaluated at "shifted" indices. Both these insights – deictic and non-quantificational tense – are combined in the following truth definition adapted from Bäuerle (1979), which illustrates at the same time the then fashionable method of double-(or even multiple) indexing.

$$[\text{PAST } \alpha]^{t,t'} = 1 \text{ iff } \exists t''(t'' \subseteq t' \text{ and } t'' < t) \text{ and } [\alpha]^{t,t^*} = 1,$$
where t^* is the greatest interval τ such that $\tau \subseteq t'$ and $\tau < t$.

The evaluation time index (in general: the speech time) is kept constant, and a second index is being shifted, which we may call the frame index for the moment, for it controls the temporal frame with respect to which the event time has to be located (remember that the theory requires α to split into "quantificational adverb + β"). But whereas we could always conceive of the evaluation time index (at which a sentence was said to be true) as a time point, this is no longer possible with the frame index, which clearly denotes a time interval. And this is indicative of a subtle change in the quality of the shifting index: t is our evaluation index at which the sentence is uttered and gets a truth value, the frame time t' and the actual event time $t(e)$ are times during which/at which the things happen or are the case which make the sentence true, and which are expressed by the proposition associated with the tenseless residual structure, the "sentence radical". In terms of our above quotation from Duncan-Jones: the sentence "Brutus killed Caesar" *is true at t* iff a killing of Caesar by Brutus *happened at some T* before *t*, where *t* may be a point but *T* has to be an interval.

The situation of the event time relative to the frame time is determined by factors outside the purely temporal realm, and before we proceed to that matter, we establish our first result:

TENSE *is a relation between evaluation index and frame index.*

The frame index introduced above was derived from the concept of "Betrachtzeit" in Bäuerle (1979). Since then, several improved concepts have been proposed to fulfill the structural role of the frame index, e.g. "topic time" in Klein (1994) or "tense time" in Musan (2000). That the relation between frame time and event time cannot be settled by purely temporal means is due to the difference between

I polished ten pairs of shoes yesterday

and

I was polishing shoes yesterday,

where only the latter, but not the former, can be continued with

... and am still doing so.

The difference would not be explicable were we to reconstuct the sentence radical, i.e. what is left of the sentence when we strip off tense and quantificational adverb, as a property of times only. The difference is reflected, however, if we distinguish properties of events *e* (see e.g. Davidson (1967); a detailed account of event semantics is given in Eckardt, this volume) from properties of states *s* and thus allow for two different types of sentence radical (see also Herweg (1990)). For then we can describe the relation between frame time and event time in the spirit of Kamp (1981b) as follows:

    a) If α is an event radical, then $[\text{ONCE } \alpha]^{\nu/t^*} = 1$ iff there is an event *e* with property α and with an event time $\tau(e)$ completely included in t^*.

    b) If α is a state radical, then $[\text{ONCE } \alpha]^{\nu/t^*} = 1$ iff there is a state *s* with property α and with an event time $\tau(s)$ overlapping t^*.

Here, τ represents a function which maps a state or event on the unique time at which the event takes place or the state holds. It may also be confusing to talk about the event time of a state in (b), so maybe the event index should now be given a different name. But what is clear enough is that we may draw a second consequence:

> *The relation between frame time and event time is not of a purely temporal nature and is often called* ASPECTUAL.

The above way of putting things is not uncontroversial, because authors like Herweg (1990) and Kamp & Reyle (1993) differ not only in ontological committment, but also in their views on the classification of Vendler's (1967) processes, but we need not dive into the matter any further (Bäuerle (1994) offers a survey of the arguments), for our main concern is with tense.

One of the putative advantages of the simplistic operator approach (i.e. in its evaluation index shifter form) was that as a quantificational element it invited for scope phenomena (as we have already seen in the context of Guenthner's attempt to account for definite tense). So there was a decided difference between the following two logical forms

> PAST (the secretary of state be a streetfighter)
> the secretary of state (PAST (be a streetfighter))

which seemed to imply the present secretary in the latter and the then secretary in the former case. This was not a very compelling advantage, because with the switch to a double indexing semantics two different indices were in principle always available. And in reality it turned out to merely camouflage a deeper problem, for there are noun phrases which have to be evaluated at indices which cannot be traced back to any shifter:

> The president invited the hostages to the White House.

The problem, first discussed in Enç (1981) and subsequently also in Bäuerle (1983) in the context of propositional attitudes, is, that the president (not the now-president, but the one at the time of the invitation: Reagan) invited a group of people, who at the time of the invitation were no longer and had already been hostages – i.e. they were hostages at a time which none of the indices can provide.

2 Second thoughts: pronominal tense

The introduction of a frame index into the operator approach had its roots in Partee's (1973) famous example

> I didn't turn off the stove.

It is evidently ridiculous to assume that this could mean that there is SOME time in the past at which I didn't turn off the stove, for there must be infinitely many such times, and therefore such a statement would neither be very informative nor require an immediate action to remedy the situation. Ever since the publication of Partee's article it has been clear that an indefinite analysis of tenses (in terms of existential quantification) in the style of Priorean tense logic was not viable. As we have seen, semanticists tried for a while to mimic the required definite tenses with the technique of double or multiple indexing, supplanting the evaluation time shifters of classical tense-logic with operators controlling a second index: the time we talk about, here called frame time. But this did not really do justice to the revolutionary impact of Partee's discovery. For Partee herself argues quite explicitly – and Kratzer (1998a) further expands the idea – that "tenses have a range of uses which parallels that of the pronouns", and in addition, the quantificational Russell-style analysis of definite descriptions had long been abandoned in favour of a renaissance of the Fregean style of analysis. The combination of these insights leads to an elegant simplification in our grammar, in that tenses are no longer a phenomenon apart, but part of the vast topic of pronominal reference. And as pronouns, they are evidently definites and denote individuals, not operators.

One of the consequences of the view that tenses *qua* definites simply denote a temporal individual, i.e. a time interval t, is that we loose the doubtful advantages of scoping. Nevertheless there is an account, within this framework, not only for the readings the operator approach produced by different scope relations between a definite description and the tense operator, but also for the readings which the operator account could not cope with. For as definite descriptions these noun phrases are definites and follow the same pattern of explanation that we shall now propose for pronouns and tenses.

A full-fledged tenses-as-pronouns theory owes its existence to the advances of dynamic semantics (discussed in detail in Kracht, this volume), proposed in the form of Discourse Representation Theory by Kamp (1981) and as File Change Semantics by Heim (1982). In dynamic semantics, sentences do not have to express propositions, they merely have to contain the information necessary to transform a given context (= conversational background) into a new one. And it is these contexts, rather than the sentences themselves, which are the bearers of truth or falsity. So it simply makes no sense to ask what proposition is expressed by

He was in the bar,

although we know easily enough what is said when the sentence is uttered in the context of

I met Harry two hours ago.

And one of the major motivations for dynamic semantics was an impasse in the explanation of the behaviour of pronouns. For there were two competing uses of pronouns, which we may call the anaphoric and the bound-variable use (notice that this is not the Government & Binding-theory's use of anaphora!):

anaphoric: Peter waited at the station. We met HIM there.
bound variable: England expects every man to do HIS duty.

And the challenge was to find a unified account which would also cope with

If a farmer owns a donkey, he feeds it

which has no straightforward account on either the anaphoric or the bound-variable theory.

As far as context-dependence is concerned, we distinguish two types of context: the utterance situation u and the conversational background c. We can thus distinguish two types of pronouns according to two different ways of fixing the reference. For there are indexical pronouns like "I" and "you", which depend for their reference only on the utterance situation:

$[\ I\ ]^{u/c} =$ the speaker in u.

And there are the third person pronouns which on their anaphoric use can be interpreted as ypresuppositional", depending only on the conversational background c:

$[\ she_i\ ]^{u/c}$ is only defined for a context c which contains a salient/ accessible female individual a. At a context c^* which satisfies the presupposition, $[\ she_i\ ]^{u/c^*} = a$. And as c can be looked upon as a variable assignment, we also have $a = c(i)$.

Tenses are surprisingly similar, albeit with a difference: as we have seen, tense is a deictic category and should thus depend on the utterance situation u for reference fixing. But not exclusively, for they are used anaphorically at the same time. And so we get a double dependence (tense is a relational category, after all), something like:

$[\ PAST\ ]^{u/c}$ is only defined for a context c which contains a unique most salient/ accessible time interval t which wholly precedes the time of utterance $\tau(u)$, and at a context c^* which satisfies the presupposition, $[\ PAST\ ]^{u/c^*} = t$.

[PRESENT]$^{w/c}$ is only defined for a context c which contains a unique most salient/accessible time interval t which overlaps the time of utterance $\tau(u)$, and at a context c^* which satisfies the presupposition, [PRESENT]$^{w/c^*} = t$.

(Another possible semantics for the present could represent it as a non-past tense)

It would in principle be possible to let this interval t serve as the restrictive term of a quantifier provided by the adverb of quantification, with the sentence radical as the quantifier's nuclear scope. We would thus arrive at another instance illustrating the all-pervasiveness of restricted (Aristotelian) quantification in natural language in contrast to the unrestricted Fregean quantifiers of predicate logic. And in the same way as we have learned to conceive of conditionals like

If a farmer has a donkey, he usually feeds it

as having the logical form

Usually (a farmer has a donkey, he feeds it)

and thus as being parallel in structure to

Every (man, snores),

we might postulate a logical form

Always (PAST, John snore)

for

John always snored.

And the claim that there always is a frequency adverb present even when there is no overt one, which would lead to the logical form

at least once (PAST, John snore)

for

John snored,

would not be an isolated ad-hoc claim, but finds a counterpart in the analysis of conditionals without overt quantificational adverb, such as

If a farmer owns a donkey, he feeds it,

where we assume an underlying universal quantification, i.e.

in all situations (a farmer owns a donkey, he feeds it).

As we shall see later on, this will be the solution to be adopted for the perfect. But it is surely more in the spirit of a pronominal analysis as definites (quantificational residues bring with them an air of indefiniteness) and also really necessary in combination with von Stechow's (1999) semantics for the perfect to interpret pronominal tense without the help of a quantificational adverb. Which amounts to interpreting it as a functor-argument structure, provided that in a structure TENSE + β, β expresses a property of times, namely the imperfective property

$$\lambda t \exists e [t \subseteq t(e) \text{ and } P(e)]$$

or the perfective property

$$\lambda t \exists e [t \supseteq t(e) \text{ and } P(e)],$$

where P stands for a property of eventualities, either state or event.

Finally, we should now come back to our problem with the hostages, which the operator approach had insurmountable problems with. We simply stipulate

> [the hostages$_i$]$^{w/c}$ is only defined for a context c if c specifies a unique pair $<X, s>$, such that X is a salient group of people, and s a salient situation, and the members of X are hostages in s. At a context c^* which satisfies the presupposition, [the hostages$_i$]$^{w/c^*} = X$.

Thus Reagan invited a group of people X that are salient in our conversational background as the hostages in the US embassy in some determinate situation, but this time belongs to the conversational background and need not be introduced by a time shifting operator.

If we now look at the bound variable use of pronouns, it may be conceivable with respect to

> England expects every woman to do her and every man to do his duty

that the two pronouns have, in accordance with what was said above, a sort of sex or gender presupposition. But this is impossible with respect to Lord Nelson's original signal

> England expects everybody to do his duty.

For the fleet at Trafalgar may, for all we know, have in fact been an all-male affair, but, and this is the point, the wording of the signal need not have been any different when hoisted at twin-Trafalgar by admiral Lady Hamilton to a British twin-fleet manned [!] by female sailors only. And the situation is even more convincing with indexical pronouns. For had Lord Nelson said

> Only I was expected to do my duty

we might consider this self-evident on a strict indexical interpretation: who else could possibly be expected to do Lord Nelson's duty? But what the good Lord would more realistically – sloppy interpretation – be complaining about is an injustice, that he was treated more severely than any other member of the fleet. This particular use of pronouns is discussed in Kratzer (1998a), and there we also find the most far-reaching conclusion: we should not try to get rid of the "normal" pronominal features in these contexts, but assume an altogether different "zero pronoun" ø at deep structure and logical form, which acquires a pronunciation on its way to phonological form from surrounding material. This latter process is the tricky part, but semantically the assumptions look very simple and elegant. And so the sloppy readings would have the following logical forms:

> England expects everybody to do ø's duty,
> Only I was expected to do ø's duty.

This suggestion immediately fills a lacuna left by both the operator approach and by the schemata of Hans Reichenbach: neither of the two lines of tradition expressly acknowledges the existence of uses of tenses in which these tenses are merely some kind of agreement phenomenon without a temporal meaning of their own. In

> Mary predicted that she would know that she <u>was</u> pregnant the minute she <u>got</u> pregnant

(a sentence discussed in Kratzer (1998a)) the preferred interpretation seems to be the nonindexical one, in which the two underlined past tenses do not necessarily denote a time before the time of utterance. If we change the tense of the higher verb, we get

> Mary will know that she is pregnant the minute she gets pregnant.

In both cases, what is expressed is simply that the times of being and getting pregnant are linked to the time of the knowing it. What surface tense expresses this relationship is only a matter of the tense of some higher verb dominating these tenses. But we should know already what the underlying tense is in this case: "zero tense" $ø^\tau$. And zero pronouns – be they personal or temporal pronouns – have a normal pronominal semantics, except that, as there is no "lexical content", they lack the presupposition that "normal" pronouns carry with them:

$$[\, ø_i \,]^{w/c} = c(i).$$

Zero tenses belong to a pronominal category which needs an antecedent (the tense in the higher sentence), but this has only consequences for the pronunciation of the zero tense and no semantic consequences, for the index of the zero tense is a binder index which is bound by a property-abstractor at complementizer level. Although we cannot give a detailed account of the binding principles for the bound variable use here, it is obvious from the examples for personal zero pronouns that there indeed is a higher quantifier ("everybody", "only I") with the pronoun in its scope. This is not so obvious in the case of the temporal zero pronouns in the above examples. We shall therefore discuss two crucial examples in more detail in an extra chapter below.

3 Temporal *de se* and *de re*

The sequence-of-tenses problem of embedded tenses has recently become a focus of interest, and the way to the above solution was paved by previous less radical accounts in the papers of Abusch (1988, 1997), Ogihara (1989, 1996), Heim (1994) and von Stechow (1995a,b). The idea that *de se* contexts are special goes back to Lewis (1979). There, Lewis argues that two Gods who inhabit the same world and know all true propositions (i.e. have all available *de dicto* knowledge) are still not omniscient, for they do not know which of the two they are. In order to learn that, they would have to self-ascribe some properties. And this proves that attitudes are not in general propositional, sometimes they are self-ascriptions of properties.

However, if the embedded tense were interpreted as an indexical in

Suzanna thought that Vashek was asleep,

the embedded sentence would express a proposition. But von Stechow (1995b) argues that attitude complements cannot occur with indexical tense, for this would create havoc: I can consistently claim at midday

John thinks that it is midnight

without any intention to ascribe to John an irrational *de dicto* belief such as

Midday is midnight

or

Midnight is at midday.

What is the intended ascription is that John takes himself to be at midnight, he is simply deluded as to the correct time and self-ascribes the wrong temporal location property. The semantics should thus lead us to a property of times as the semantic correlate of the embedded sentence. And the attitude verb becomes a function from properties of times to properties of individuals. So we first abstract

$[\emptyset_i, \text{asleep(Vashek)}]$

at the complementizer position to

$\lambda i\, [\emptyset_i, \text{asleep(Vashek)}]$

to have an argument of the correct type for the function

[think] $(P)(a)(t)(w) = 1$ iff for all of a's doxastic alternatives $<w^*,$ $t^*>$ in w at t it is the case that [P] $(t^*)(w^*) = 1$.

The combination of the two then yields

[think that Vashek is asleep] $(a)(t)(w) = 1$ iff for all of a's doxastic alternatives $<w^*, t^*>$ in w at t it is the case that
[$\lambda i\, [\emptyset_i, \text{asleep(Vashek)}]](t^*)(w^*) = 1$.

And even more simple:

> [think that Vashek is asleep] $(a)(t)(w) = 1$ iff for all of a's doxastic alternatives $<w^*, t^*>$ in w at t it is the case that Vashek is asleep in w^* at t^*.

As was already hinted at at the end of the last chapter, the zero tense is bound lexically by the attitude verb in this example and not at all by the higher tense which contributes the phonetic form of the zero tense. The claim thus is that the highest tense embedded under an attitude verb is always empty and never coreferential to a higher tense, because bound at the level of the complementizer. But then there are sentences which are acceptable to some speakers and seem to contradict this analysis, e.g.

> John thought that Mary is pregnant

with a present tense which cannot at first sight be a zero tense spelled out as present, because it is embedded under a past tense. If it were an indexical tense, however, the complement of the attitude verb would be a proposition and not a property of times. Kratzer (1998b) now argues that certain cases of knowledge ascriptions are to be understood *de re* with respect to the event or state described. In this case, the attitude verb would take the *res* and a property of times (converted into a property of eventualities) as arguments to form a property of individuals. In Kratzer's counterpart-theoretic notation this becomes:

> [think that Mary is pregnant] $(a)(t)(w) = 1$ iff there is a state s of Mary in w at t such that for all of a's doxastic alternatives $<s^*, w^*>$ of s in w at t it is the case that $*[\lambda t \lambda w$ Mary is pregnant in w at $t](s^*)(w^*) = 1$.

where $*P$ indicates the transformation of P into a property of eventualities:

$$*P = [\lambda e \lambda w \forall w^* \ (P(\tau(e))(w^*) = 1]$$

i.e. the property of times $[\lambda t \lambda w$ Mary is pregnant in w at $t]$ is mapped onto the property of eventualities $*P$ which is true of an eventuality e and world w iff the time $\tau(e)$ is in all worlds a time when Mary is pregnant. Such a solution is, of course, again based on zero tense, which this time takes the transparent *res*-argument for its antecedent, which is thus supposed to somehow contribute the correct tense features that spell out the phonetic form.

4 The compound tenses

The three chapters above very consciously restricted themselves to simple tenses, which were found to be anaphoric and dependent on only two contextual parameters: the utterance context for a determination of "now" and the conversational background for a determination of the time about which a claim is made. We now have to look at compound tenses, and in accordance with a basic principle of semantics, we shall take it for granted here that compound tenses have a compositional semantics. Our attention will focus on a recalcitrant phenomenon, which, unlike "zero tenses", has always received attention, but with at best uncertain results: the perfect tenses, especially the present perfect. Classical tense logic did not have the tools to even adress the problem sensibly, for iteration of operators did not work for the present perfect (for want of a present tense operator), and to render the pluperfect as PAST PAST p was somewhat nonsensical, for, given the denseness of time, this simply turns out to be equivalent to PAST p. For the German perfect, the search for a compositional explanation has a special significance, because the German perfect was often deemed ambiguous (see e.g. Bäuerle (1979)) between a compositional "perfect" reading and a noncompositional "preterite" reading. The reason for this is the possibility of combining the German present perfect with a point adverb which in English would require simple past:

> Ich habe ihn um vier getroffen (I have him at four met),
> I met him at four.

Just recently, however, two ambitious accounts have been proposed which promise to do without the ambiguity hypothesis for German: Musan (2000) and von Stechow (1999). These two represent two different traditions of thinking about the perfect.

Von Stechow's theory purports to be a version of what McCoard (1978) dubbed *Extended Now Theories* (Dowty (1979) offers an early version). His more immediate motivation derives from the seminal work of Fabricius-Hansen (1986) and Iatridou et al. (1997). Fabricius-Hansen proposed the denotation of "unechter Vergangenheitsbereich" (i.e. a past interval which ends with and includes the evaluation time) for the perfect and a symmetric "unechter Zukunftsbereich" (i.e. a future interval which begins with and includes the evaluation time) for the future. And Iatridou et al. are not only concerned with the morphosyntactic representation required for a compositional interpretation, they also urge, against Klein (1994), that the universal and the existential readings of the perfect arise from a genuine semantic ambiguity [2]:

> I have been sick (= not now),
> I have been sick since last year (= maybe now, maybe not),
> I have been sick ever since (= now!).

This latter reading, by the way, contradicts Reichenbach's (1947) assumption

---

[2] On the grounds that the universal perfect is not a special case of the existential perfect. Otherwise

> Mary has lived in Boston for three years

should keep its existential reading rather than the universal interpretation when the adverb is fronted:

> For three years, Mary has lived in Boston

that the semantics of the present perfect requires event time to precede reference time and speech time.

The setup is now as follows: let anaphoric tense provide some time t, the perfect will then denote an interval which has t as its final subinterval, say t^*. t^* will in turn act as the restrictor of a quantification adverb which takes the sentence radical for its nuclear scope and accounts for the universal or existential reading. The existential quantifier may again be a silent one, which in turn means that universal readings must be overtly quantified. Given an existential quantification, the result finally is that there is some $t' \subseteq t^*$ at which an eventive sentence radical is true iff $e \subseteq t'$, and at which a stative sentence radical is true iff $t' \subseteq s$. Therefore the phenomena dubbed *aspectual* above (i.e. perfective/imperfective) belong to a different category: the perfect is not an aspect, the explanation here is purely temporal. And this is justified by the fact that on a truly universal reading, available only for statives, the perfect has no implication of perfectivity. On the other hand, an existentially interpreted eventive, such as

> I have read this book

acquires the air of perfectivity simply through the perfective interpretation of eventives in general, in that the event is included in t' and thus by transitivity in t^*. On the other hand, the perfect cannot be a tense as defined above either, for perfect occurs syntactically in the scope of tense. Thus "perfect" is not indexical, and through the quantificational interpretation it is truly indefinite.

The constructions (*have* + Participle) and (*shall/will* + Infinitive) are thus seen as a category apart: the two possible extended now intervals with "now" being either the left or the right border, XNP and XNF (strictly speaking, the term "extended now" is a misnomer, given that the perfect is not indexical; what is "extended" is some reference time provided by tense). Von Stechow does not nearly talk about the "future tense" as much as about the perfect, but the categorization does not seem unproblematic, for now we have to account for the perfect *have*-construction in the scope of the futurate *will/shall*-construction in

> I shall have read the book.

Furthermore, von Stechow explains German perfect constructions like

> Arnim hat gestern geschlafen (Arnim has yesterday slept)

by means of a logical form

> $\exists t$: t is in XNP(pres) & Arnim schläft zu t & $t \subseteq$ gestern

where XNP stands for "extended now past" (XPF would be the future counterpart). Evidently, he says, there can be a time of Arnim sleeping which is both within yesterday and within XNP. This is as we want things to be for the German perfect. It is not obvious from the theory, however, why the same context does not go well with the perfect in English (for an attempt to derive the difference from morpho-syntactic structure see Giorgi and Pianesi (1997)).

But this latter problem points to a conceptual difficulty: any past interval can trivially be a subinterval of an XNP-interval. In addition, von Stechow explicitly rejects what he takes to be Herweg's (1990) proximity interpretation, i.e. that there must be some sort of temporal proximity between event time and utterance time[3]. This leaves us basically with definite indexical past tense vs. perfect as indefinite relative anterior "tense". This is enough to explain the difference in context between

> Vor 20 Jahren war ich zum letzten Mal in Rom
> (Ago 20 years was I for the last time in Rome.)

and

> Vor 20 Jahren bin ich zum letzten Mal in Rom gewesen
> (Ago 20 years have I for the last time in Rome been),

but it deprives the perfect of any "current relevance"-meaning. But a sentence like

> Ich habe gegessen (I have eaten)

simply does not express – given my age –a trivial biological necessity, it explains why I am not hungry at the moment. Is there an additional pragmatic story to be told? It thus seems that the account is geared to examples like

> Ich habe gesündigt (I have sinned),

where the truth really merely depends on some past sin, no matter which.

Musan (2000) works with a variant of the sort of theory we discussed at the end of chapter 1. Tense locates TT (tense time) relative to TU (time of utterance), and aspect locates a truth interval of the poststate relative to TT. But this aspect is the one we discussed above (perfective/imperfective), not the Reichenbachian precedence relation also found in Klein (1994). For there is a third component, which is linked to (*have* + Participle) and which, roughly speaking, assigns a poststate to every event or state. This poststate is the relevant situation which overlaps TT. And these poststates are combined with contextually restricted frequency quantifiers that quantify over times contextually contributed, which may correspond to von Stechow's extended now intervals.

The idea needs, however, a cunning formulation, for prima facie being at the poststate of some eventuality y means that y itself, the TS of y, is anterior. And correct as this would be for

> Ich habe schon gegessen (I have already eaten),

it is not applicable to

> Ich habe sie schon gekannt (I have her already known).

---

[3] But this is a misunderstanding anyway. What Herweg claims for the present perfect is that *qua* perfect the post-state must be proximal to the event which gives rise to it, and that the poststate must in turn *qua* present tense be proximal to the utterance time. This is reminiscent of Musan's account, and it does not warrant the conclusion that event time and utterance time have to be temporally proximal.

Here Musan exploits the subinterval properties of states to argue that as events have only one subinterval, i.e. the event itself, their poststate begins after the event is over or has culminated. But as statives have infinitely many subintervals, the poststate of a state begins after the first subinterval. Quite literally, it would probably be more precise to say that any one of the subintervals has its own poststate. For in effect – returning to our less fine-grained idiom – this means that a state can co-exist with its poststate. And so – the reader may find this a little perplexing – we find ourselves both at a time of knowing her and at a time of having known her when we utter the above present perfect sentence, but presumably only the latter is asserted. The former seems to be at best a pragmatic implicature.

This alone does not yet account for universal perfects, and for a sentence like

Lola hat immer Donald geliebt (Lola has always Donald loved),

Musan postulates a contextual restriction of the frequency adverb, for instance to Lola's lifetime up till and including now (or else to Lola's lifetime *tout simple*, if we are talking about a past Lola). All subintervals of this interval are then said to be intervals at which Lola loves Donald, provided they are before or abut some subinterval of the utterance time. This comes close to von Stechow's "love at utterance time", but only close, as far as I can make out, for "now" is not necessarily included. Therefore it seems fair to say that Musan opts for a pragmatic view of the "now-inclusion"-interpretation of the universal readings, whereas von Stechow prefers to anchor it in the semantics. We shall soon see that this may be a decisive advantage for Musan's approach.

A further superficial similarity between the two approaches is that – metaphor aside – their formal definitions are strictly in terms of time relations. For von Stechow, this is stated policy, but if the relation between state and poststate is simply a temporal relation "being before or abut" in Musan, both theories seem to offer a "definitely before now" past tense and a "before now or abut/overlap now" present perfect. The latter then does not express, but allow proximity. But Musan is open to a contextual determination of what a suitable post-state could be (e.g. lexically or pragmatically or otherwise invited result states) in a way that von Stechow is not (perhaps not yet, given that his article is very brief; but there seems to be a principled difficulty which will be discussed below). And in this sense she offers more than a purely temporal account, because she has at least two parameters at her disposal (eventuality and poststate of eventuality), which decide between a "perfect as present relevance" reading and a sort of "preterite" reading according to which of the two is focussed. These readings are our old friends from the ambiguity hypothesis, and we see here how both have been absorbed into Musan's unified reading.

I think that von Stechow's problem in the Extended-Now-framework, which speaks against an easy pragmatic elaboration, has to do with a very different way of specifying the crucial interval. Von Stechow postulates a truly indefinite event in a vague XNP time with an indefinite left border. This creates a variant of Partee's indefinite tense problem. For the truth conditions have it that it is true that

> I have eaten

iff there is an event of eating by myself in XNP. But there may be many such events, and in order to express that I am not hungry, it should probably be the last one(s), the one(s) that caused my feeling of not wanting any more food. Von Stechow's account may be too indefinite. Instead of XNP as a function of "now", Musan introduces poststates as a function of previous events/states. This is a little less indefinite, for we are talking about a present state (the poststate), which has been caused or produced by another state or event. And presumably by a unique, not indefinite, (set of) event(s) or state(s).

It is not easy to adjudge the relative merits of two approaches when one is presented in a short article and the other in a full-fledged *Habilitationsschrift*. But I think that the account offered by von Stechow suffers from a curious flaw in its present formulation. Von Stechow insists that the universal readings of the perfect be given semantic status (for arguments why this is desirable see Iatridou (1997)), but this could be detrimental. For if the present validity of the universal perfect rests on the truth of the sentence radical at all subintervalls, including those containing "now", these latter intervals might as well serve as truth intervals for an existential perfect. Von Stechow therefore has to add a further qualification which ensures that the universal perfect does in fact quantify over $XNP(r)$ including r, whereas the existential perfect has to quantify over the different interval $XNP(r)$ excluding r[4] (the first interval is said to be denoted by the auxiliary, where do we get the second from?). So we have to do with two theories: the "extended now for the universal perfect", and the "extended before-now for the existential perfect". To the extent that this now reverses the situation refuted by Iatridou and makes the existential interpretation look like a special case of the universal interpretation, we may consider it strange that it is the more general universal case which has to be explicitly quantified. Some people (Rathert (1999)) have argued that the approach can be watered down to a XNP just before the present moment. This provides a unified theory at the cost of sacrificing the problem the XNP-theory was originally designed for. And we are edging even closer to Musan's account for universal readings. Musan succeeded to absorb the "preterite" and the "perfect" readings of the present perfect into one single meaning ascription plus focus (not a trivial move at all!). But strangely enough this might now inspire the ambiguity hypothesists again, who will perhaps return with a more sophisticated form of the ambiguity hypothesis some day, e.g. in a form comparable to Kratzer's (1998a) proposal with respect to the English preterite. For Kratzer observes that German

> Wer hat die Kirche gebaut? (Who has the church built?)

---

[4] r stands for reference time here, which is the time, provided by tense, from which the extended-r-interval is figured out.

is rendered as

> Who built the church?

in English and argues for a more indirect matching of abstract tense features onto surface tense forms. In that sense, the perfect puzzle survived, has survived, and survives – whichever is applicable.

Bibliography

Abusch, D. (1988): "Sequence of Tense, Intensionality and Scope", in: H. Borer (ed.), Proceedings of WCCFL 7, p. 1–14.

Abusch, D. (1997): "Sequence of Tense and Temporal *De Re* ", in: Linguistics and Philosophy 20/1, 1–50.

Bäuerle, R. (1979): Temporale Deixis, temporale Frage, Tübingen: Narr.

Bäuerle, R. (1983): "Pragmatisch-semantische Aspekte der NP-Interpretation", in: Faust/Lehfeldt/Wienold (eds.), Allgemeine Sprachwissenschaft, Sprachtypologie und Textlinguistik, Tübingen: Narr, p. 121–131.

Bäuerle, R. (1994): "Zustand – Prozeß – Ereignis. Zur Kategorisierung von Verb(al-phras)en", in: Wuppertaler Arbeitspapiere zur Sprachwissenschaft 10, p.1–32.

Davidson, D. (1967): "The logical form of action sentences", in: N. Rescher (ed.), The Logic of Decision and Action, Pittsburgh: The University of Pittsburgh Press, p. 81–95.

Dowty, D. (1979): Word Meaning and Montague Grammar, Dordrecht: Reidel.

Duncan-Jones, A. (1949): "Fugitive Propositions", in: Analysis 10/1, p. 21–23.

Enç, M. (1981): Tense without Scope: An Analysis of Nouns as Indexicals, PhD-Dissertation, University of Wisconsin at Madison.

Fabricius-Hansen, C. (1986): Tempus fugit, Düsseldorf: Schwann.

Fabricius-Hansen, C. (1991): "Tempus", in: A. von Stechow & D. Wunderlich (eds.), Semantik – Ein internationales Handbuch der zeitgenössischen Forschung, Berlin: de Gruyter, p. 722–748.

Gabbay, D. (1976): Investigations in Modal and Tense Logics with Applications to Problems in Philosophy and Linguistics, Dordrecht: Reidel.

Galton, A. (1984): The Logic of Aspect, Oxford: Clarendon Press.

Giorgi, A. & F. Pianesi (1997): Tense and Aspect. From Semantics to Morphosyntax, New York/Oxford: OUP.

Guenthner, F. (1979): "Time Schemes, Tense Logic and the Analysis of English Tenses", in: F. Guenthner & S. J. Schmidt (eds.), Formal Semantics and Pragmatics for Natural Languages, Dordrecht: Reidel, p. 201–222.

Heim, I. (1982): The Semantics of Definite and Indefinite Noun Phrases, PhD-Thesis, Amherst: UMass.

Heim, I. (1994): "Comments on Abusch's Theory of Tense", in: Hans Kamp (ed.), Ellipsis, Tense and Questions, Dyana 2 Deliverable, p. 143–170.

Herweg, M. (1990): Zeitaspekte. Die Bedeutung von Tempus, Aspekt und temporalen Konjunktionen. Wiesbaden: DeutscherUniversitätsVerlag.

Iatridou, S., Anagnostopoulou, E. & R. Izvorski (1997): "Some Observations about the Form and Meaning of the Perfect". Manuscript, MIT.

Kamp, H. (1981a): "A Theory of Truth and Semantic Representation", in: Groenendijk/ Janssen/Stokhof (eds.), Formal Methods in the Study of Language, Mathematical Centre Tract 135, Amsterdam, p. 277–322.–repr. in: Groenendijk/Janssen/Stokhof (eds.) (1984): Truth, Representation and Information, Dordrecht: Foris, p. 277–322.

Kamp, H. (1981b): "Evénements, représentations discursives et référence temporelle", in: Langages 64, p. 39–64.

Kamp, H. & U. Reyle (1993): From Discourse to Logic, Dordrecht: Kluwer.

Klein, W. (1994): Time in Language, London: Routledge.

Kratzer, A. (1998a): "Some further Analogies between Pronouns and Tenses", paper delivered at SALT VIII.

Kratzer, A. (1998b): "Scope or pseudoscope? Are there wide-scope indefinites?", in: Susan Rothstein (ed.), Events and Grammar, Dordrecht: Kluwer, p. 163–196.

Kuhn, S.T. (1989): "Tense and Time", in: D. Gabbay and F. Guenthner (eds), Handbook of Philosophical Logic, vol. IV, Dordrecht: Kluwer, p. 513–552.

Lewis, D. (1979): "Attitudes De Dicto and De Se", in: The Philosophical Review 88, p. 513–543.

McCoard, R. (1978): The English Perfect: Tense Choice and Pragmatic Inferences, Amsterdam: North Holland.

Musan, R. (2000): The Semantics of Perfect Constructions and Temporal Adverbials in German, Habilitationsschrift, Humboldt-Universität Berlin.

Ogihara, T. (1989): Temporal Reference in English and Japanese, PhD-dissertation, University of Texas.

Ogihara, T. (1996): Tense, Attitudes, and Scope, Dordrecht: Kluwer.

Øhrstrøm, P. & P.F.V. Hasle (1995): Temporal Logic, Dordrecht: Kluwer.

Partee, B. (1973): "Some Structural Analogies between Tenses and Pronouns in English", in: Journal of Philosophy 70, p. 601–609.

Rathert, M. (1999): Einfache Temporalitätsphänomene. Die Kompositionalität von Tempus (Perfekt) und Temporalitätsadverbien (bis und seit) in geraden Kontexten. MA-Thesis, Tübingen University, Seminar für Sprachwissenschaft.

Reichenbach, H. (1947): Elements of Symbolic Logic, New York.

Stechow, A. von (1995a): "Tense in Intensional Contexts: Two Accounts of Abusch's Theory of Tense", in: Hamm & von Stechow (eds.), The Blaubeuren papers: Proceedings of the Workshop on Recent Developments in the Theory of Natural Language Semantics, vol. II, Universität Tübingen, Seminar für Sprachwissenschaft, Report 09-95, p. 379-433.

Stechow, A. von (1995b): "On the Proper Treatment of Tense", in: Simons & Galloway (eds.), Proceedings of SALT V.

Stechow, A. von (1999): "Eine erweiterte Extended-Now-Theorie für Perfekt und Futur", in: Zeitschrift für Literaturwissenschaft und Linguistik, Heft 113, p. 86–117.

Steedman, M. (1997): "Temporality", in: J.van Benthem & A. ter Meulen (eds.), Handbook of Logic and Language, Cambridge: MIT-Press, p. 895–938.

Vendler, Z. (1967): Linguistics in Philosophy, Ithaca: Cornell University Press.

Stuttgart   Rainer Bäuerle

Institut für Maschinelle Sprachverarbeitung, Universität Stuttgart, Azenbergstr. 12, D-70174 Stuttgart, rainer@ims.uni-stuttgart.de

Lexical Semantics and Pragmatics

Reinhard Blutner

1 Introduction

In the view of Katz & Fodor (1963) the scope of a language description covers the knowledge of a fluent speaker "about the structure of his language that enables him to use and understand its sentences". The scope of a semantic theory is then the part of such a description not covered by a theory of syntax. There is a second aspect which Katz and Fodor make use of in order to bound the scope of semantics. This is the pragmatic aspect of language and it excludes from the description any ability to use and understand sentences that depends on the "setting" of the sentence. *Setting*, according to Katz & Fodor (1963) can refer to previous discourse, socio-physical factors and any other use of "non-linguistic" knowledge. A nice demonstration of the essence of "non-linguistic" knowledge in the understanding of sentences has been provided by psychologists in the 70's (e.g. Kintsch 1974, Bransford et al. 1972). Let's consider the following utterance:

(1)   The tones sounded impure because the hem was torn.

I guess we do not really understand what this sentence means until we know that this sentence is about a bagpipe. It is evident that this difficulty is not due to our insufficient knowledge of English. The syntax involved is quite simple and there are no unknown words in the sentence. Instead, the difficulty is related to troubles in accessing the relevant conceptual setting. The idea of *bagpiping* is simply too unexpected to be derived in a quasi-neutral utterance context. The example demonstrates that we have to distinguish carefully between the linguistic aspects of representing the (formal) meaning of sentences and the pragmatic aspects of utterance interpretation (speaker's meaning).

In this paper I restrict myself to the semantics of lexical units and intend to explain the interaction of lexical meaning with pragmatics. Already Katz & Fodor (1963) have stressed the point that a full account of lexical meaning has to include more information than that which allows one to discriminate the meanings of different words. In one of their examples they argue that *take back* is used in very different ways in the sentences (2a,b), although the relevant lexical entries are semantically unambiguous.

(2)   a. Should we take the lion back to the zoo?
        b. Should we take the bus back to the zoo?

An obvious difference between these sentences is that the lion is the *object* taken back to the zoo in (2a), but the bus is the *instrument* that takes us back to

Linguistische Berichte Sonderheft 10 · © Helmut Buske Verlag 2002 · ISSN 0935-9249

the zoo in (2b). The problem for the pragmatic component of utterance interpretation is to explain the difference in terms of different conceptual settings
("world knowledge"), starting from a lexicon that doesn't discriminate the two
occurrences of *take back* semantically and from a syntax that is completely
parallel for the two sentences.

As a third introductory example let's consider the perception verbs in English (cf. Sweetser 1990). This example may be helpful for demonstrating a way
of how to discriminate between the purely lexical semantic component of language and the pragmatic component in more practical terms. If Saussure is right,
there is an essentially arbitrary component in the association of words or mor-
phemes with what they mean. Consequently, the feature of arbitrariness could be
taken at least as a sufficient condition for the presence of semantic information.
It is certainly an arbitrary fact of English that *see* (rather than, say, *buy* or *smell*)
refers to visual perception when it is part of the utterance (3a). Given this arbitrary association between a phonological word and its meaning, however, it is
by no means arbitrary that *see* can also have an epistemic reading as in (3b).

(3)   a. I see the tree.
        b. I see what you're getting at.

Moreover, it is not random that other sensory verbs such as *smell* or *taste* are not
used to express an epistemic reading. Sweetser (1990) tries to sketch an explanation for such facts and insists that they have to do with conceptual organization. It is our knowledge about the inner world that implicates that vision and
knowledge are highly related, in contrast to, say smell and knowledge or taste
and knowledge, which are only weakly related for normal human beings. If this
claim is correct, then the information that *see* may have an epistemic reading but
smell and *taste* do not must no longer be stipulated semantically. Instead, this
information is pragmatic in nature, having to do with the utterance of words
within a conceptual setting, and can be derived by means of some general
mechanism of conceptual interpretation.

Considerations of this kind raise a standard puzzle for lexical semantics
when we ask how to separate the (mental) lexicon from the (mental) encyclopedia. How should we separate information about the meaning of words from
information about the (supposed) reality associated with these words? Admit-
tedly, it may be rather difficult to discriminate these two kinds of information.
Tangible, theory-independent empirical tests simply don't exist. There are two
principal possibilities of dealing with this situation. First, the distinction between the lexicon and the encyclopedia is said to be illusory (as it has sometimes be suggested by representatives of Cognitive Semantics, e.g. Lakoff
1987). In this case all the relevant information has to be put into the lexicon. It
will be argued in what follows that this view leads to a highly non-compositional account of meaning projection. The second possibility is to take the
distinction as an important one. As a consequence, we are concerned with two
different types of mechanisms: (i) a mechanism that deals with the combinato-

rial aspects of meaning and (ii) a pragmatic mechanism that deals with conceptual interpretation. Once we have adopted such theoretical mechanisms, the problem of discriminating lexical semantic information from encyclopedic information need no longer look so hopeless, and we really may profit from a division of labor between semantics and pragmatics. It is the position of this paper to argue in favor of the second option.

The aims of this paper are threefold. First, I want to demonstrate some general problems we are confronted with when trying to analyze the utterance of words within concrete conceptual and contextual settings and to go beyond the aspects of meaning typically investigated by a contrastive analysis of lexemes within the Katz-Fodor tradition of semantics. Second, I want to discuss and criticize some extensions of the standard theory. The models considered include Bartsch's indexical theory of polysemy, Bierwisch's two-level semantics and Pustejovsky's generative lexicon. Finally, I would like to argue in favor of a particular account of the division of labor between lexical semantics and pragmatics. This account combines the idea of (radical) semantic underspecification in the lexicon with a theory of pragmatic strengthening (based on conversational implicatures).

The organization of this paper is as follows. In the next section I will emphasize some important consequences of the traditional view of (lexical) semantics. In the third section some phenomena are collected that have a *prima facie* claim on the attention of linguists, and I will show that most of these phenomena conflict with the theoretical assumptions made by the traditional view. The fourth section aims to demonstrate that several simple extensions of the traditional view which are suggested in the literature can't deal with these problems in a systematic and theoretically satisfactory way. In the fifth section I introduce a particular way of combining (radical) semantic underspecification with a theory of pragmatic strengthening.

2 Three features of the standard view of (lexical) semantics

In this section I will remain neutral about what sort of thing a semantic value should be taken to be: an expression in some language of thought, a mental structure as applied in cognitive semantics or a model-theoretic construct. To be sure, there are important differences between conceptualistic accounts à la Katz & Fodor and realistic accounts as developed within model-theoretic semantics. These differences become visible, first at all, when it comes to substantiate the relationship between individual and social meaning (see Gärdenfors 1993). For the purpose of the present paper, however, the question of whether semantics is realistic or conceptualistic doesn't matter. In the following I will concentrate on some general features that can be ascribed to both accounts in their classical design. These features are not intended to characterize the family of theories called *the standard view* in any sense completely. Rather, their selection is intended to emphasize several properties that may become problematic when a broader view of utterance meaning is taken. In section 5, I will use these features for making out the borderline between semantics and pragmatics.

2.1 Systematicity and compositionality

One nearly uncontroversial feature of our linguistic system is the *systematicity of linguistic competence*. According to Fodor & Pylyshyn (1988: 41–42) this feature refers to the fact that the ability to understand and produce some expressions is intrinsically connected to the speaker's ability to produce and understand other expressions that are semantically related. The classical solution to account for the systematicity of linguistic competence crucially makes use of the *principle of compositionality*. In its general form this principle states the following:

(4)   The meaning of a complex expression is a function of the meanings of its parts and their syntactic mode of combination.

In an approximation that is sufficient for present purposes, the principle of compositionality states that "a lexical item must make approximately the same semantic contribution to each expression in which it occurs" (Fodor & Pylyshyn 1988). As a simple example consider adjective-noun combinations as *brown cow* and *black horse*. Let's take "absolute" adjectives (such as *brown* and *black*) as one-place predicates. Moreover, non-relational nouns are considered as one-place predicates as well. Let's assume further that the combinatorial semantic operation that corresponds to adjectival modification is the intersection operation. Fodor & Pylyshyn (1988) conclude that these assumptions may explain the feature of systematicity in the case of adjectival modification. For example, when a person is able to understand the expressions *brown cow* and *black horse*, then she should understand the expressions *brown horse* and *black cow* as well. Note that it is the use of the intersection operation that is involved in explaining the phenomenon, not compositionality *per se*. Nevertheless the principle of compositionality is an important guide that helps us to find specific solutions to the puzzle of systematicity.

Lexical semantics is concerned with the meanings of the smallest parts of linguistic expressions that are assumed to bear meaning. Assumptions about the meanings of lexical units are justified empirically only in so far as they make correct predictions about the meanings of larger constituents. Consequently, though the principle of compositionality clearly goes beyond the scope of lexical semantics, it is indispensable as a methodological instrument for lexical semantics. I state the principle of compositionality as the first feature characterizing the standard view of (lexical) semantics.

2.2 The monotonicity of the lexical system

Another general characteristic of the standard view is connected with the idea of analyzing the meanings of lexical items as a complex of more primitive elements. The main motivation for a componential (decompositional) analysis is connected with the explanation of certain semantic relations such as antonymy, synonymy, and semantic entailment. If the meaning of a lexical item were not analyzed into components, the lexical system of grammar would have to simply enumerate the actually realized relations as independent facts. This procedure would not be descriptively very economical. More important, it would miss the point that these facts are *not* independent of each other. The componential approach can be found both in theories of meaning in generative semantics (cf. Fodor 1977) and in model-theoretic based (especially Montagovian) semantic work (cf. Dowty 1979).

Defining the meaning of lexical items in terms of a repertoire of more primitive elements leads to a second order property which I will call the *monotonicity* of the lexical system. In short, the monotonicity restriction refers to the fact that we can incrementally extend the lexical system (by adding some definitions for new lexical material) without influencing the content of elements already defined.

At first glance, the monotonicity of the lexical system looks quite natural as a constraint within formal semantics. Of course, it would be very surprising if the content of ... *is a bachelor* would change if the system learns what a spinster is (by acquiring the corresponding definition). Similarly, the meaning of *prime, even, odd (number)* should be independent of whether the system knows the meaning of *rational number* or *perfect number*[1].

It should be stressed that it is not the idea of decomposition (definition) *per se* that leads to the monotonicity feature of the lexical system. Instead, it is its classical treatment within a formal metalanguage that exhibits all features of a deductive system in the sense of Tarski.[2]

---

[1] A perfect number is a natural number that is identical to the sum of its proper divisors; e.g. $6 = 1+2+3$ or $28 = 1+2+4+7+14$.

[2] Within a deductive system a consequence relation $\vDash$ is defined. $\Gamma \vDash \phi$ explicates the notion of a logical consequence: the formula ϕ (of a particular formal language $\mathcal{L}$) is a logical consequence of the set of premises Γ (of $\mathcal{L}$). For the present purpose it isn't essential to consider the details of constructing the consequence relation. What is essential, however, is to remember what Tarski stated quite generally as some minimal requirements which a deductive consequence relation $\vDash$ must fulfill if it is to be a truly logical notion:

A logical consequence relation $\vDash$ has to satisfy the following principles (here Γ and Γ' range over sets of formulas and ϕ over isolated formulas of $\mathcal{L}$):

a. REFLEXIVITY: $\Gamma \vDash \Gamma$
b. CUT: if $\Gamma \vDash \Gamma'$ and $\Gamma \cup \Gamma' \vDash \phi$, then $\Gamma \vDash \phi$
c. MONOTONICITY: if $\Gamma \vDash \phi$, then $\Gamma \cup \Gamma' \vDash \phi$

In the simplest case, definitions are explicit and can be represented as $Q(x) \leftrightarrow C(x)$, where Q is the definiendum and C the definiens (an expression constructed in terms of a given system of lexical "primes"). In other cases, for example when we have to define disposition-like expressions like *soluble*, Carnap's (1936) reduction pairs may be used. An interesting case are bilateral reduction sentences. They have the form $F(x) \rightarrow (Q(x) \leftrightarrow C(x))$, with definiendum Q and definies C (under condition F). In both cases, the system of (explicit or implicit) definitions bears the feature of monotonicity.

The following picture illustrates the difference between monotonic systems and non-monotonic ones in a schematic way. The picture simplifies matters by identifying meanings with extensions (represented by Venn-diagrams). In the case of a monotonic system, the addition of a new predicate R doesn't change the extensions of the old predicates P and Q. However, the same doesn't hold in the case of a non-monotonic system. In this case we have "field"-effects: there seem to be attracting and repelling "forces" that shift the extensions of old predicates in a particular way when new lexical material comes into play.[3]

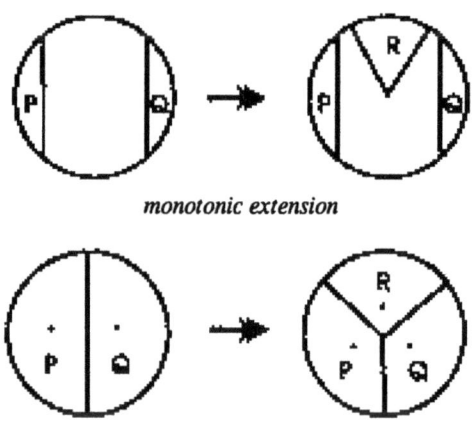

monotonic extension

non-monotonic extension

Figure 1: monotonic and non-monotonic extensions
of a (lexicalized) system of concepts

The most important characteristics is MONOTONICITY. Informally, this principle states that the old theorems remain valid when the system Γ of axioms (definitions, meaning postulates, factual knowledge) has been augmented by adding some new axioms.

[3] The non-monotonic system I have in mind corresponds to the so called *Voronoi tesselation* defining a partitioning of some (abstract) space in terms of a given set of prototypes. The construction stipulates that the element x belongs to the same category as the closed prototype of the given set of prototypes. It is evident that previously defined categories may change when we add new prototypes. (For more details and for the cognitive significance of this construction, see Gärdenfors 2000.)

The example may also be used for demonstrating that it is not the notion of decomposition *per se* that leads to the non-monotonicity of the system. This results from the fact that we define prototypes in terms of certain (binary or continuous) features.

2.3 The persistence of anomaly

Lexical semantics has to account for semantic contradictions as *married spin-ster, *female bachelor, *reddish green* and for other types of semantic anoma-lies as exemplified by the famous *colorless green ideas sleep furiously*. Usu-ally, semantic anomaly of an expression is defined as logical incompatibility of (some part of) the formal translation of the expression taken in union with a given system Γ of definitions and/or meaning postulates (e.g. McCawley 1971). Explicating incompatibility in terms of inconsistency and inconsistency in terms of contradictory entailments makes it possible to derive a second order property which I call the *persistence of anomaly*.

The persistence of anomaly comes in two variants: (i) if we add some new axioms to Γ, then any former anomaly persists; and (ii) if a (propositional) for-mula is anomalous, then every other formula that implies it is anomalous as well.[4] Both varieties seem to be satisfied empirically. It would be very surpris-ing if the anomaly of *married bachelor* could be cancelled by learning the meaning of several new words. Once an anomaly is established it seems to per-sist when the system is extended. In a similar sense it would be perplexing if the anomaly of the expression *the idea sleeps* did not persist if the expression is made more specific, e.g. *the new idea sleeps*.

It is straightforward that the notion of semantic anomaly can be converted to a notion of pragmatic anomaly if the system Γ of axioms is assumed to include other sources of knowledge, such as conceptual and ontological knowledge. Not surprisingly, the persistence of anomaly persists in this case.

3 Beyond the standard view: some inexplicable phenomena

In this section I will present several phenomena which may raise some doubts about the validity of the three principles just sketched. The phenomena suggest that we take a broader perspective on meaning and include various aspects of utterance interpretation. The examples address the whole spectrum of informa-tion shared between lexicon and encyclopedia.

3.1 Challenging the principle of compositionality

In the previous section we have taken adjectives like *red, interesting,* or *straight* as intersective adjectives, and I have illustrated how this pretty simple analysis brings together systematicity and compositionality. Unfortunately, the view that a large range of adjectives behaves intersectively has been shown to be ques-

---

[4] Again, it is the classical, deductive character of the entailment relation that leads to this con-clusion.

tionable. For example, Quine (1960) notes the contrast between *red apple* (red on the outside) and *pink grapefruit* (pink on the inside), and between the different colors denoted by *red* in *red apple* and *red hair*. In a similar vein, Lahav (1989, 1993) argues that an adjective like *brown* doesn't make a simple and fixed contribution to any composite expression in which it appears.

In order for a cow to be brown most of its body's surface should be brown, though not its udders, eyes, or internal organs. A brown crystal, on the other hand, needs to be brown both inside and outside. A brown book is brown if its cover, but not necessarily its inner pages, are mostly brown, while a newspaper is brown only if all its pages are brown. For a potato to be brown it needs to be brown only outside, ... Furthermore, in order for a cow or a bird to be brown the brown color should be the animal's natural color, since it is regarded as being 'really' brown even if it is painted with all over. A table, on the other hand, is brown even if it is only painted brown and its 'natural' color underneath the paint is, say, yellow. But while a table or a bird are not brown if covered with brown sugar, a cookie is. In short, what is to be brown is different for different types of objects. To be sure, brown objects do have something in common: a salient part that is wholly brownish. But this hardly suffices for an object to count as brown. A significant component of the applicability condition of the predicate 'brown' varies from one linguistic context to another. (Lahav 1993: 76)

Some authors – for example, Keenan (1974), Partee (1984), Lahav (1989, 1993) – conclude from facts of this kind that the *simplistic view* mentioned above must be abolished. As suggested by Montague (1970), Keenan (1974), Kamp (1975) and others, there is a simple solution that addresses such facts in a descriptive way and obeys the principle of compositionality. This solution considers adjectives essentially to be adnominal functors. Such functors, for example, turn the properties expressed by *apple* into those expressed by *red apple*. Of course, such functors have to be defined disjunctively in the manner illustrated in (5):

(5)   RED(X) means roughly the property
        a. of having a red inner volume if X denotes fruits only the inside of
           which is edible
        b. of having a red surface if X denotes fruits with edible outside
        c. of having a functional part that is red if X denotes tools
        ..

Let us call this view the *functional view*. It should be stressed that the functional view describes the facts mentioned above only by enumeration. Consequently, it doesn't account for any kind of systematicity concerning our competence to deal with adjective-noun combinations in an interesting way. Another (notorious) problem of this view has to do with the treatment of predicatively used adjectives. In that case the adjectives must at least implicitly be supplemented by a noun. Various artificial assumptions are necessary which make such a theory inappropriate (cf. Bierwisch 1989 for more discussion of this point). We may conclude that compositionality doesn't necessarily lead to systematicity.

There is a third view about treating the meanings of adjectives, which I call the *free variable view*. In a certain sense, this view can be seen as preserving the advantages of both the simplistic as well as the functional view, but as overcoming their shortcomings. The free variable view has been developed in considerable detail in case of gradable adjectives (see for example, Bierwisch 1989, and the references given therein). It is well known that the applicability conditions of restricting adjectives that denote gradable properties, such as *tall, high, long, short, quick, intelligent* vary depending upon the type of object to which they apply. What is high for a chair is not high for a tower and what is clever for a young child is not clever for an adult. Oversimplifying, I can state the free variable view as follows. Similarly to the first view, the meanings of adjectives are taken to be one-place predicates. But now we assume that these predicates are complex expressions that contain a free variable. Using an extensional language allowing λ-abstraction, we can represent the adjective *long* (in its contrastive interpretation), for example, as $\lambda x \; \text{LONG}(x,X)$, denoting the class of objects that are long with regard to a comparison class, which is indicated by the free variable X. At least on the representational level the predicative and the attributive use of adjectives can be treated as in the first view: *The train is long* translates to (after λ-conversion) $\text{LONG}(t,X)$ and *long train* translates to $\lambda x \; [\text{LONG}(x,X) \wedge T(x)]$. In these formulas t is a term denoting a specific train and T refers to the predicate of being a train.

Free variables are the main instrument for forming underspecified lexical representations. To be sure, free variables simply have the status of place holders for more elaborated subpatterns and expressions containing free variables should be explained as representational schemes. Free variables not only stand as place holders for a comparison class X as just indicated. The view can be generalized to include other types of free variables as well, for example a type of variable connected with the specification of the dimension of evaluation in cases of adjectives like *good* and *bad* or a type of variable connected with the determination of the object-dependent spatial dimensions in cases of spatial adjectives like *wide* and *deep*. In what follows, a variety of other kinds of variables will be considered, leading to rather complex types of lexical underspecification.

Of course, it is not sufficient to postulate underspecified lexical representations and to indicate what the sets of semantically possible specifications of the variables are. In order to grasp natural language interpretation ("conceptual interpretation"), it is also required to provide a proper account of contextual enrichment, explaining how the free variables are instantiated in the appropriate way. Obviously, such a mechanism has to take into consideration various aspects of world and discourse knowledge. We are presented here with a kind of *selection task*: how to select from a set of possibilities an appropriate one where (weak) restrictions are given in the form of world and discourse knowledge.

In some particular cases the instantiation of free variables may be done using ordinary (monotonic) unification. If that works fine, it may be concluded that the mechanism of contextual enrichment has the feature of compositionality. In other words, the principle of compositionality stated for semantic representations can be transferred to the level of contextually enriched forms. In section

4.3 I will consider some examples that demonstrate that monotonic unification doesn't suffice for contextual enrichment.

There is a variety of other examples that demonstrate that our comprehension capacities have salient non-compositional aspects. The most prominent class of examples may be found within the area of *systematic polysemy*. This term refers to the phenomenon that one lexical unit may be associated with a whole range of senses which are related to each other in a systematic way.[5] The phenomenon has traditionally been thought intractable, and in fact it *is* intractable when considered as a problem of lexical semantics in the traditional sense.

There are two central possibilities of how to account for the interpretation of utterances containing polysemous elements. The first possibility – call it the *sense enumeration view* – is to handle polysemy similar to homonymy, i.e. to state separate word senses for a polysemous word in a context-independent way. This view requires a second computational step – a procedure that eliminates the contextually inappropriate interpretations.

The second possibility – call it the *selective generation view* – is to take systematic polysemy as a generative device that *calculates* the contextually appropriate senses starting from a unique, non-ambiguous meaning representation of the relevant linguistic expression. Given a polysemous lexeme, its meaning representation may either refer to a primary conceptual variant (representing its base sense), or it may be a more abstract unit referring to some form of underspecified structure. In both cases, a unique meaning representation may be calculated for longer expressions in a compositional way. The restricted generative device that has to be postulated for interpreting such expressions, however, lies outside the mode of compositionality.

I will postpone a more detailed illustration of these views until section 4, where some extensions of the standard view are considered. In section 4 and 5, the principal advantage of the selective generation view will be demonstrated and several ways of dealing with the non-compositional aspects of the interpretation will be discussed.

A lot of related problems with compositionality come to mind. They arise in connection with word formation in general (e.g. Aronoff 1976, Bauer 1983) and the interpretation of compounds in particular (e.g. Meyer 1993, Wu 1990). Moreover, the investigation of different kinds of polysemy may be helpful in order to see the ubiquity of the problem (cf. Lakoff's (1987) study on English prepositions and Sweetser's (1990) investigation of English perception verbs). Furthermore, Fabricius-Hansen's (1993) research on how the interpretation of noun-noun compounds is affected by a genitive attribute may raise the same problems in a more complex area.

---

[5] Unfortunately, the term *systematic polysemy* covers a whole family of empirically different subphenomena for which no unified terminology is available. Expressions as *open and closed polysemy* (Deane 1988), *conceptual specification* and *conceptual shift* (Bierwisch 1983), *sense modulation* and *sense change* (Cruse 1986), *constructional polysemy* and *sense extension* (Copestake and Briscoe 1995) may be convenient to indicate a rough outline of the classification.

3.2 Blocking and the non-monotonicity of the lexical system

A general problem that lexical semantics has to address is the phenomenon of *(partial) lexical blocking*. This phenomenon has been demonstrated by a number of examples where the appropriate use of a given expression formed by a relatively productive process is restricted by the existence of a more "lexicalized" alternative to this expression. One case in point is due to Householder (1971). The adjective *pale* can be combined with a great many color words: *pale green, pale blue, pale yellow*. However, the combination *pale red* is limited in a way that the other combinations are not. For some speakers *pale red* is simply anomalous, and for others it picks up whatever part of the pale domain of red *pink* has not preempted. This suggests that the combinability of *pale* is fully or partially blocked by the lexical alternative *pink*.

Another standard example is the phenomenon of blocking in the context of derivational and inflectional morphological processes. Aronoff (1976) has shown that the existence of a simple lexical item can block the formation of an otherwise expected affixally derived form synonymous with it. In particular, the existence of a simple abstract nominal underlying a given -*ous* adjective blocks its nominalization with -*ity*:

(6)   a. curious – curiosity
           tenacious – tenacity
        b. furious – *furiosity – fury
           fallacious – *fallacity – fallacy

While Aronoff's formulation of blocking has been limited to derivational processes, Kiparsky (1982) notes that blocking may also extend to inflectional processes and he suggests a reformulation of Aronoff's blocking as a subcase of the *Elsewhere Condition* (special rules block general rules in their shared domain). However, Kiparsky cites examples of *partial blocking* in order to show that this formulation is too strong. According to Kiparsky, partial blocking corresponds to the phenomenon that the special (less productive) affix occurs in some restricted meaning and the general (more productive) affix picks up the remaining meaning (consider examples like *refrigerant - refrigerator, informant - informer, contestant - contester*). To handle these and other cases Kiparsky (1982) formulates a general condition which he calls *Avoid Synonymy*: "The output of a lexical rule must not be synonymous with an existing lexical item".

Working independently of the Aronoff-Kiparsky line, McCawley (1978) collects a number of further examples demonstrating the phenomenon of partial blocking outside the domain of derivational and inflectional processes. For example, he observes that the distribution of productive causatives (in English, Japanese, German, and other languages) is restricted by the existence of a corresponding lexical causative. Whereas lexical causatives (e.g. (7a)) tend to be restricted in their distribution to the stereotypic causative situation (direct, unmediated causation through physical action), productive (periphrastic) causatives tend to pick up more marked situations of mediated, indirect causation. For example, (7b) could be used appropriately when Black Bart caused the sheriff's gun to backfire by stuffing it with cotton.

(7)   a. Black Bart killed the sheriff
        b. Black Bart caused the sheriff to die

The phenomenon of blocking can be taken as evidence demonstrating the apparent non-monotonicity of the lexical system. This becomes pretty clear when we take an ontogenetic perspective on the development of the lexical system. Children overgeneralize at some stage while developing their lexical system. For example, they acquire the productive rule of deriving adjectives with -*able* and apply this rule to produce *washable, breakable, readable*, but also *seeable* and *hearable*. Only later, after forms like *seeable* and *visible*, *hearable* and *audible* have coexisted for a while, the meanings of the specialized items block the regularly derived forms. Examples of this kind suggest that the development of word meanings cannot be described as a process of accumulating more and more denotational knowledge in a monotonic way. Instead, there are highly non-monotonic stages in lexical development. At the moment, it is not clear whether this ontogenetic feature must be reflected in the logical structure of the mental lexicon. Rather, it is possible that pragmatic factors (such as Gricean rules of conversation) play an important role in determining which possible words are actual and what they really denote (McCawley 1978, Horn 1984, Dowty 1979; see also section 5).

3.3 The non-persistence of (pragmatic) anomaly

Take the well-known phenomenon of "conceptual grinding", whereby ordinary count nouns acquire a mass noun reading denoting the stuff the individual objects are made of, as in *Fish is on the table* or *Dog is all over the street*. There are several factors that determine whether "grinding" may apply, and, more specific, what kind of "grinding" (meat grinding, fur grinding, universe grinding, ...) may apply. Some of these factors have to do with the conceptual system, while others are language-dependent (cf. Nunberg & Zaenen 1992, Copestake and Briscoe 1995, Leßmöllmann 1996).

     One of the language-dependent factors affecting the grinding mechanism is lexical blocking. For example, in English the specialized mass terms *pork, beef, wood* usually block the grinding mechanism in connection with the count nouns *pig, cow, tree*. This explains the contrasts given in (8).

(8)   a. I ate pork/?pig
        b. Some persons are forbidden to eat beef/?cow
        c. The table is made of wood/?tree

The important point is the observation that blocking is not absolute, but may be canceled under special contextual conditions. That is, we find cases of *deblocking*. Nunberg & Zaenen (1992) consider the following example:

(9)   Hindus are forbidden to eat cow/?beef

They argue that "what makes *beef* odd here is that the interdiction concerns the status of the animal as a whole, and not simply its meat. That is, Hindus are forbidden to eat beef only because it is cow-stuff." (Nunberg & Zaenen 1992: 391). Examples of this kind strongly suggest that the blocking phenomenon is pragmatic in nature. Furthermore, these examples suggest that (pragmatic) anomaly does not necessarily persist when specific contextual information is added. Copestake & Briscoe (1995) provide further examples that substantiate this claim.

In section 2.3 I introduced a second variant of the notion of persistent anomaly. It concerns the specificity of linguistic information, and less that of contextual information. There is a variety of examples showing that this variant of the persistence of (pragmatic) anomaly likewise must fail (cf. Nunberg & Zaenen 1992):

(10)   a. This wine is particularly good with ?mammal/lamb
        b. ?mammal/canine is healthy food
        c. She likes to wear ?mammal/?sheep/angora

4   Some extensions of the standard view

In this section I will consider some approaches that go beyond the aspects of meaning typically investigated by a contrastive analysis of lexemes within the standard view. These approaches deal with the meaning of words within concrete conceptual and contextual settings, and they can be seen as different ways of closing the gap between lexical semantics and pragmatics. In the discussion I will concentrate on the problems and phenomena descibed above, and I will offer a critique of these proposals. It goes without saying that this discussion has to be necessarily unbalanced, and doesn't pretend to provide a comprehensive impression of the work under discussion. Further, the order of presentation is determined exclusively by didactic considerations and does not intend to reflect the historical development of the ideas presented.

4.1   Context-dependent semantics

In the late 70's a renewed interest in the formal treatment of indexical expressions (like *I, you, he, here, now, that, that book,* etc.) within model-theoretic semantics can be observed, inspired primarily by the work of Montague (e.g. Montague 1970). The basic idea was to overcome the fallacies of the traditional possible-world semantics *à la* Kripke by introducing aspects of context into formal semantics. As a result of these efforts, something like a classical theory of context-dependency originated.[6]

Within this theory, the connection between meaning and extension is established in two steps. The meaning (or the *character*) $[\alpha]$ of an expression α (in a model M) is a two-place function of *context* (utterance situation) and *index* (possible world). Applying the character $[\alpha]$ to a context c, the intension $[\alpha]<c>$ of α in this context results. The intension itself can be understood as a function which applied to a index w results in the extension $[\alpha]<c><w>$.

So-called *Kaplan contexts* c include a specification of factors chacterizing the speech situation, such as the agent c_{ag} (speaker), the audience c_{aud}, the time of utterance c_T, the place of utterance c_p, and a characterization of the reference situation c_w (the world of utterance). Formally, they can be considered 5-tuples $c = <c_{ag}, c_{aud}, c_T, c_p, c_w>$. As an example let's consider the semantic interpretation of the deictic expressions *I* and *you*.

(11)   a. $[I]<c><w>$ $= c_{ag}$
        b. $[you]<c><w>$ $= c_{aud}$

The characters defined in (11) are functions whose values vary only with context. With regard to the index they are constant functions, like rigid designators. This explains that deictic expressions, when embedded in intensional contexts, behave very similar to proper names.

It is straightforward that a Kaplan context can be augmented by including further components into the list of contextual elements. Before I consider some examples of interesting augmentations, I want to comment about the nature of compositionality, the monotonicity of the lexical system, and the persistence of anomaly. Clearly, within context-dependent semantics, the principle of compositionality is required to apply to characters. In the case of descriptive expressions, where the characters don't really depend on context, the principle of compositionality can be transferred to the level of intensions. However, compositionality with respect to intensions may be violated when true context-dependencies come into play. Since the apparent violations of compositionality discussed in section 3.1 don't concern characters, but rather intensions (and extensions), the challenge is to deal with the relevant facts by considering the context-dependency of the expressions involved. The important question is whether a systematic and explanatory solution may be found in this way.

Similarly, it can be argued that the persistence of anomaly only applies in case of context-independent expressions. The introduction of true context-dependencies may abolish the persistence of anomaly, and this mechanism may be used to describe the phenomenon of deblocking considered in section 3.3.

---

[6] At this place, it is possible only to give a rough outline of the formal skeleton of this theory. For motivation, explanation, and discussion, I refer to the original literature, e.g. Kaplan (1978, 1979), and to a review article by Zimmermann (1991).

With respect to the violation of the monotonicity feature of the lexical system, exemplified by the blocking phenomenon in section 3.2, I cannot see a real possibility of treating the problems by using the framework of context-dependent semantics. Of course, it would be possible to augment the context by a component c_{lex} characterizing a whole lexical system. Blocking then might be described as resulting from the existence of a certain lexical item within the lexical system c_{lex}. Of course, this approach would be purely stipulative, and, fortunately, nobody has made a proposal in this direction. Instead, another pragmatic mechanism has been highly recommended in order to deal with the blocking phenomenon: the mechanism of conversational implicature (see section 3.2 and section 5).

Let's now consider two examples that demonstrate how context-dependent semantics may explain violations of compositionality at the intensional level. First, consider the phenomenon of predicate transfer (Nunberg 1979, Sag 1981, Nunberg 1995), exemplified by examples as the following:

(12)   a. The <u>ham sandwich</u> is sitting at table 9. (Preferred Interpretation: *The one who ordered a ham sandwich is sitting at table 9*)
       b. There are five <u>ham sandwich</u>es sitting at table 9. (Preferred Interpretation: *There are five people who ordered ham sandwich sitting at table 9*)
       c. Every <u>ham sandwich</u> at the table is a woman. (Preferred Interpretation: *Everyone who ordered a ham sandwich is a woman*).

Sag (1981) and Nunberg (1995) assume that the intension of the head noun (*ham sandwich*) has to be transfered to another property in order to get the intended (Nunbergian) interpretation (preferentially to the property of being the orderer of the ham sandwich). Sag (1981) proposes to augment Kaplan contexts by adding a sense transfer function, c_{ST}, which maps one-place predicate senses to one-place predicate senses. Sag's interpretation of a predicate symbol P deviates from the standard interpretation (13a) and is presented in (13b).

(13)   a. $[P]<c> = I(P)$, where $I(P)$ designates the intension of P
       b. $[P]<c> = c_{ST}(I(P))$

We obtain the new, transferred intension of P by applying c_{ST} to the intension of P. According to this view, different contexts may trigger different transfers, and the selection of the "appropriate" context is crucial for determining the preferred (intended) interpretation. Consider the following contexts in which the head noun *ham sandwich* may be interpreted:

(14)   a. $c^0_{ST}(I(ham\ sandwich)) = I(ham\ sandwich)$
       b. $c^1_{ST}(I(ham\ sandwich)) = I(orderer\ of\ the\ ham\ sandwich)$
       c. $c^2_{ST}(I(ham\ sandwich)) = I(customer\ of\ the\ ham\ sandwich)$
       d. $c^3_{ST}(I(ham\ sandwich)) = I(son\ of\ the\ cook\ of\ the\ ham\ sandwich)$

The context c^0 leaves the intension of the head noun unaffected. The intensions of the sentences in (12) in this context would suffer from sort conflicts and therefore should be excluded. Straightforwardly, more plausible results of comprehension correspond to the intensions in c^1 or c^2 (*the orderer / the customer of the ham sandwich is sitting at table 9*). The intensions in c^3 (*the son of the cook of the ham sandwich is sitting at table 9*) is completely improbable.

At this point it becomes pretty clear – at least for the phenomenon of predicate transfer – that the classical theory of context-dependency provides no real explanation of the phenomenon. The theory simply doesn't give any hints of how to separate the adequate from the less adequate transfers. "Which sense-transfer can be affected by $c_{ST}(P)$ is again to be explicated by pragmatic theory" (Sag 1981: 286). This means that it needs an independently stated "pragmatic theory" in order to decide the question whether an explanation of the phenomenon may be found in this way.[7]

Consider next the indexical theory of systematic polysemy proposed by Bartsch (1989). In a nutshell, Bartsch proposes to augment Kaplan contexts by adding a *thematic dimension* c_{them}, which determines "what the text is about, in the sense of, to which goal of the speaker or hearer this part of the text is directed" (Bartsch 1989: 1). The lexical material Bartsch investigates are adjectives like *good, strong, satisfactory* in English and *flink* in Dutch which she calls *thematically weakly determined expressions*. All these expressions require a specification as to which aspect of qualification they apply. For example, *flink* in Dutch expresses something like "strong under aspect X" where X refers to a specific thematic dimension d which Bartsch (1989: 2) exemplifies by

$d_{1,1}$: degree of readiness to get into possible adverse situations for the sake of something good.
$d_{1,2}$: degree of endurance in adverse situations
d_3: size of volume or circumference
d_4: degree of physical ability and strength

There is a series of adjectives in Dutch which are equivalent with *flink* in specific contexts, such as *dapper* ('brave'), *volhardened* ('enduring' or 'persistent'), *dik* ('big'), *sterk* ('strong') (see table 1).

thematic dimension		flink	dapper	volhardened	dik	sterk
risk taking	$d_{1,1}$	●	●			
endurance	$d_{1,2}$	●		●		
circumference/vol.	d_3	●			●	
physical strength	d_4	●				●

Table 1: Dutch adjectives which are equivalent with *flink*
in specific thematic dimensions

[7] Sag (1981) doesn't give any hints about the intended kind of "pragmatic theory". Nunberg (1979, 1995) discusses different factors like familiarity, accessibility, and probabilistic parameters like cue validy and noteworthiness that seem to affect predicate transfer. He makes clear that it is such non-representational factors that substantiate a general pragmatic theory of contextual selection.

Simplifying matters, the characters associated with these adjectives may approximately be defined as in (15). As a consequence, the equivalences illustrated in table 1 may be derived from these entries.

(15)   a. $[\textit{flink}]<c>$ =   the property of being strong under aspect c_{them}, (undefined for $c_{them} \notin \{d_{1,1}, d_{1,2}, ...\}$)

       b. $[\textit{dapper}]<c>$ =   the property of being strong under aspect $c_{them} = d_{1,1}$ (undefined for $c_{them} \neq d_{1,1}$)

       c. $[\textit{volhardened}]<c>$ =   the property of being strong under aspect $c_{them} = d_{1,2}$ (undefined for $c_{them} \neq d_{1,2}$)

       d. $[\textit{dik}]<c>$ =   the property of being strong under aspect $c_{them} = d_3$ (undefined for $c_{them} \neq d_3$)

       e. $[\textit{sterk}]<c>$ =   the property of being strong under aspect $c_{them} = d_4$ (undefined for $c_{them} \neq d_4$)

It is obvious that we can list the families of senses related to particular lexical items when we use context-dependent semantics in the way illustrated. However, as in the case discussed before, there remains a series of questions which can be answered only with respect to a proper pragmatic theory. These questions concern the nature of the thematic dimension, the problem of blocking, and the problem of restricting the possible sense families in a systematic way (for some ideas of what such restrictions might look like, cf. Lehrer 1978).[8]

4.2 Two-level semantics

In a series of papers, Bierwisch has developed a conception which is known as *two-level semantics* (e.g. Bierwisch 1983, 1989). This approach can be discussed under two perspectives. First, there is a broader perspective that directs our attention to the leitmotif of the conception. Second, there is a narrower and more tangible perspective that directs our attention to the proposed mechanisms

---

[8] Of course, this doesn't mean that context-dependent semantics is useless in the domain under discussion. As Bartsch (1989) has shown, context-dependent semantics may be a proper framework for analyzing thematic operators (such as *in every respect*), restrictions in term-interpretation (*John, as a teacher, is good*), and sentential adverbials (such as *as far as his health is concerned, John is alright*). However, as Bartsch herself admits, questions about the correctness of texts, about the establishment of thematic dimensions, about the restricted interpretations of polysemic expressions, and so on can be answered only with respect to an adequate pragmatic background theory.

and details of knowledge representation (insofar as they are essential to the whole approach).

Let's first adopt the broader perspective. I guess it is correct to say that two-level semantics is the representational counterpart of the classical theory of context-dependency. As context-dependent semantics discriminates between *character* and *sense*, two-level semantics makes a difference between (the representation of) linguistic meaning (called *semantic representation*) and (the representation of) utterance meaning (called *conceptual representation*). Conceptual representations result from semantic representations by evaluating them with regard to a particular (representation of a) context. The question whether the two kinds of representation really correspond to different levels (in the sense Generative Grammar differentiates between different levels of representation) has proven to be very difficult to decide. Fortunately, this question seems not to be essential to the approach. For example, Jackendoff (1983) claims that semantic representation and conceptual representation belong to the same level.

At the beginning of section 4.1 I considered context-dependent semantics under a broad perspective, and I made some general claims concerning the nature of compositionality, the monotonicity of the lexical system, and the persistence of anomaly. These claims can be straightforwardly transferred to two-level semantics.

Next, let's adopt the narrower perspective. In Bierwisch (1983, 1989) and Lang (1989) we find many proposals which deserve our critical attention. Some of these proposals, such as the use of monotonic unification and the idea of type and sort coercion for calculating conceptual interpretations, may also be found in the work of other authors (e.g. Partee & Rooth 1983, Klein & Sag 1985, Jackendoff 1983). Most of these ideas were picked up and refined by Pustejovsky. I will postpone a critical discussion of these ideas until the next subsection.

An important problem in the research field of systematic polysemy concerns the question of how to constrain the possible senses that are associated with a polysemous lexical expression. Whereas context-dependent semantics appears to relegate such constraints to pragmatics (cf. Sag 1981, Nunberg 1995, Bartsch 1989), Bierwisch (1983) has his eyes on the idea of treating such restrictions semantically. He explicitly considers the restriction problem in connection with words like *institute, school, university, government, parliament,* and alike. For these nouns, Bierwisch has proposed semantic entries of the following general form:

(16) $\lambda x \, [\text{PURPOSE}(x,w) \wedge \text{CC}(w)]$

"PURPOSE" is a semantic prime, "x" a bound variable and "w" a free variable that refers to a conceptual complex to which the condition CC (a predicate constant) applies. It is this semantic condition which discriminates school from university, parliament from government, and so on. In the case of *school*, CC is LEARNING_&_TEACHING (Bierwisch 1983: 86). This leads us to the following semantic entry for *school*:

(17) λx [PURPOSE(x,w) $\wedge$ LEARNING_&_TEACHING(w)]

Bierwisch (1983: 88) stresses that the semantic entry for *school* is underspecified with regard to the level of conceptually salient senses. He proposes several
functions or "templates" (Bierwisch 1983: 87):

(18)   a. $\lambda P \lambda x$ [INSTITUTION(x) $\wedge$ $P(x)$]
        b. $\lambda P \lambda x$ [BUILDING(x) $\wedge$ $P(x)$]
        c. $\lambda P \lambda x$ [PROCESS(x) $\wedge$ $P(x)$]

Applying these λ-expressions to the semantic entry (17) for *school*, we get the
following representations identifying three conceptual variants for *school*, the
institution-, building-, and process-reading:

(19)   a. λx [PURPOSE(x,w) $\wedge$ LEARNING_&_TEACHING(w) $\wedge$ INSTIT(x)]
        b. λx [PURPOSE(x,w) $\wedge$ LEARNING_&_TEACHING(w) $\wedge$ BUILD-
           ING(x)]
        c. λx [PURPOSE(x,w) $\wedge$ LEARNING_&_TEACHING(w) $\wedge$ PRO-
           CESS(x)]

The uniform semantic entry of *school* thus comes to be interpreted as a kind of
institution, a kind of building, or a kind of process. For some institution words,
however, the range of interpretations is more restricted. Bierwisch compares
Regierung (English *government*) and *Parlament* (*parliament*). Whereas the
latter may have both the institution and the building interpretation (in German
and English), the former lacks the building interpretation (cf. Bierwisch 1983: 83):

(20)   a. Das Parlament hat die Frage bereits entschieden.
           The parliament has already come to a decision on the issue.
        b. Das Parlament liegt am Stadtrand.
           The parliament is situated on the outskirts of the city.

(21)   a. Die Regierung hat die Frage bereits entschieden.
           The government has already come to a decision on the issue.
        b. ?Die Regierung liegt am Stadtrand.
           ?The government is situated on the outskirts of the city.

Here we are confronted with the restriction problem of polysemy. Bierwisch
solves it by stipulating a corresponding constraint in the lexicon, giving *Regierung* a more restricted representation than *Parlament*:

(22)   a. Parlament $\rightarrow$ λx [PURPOSE(x,w) $\wedge$ CC$_{parliament}(w)$]
        b. Regierung $\rightarrow$ λx [PURPOSE(x,w) $\wedge$ INSTITUTION(x) $\wedge$
           CC$_{government}(w)$]

Using (22b) as the semantic entry for *Regierung* excludes the templates (18b,c)
from being applied, for applying them would result in sortal incorrectness. Generally speaking, Bierwisch's restrictions on interpretation are determined exclusively by the lexical system of grammar and certain conditions on sortal cor-

rectness. As a consequence, the anomaly of utterances like (21b) comes out as a semantic anomaly.

The view to treat the restriction problem as a purely linguistic problem has been criticized by various authors (e.g., Meyer 1994, Taylor 1994, Blutner 1995). Taylor (1994), for example, argues that the different restrictions for *Parlament* and *Regierung* are

closely linked to conceptual knowledge of what a parliament and a government actually are. A parliament is primarily a legislative institution, whose members are housed in a specially dedicated building; while a government is primarily a group of people with executive authority, but who do not necessarily or typically congregate in a special building to carry out their duties. (Taylor 1994: 16).

A proper way to check the view whether conceptual knowledge may restrict the range of polysemous variants might be to consider the influence of "social-cultural" factors on the realization of polysemy. A nice illustration is provided by the way people in Munich and Saarbrücken use these words. Contrary to the normal situation just mentioned, in Munich and Saarbrücken the government typically congregates in a special building that is well-known to the people. Surprising only for advocates seeing the restrictions on polysemy as "rein sprach-lich", it turns out that utterances like

(23)   ?Die Regierung liegt nicht weit vom Stadtzentrum.
          ?The government is situated not far from the center of the city.

are not deviant for most people in Munich and Saarbrücken.[9]

If this line of argumentation is correct, then it can be concluded that the restriction problem must be solved by finding a systematic explanation of pragmatic anomalies within a proper pragmatic setting.

4.3 Generative lexicon

In section 3.1 I mentioned two different views on how to handle the interpretation of polysemous expressions: the *sense enumeration view* and the *selective generation view*. Pustejovsky's disapproval with the sense enumeration analysis of polysemy led him to his theory of the *generative lexicon* (cf. Pustejovsky 1989, 1991, 1993, 1995), which may be seen as a particular variant of the selective generation view. According to Pustejovsky, sense enumeration lexicons simply miss the fact that the different senses of a polysemous expression are semantically related. Moreover, the process of sense selection on the basis of

---

[9] In a similar vein, Taylor (1984: 16) argues that the contrast between German *Palast* and English *palace* seems to reflect facts of a "social-cultural" nature: "The institution reading of *palace* is surely sanctioned by the fact that speakers of (British) English are citizens of a still extant monarchy, while the absence of an institution reading of *Palast* follows from the fact that for German speakers a "palace", probably, is no more than just another kind of historical monument."

various contextual factors becomes computationally undesirable, particularly when it has to account for longer phrases involving different sources of polysemy.

One of Pustejovsky's typical examples concerns the ambiguity and context dependence of adjectives such as *fast* and *slow*, where the interpretation of the adjective varies depending on the noun being modified (cf. Pustejovsky & Bogurajev 1993).

(24) a. a fast car   [one that moves quickly]
      b. a fast typist   [a person that performs the act of typing quickly]
      c. a fast book   [one that can be read in a short time]
      d. a fast driver   [one who drives quickly]

With regard to these examples, it can be argued that the four different interpretations of *fast* can all be derived from a single word meaning, and there is no need for enumerating the different senses (cf. Pustejovsky & Bogurajev 1993, Pustejovsky 1995). The basic idea is the following. The adjective modifies a specific conceptual component connected with the noun, namely its purpose or function. With regard to this component, the adjective seems to make an uniform contribution: it qualifies this component (the act of moving, typing, reading or driving) in a specific and predictable way.

In order to illustrate this idea more precisely, let us calculate the interpretation of the expression *fast car*. In (25a) the semantic analysis of the noun *car* (its *qualia structure*) is sketched in some relevant aspects. The analysis states that the concept related to cars is characterized (besides other things) by a *telic role* (purpose or function) that qualifies a situation s associated with cars as a moving process. The semantic analysis of the adjective *fast* given in (b) expresses that it affects the telic role only. From a technical point of view, the free variables s and s' introduce elements of underspecification into the lexical representations of *car* and *fast*. In (c) the expressions given in (a) and (b) are combined by the intersection operation, and in (d) the resulting interpretation (*a car that moves quickly*) is obtained by unifying the free variables.

(25) a. *car*: $\lambda x \, [CAR(x) \wedge TELIC(x,s) \wedge MOVE(s) \wedge ...]$
      b. *fast*: $\lambda x \, [TELIC(x,s') \wedge FAST(s')]$
      c. *fast car*: $\lambda x \, [CAR(x) \wedge TELIC(x,s) \wedge MOVE(s) \wedge$
                             $TELIC(x,s') \wedge FAST(s') \wedge ...]$
      d. unification → $\lambda x \, [CAR(x) \wedge TELIC(x,s) \wedge MOVE(s) \wedge FAST(s) \wedge ...]$

It is straightforward to extend the analysis to the other cases given in (24). At first glance, this kind of analysis seems to work well for the examples under discussion. However, there is a problem. Clearly, the analysis establishes a kind of inferential relationship, namely the inference from *a fast car* to *a car that moves quickly*, or from *a fast book* to *a book that can be read in a short time*. Since the analysis rests on non-defeasible lexical information and the operation of monotonic unification, these inferences come out as strictly necessary entailments. However, from an intuitive point of view, such inferences are defeasible, hence not strictly necessary, as shown by the following example for contextual canceling.[10]

(26)   Yesterday, my friend had some trouble with his wife, and she threw his books out of the window. Unfortunately, I was struck by a <u>fast book</u>. [preferentially, one that moved quickly]

Another problem of the account becomes visible when we try to generalize the account to other types of adjectives, e.g. to color and taste adjectives. Suppose that we want to describe that a red apple is one whose peel is red (but not necessarily its inside), and a red grapefruit is one having a red inside (but not necessarily a red peel). According to the account just sketched, we can try to describe this by assuming an application condition for *red* saying that a salient part of the object (with regard to color) is wholly reddish. Furthermore, we have to characterize the noun *apple* with respect to its mereological structure. Perhaps Pustejovsky's *constitutive qualia* could be (mis)used for this purpose, and we could postulate that the salient part of an apple is its peel and the salient part of a grapefruit is its inside. However, what counts as a salient part with regard to color is not necessarily salient with regard to other aspects. What counts as the salient part of an apple with regard to taste, for example, seems to be the inside and not the peel. Consequently, what is needed is a mechanism for assigning, manipulating and comparing saliencies. I think it is not unfair to say that monotonic unification is a completely unsuitable mechanism in this connection.

Most of this criticism also applies to two-level semantics, because this approach makes extensive use of (some variant of) monotonic unification as well. Although the two-level semantics makes a careful distinction between lexical and encyclopedic information – I see that as an advantage over Pustejovsky's account – this doesn't help very much as soon as it uses the very same mechanism of monotonic unification. Paradoxically, the general claim made by two-level semantics – that the principle of compositionality cannot be transferred to the level of utterance interpretation – conflicts with the specific proposals made for calculating utterance meanings.

Let's next consider the case of *logical polysemy*, another typical example which Pustejovsky uses to argue against the sense enumeration view. The phenomenon of logical polysemy brings to the foreground some new ideas and mechanisms of the "generative capacity" of the lexicon. Pustejovsky (1989, 1991, 1993, 1995) considers examples such as those illustrated in (27) and argues that it would seem arbitrary to create separate word senses for a lexical item just because it can participate in distinct syntactic realizations.

---

[10] For a similar argument, cf. Fodor & Lepore (1998).

(27)   a. Mary began to read a novel
       b. Mary began to write a novel
       c. Mary began a novel

The type for *begin* in (27a,b) is <VP,<NP,S>> and appears to be <NP,<NP,S>>
in (27c). Pustejovsky suggests that it is sufficient to assume one basic type,
namely <VP,<NP,S>>, and that the well-formed construction (27c) is the result
of *coercing* the complement (the NP *a novel*) to another type. In general, type
coercion is realized by "a semantic operation that converts an argument to the
type which is expected by a function, where it would otherwise result in a type
error" (Pustejovsky 1993: 83). Type coercion leads to the derivation tree shown
in (28) for (27c).

(28)   Mary   begin   a   novel

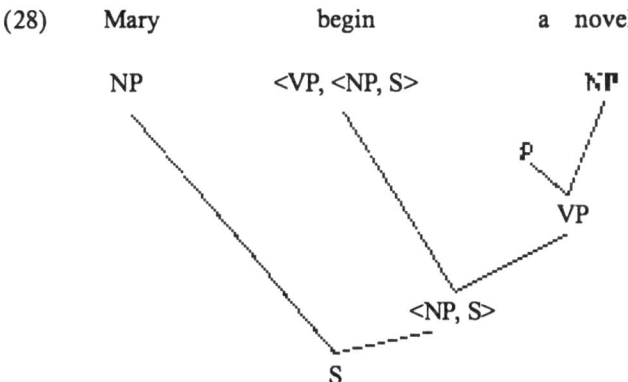

Here ρ denotes a shifting-operator. In its most general form, this shifting operator is called the *relate*-operator. It has the following form (when applied to the
semantic representation of *a novel*):

(29)   ρ(A NOVEL) = $\lambda x \exists P[P(\text{A NOVEL})(x)]$

Using this operator, the combinatorial derivation shown in (28) leads to the
result (30) (after performing several conversions explained in Pustejovsky
(1993: 86)). This expression leaves the relation between JOHN and A NOVEL
underspecified (the existential quantifier should not be taken too literally).

(30)   BEGIN($\exists P[P(\text{A NOVEL})(\text{JOHN})]$)(JOHN)

Pustejovsky uses such underspecified forms only for the interpretation of *contextually dependent* cases of (27c). Such a case can be exemplified by the following question-answer pair:

(31)   What about Mary's restoring?
          He began the novel.

For the usual, so-called *contextually independent* interpretation of (27c), where *write* or *read* stand for the intended relations, Pustejovsky (1989, 1991, 1993) suggests another mechanism. This mechanism doesn't make use of the general *relate*-operator (29). The idea is to make use of a system of basic roles that characterize the semantics of nominals, the *qualia structure*. For the present purposes, these roles can be defined as operators that affect the semantic content of the NP. Two of these operators, the telic role and the agentive role, are given in (32):

(32)   a. $Q_T(A\ NOVEL) = \lambda x\ READ(A\ NOVEL)(x)$
       b. $Q_A(A\ NOVEL) = \lambda x\ WRITE(A\ NOVEL)(x)$

In a certain sense, these operations may be seen as default realizations of the "underspecified" operator ρ and we may make use of the general doctrine to follow default options before applying stricter options, in case the former can be applied consistently. By applying the operators (32a,b), the expressions (33a,b) result; they are conform to the interpretations of (27a,b).

(33)   a. BEGIN([READ(A NOVEL)(JOHN)])(JOHN)
       b. BEGIN([WRITE(A NOVEL)(JOHN)])(JOHN)

Pustejovsky (1991) tries to illustrate the restrictiveness of this mechanism by considering the qualia structure of the noun *dictionary*, which lacks a realization of the telic role, and by considering the noun *rock*, which lacks a realization of both the telic role and the agentive role. Consequently, the distribution presented in (34) falls out rather naturally.

(34)   a. Mary began a dictionary (Agentive)
       b. ? Mary began a dictionary (Telic)
       c. ?? Mary began a rock

However, the approach loses much of its initial fascination and becomes rather questionable when confronted with examples like the following (borrowed from Fodor & Lepore, 1998):

(35)   a. John began a car
       b. John wants a dictionary

The predictions Pustejovsky's account makes (due to the corresponding qualia structures of *car* and *dictionary*) are that (35a) means *John began to drive a car*, and (35b) means *John wants to write a dictionary*. Both predictions clearly are wrong.

   This problem of the *restrictiveness* of the coercion mechanism is only one problem that is connected with Pustejovsky's account. Another one looks like a technical problem and is perhaps avoidable. The problem is connected with the apparent inflation of shifting operations. Certainly we need the information provided by the telic and agentive role of nouns like *novel* that express two salient and highly context-independent properties of novels: that they are typically created by the process of writing and that their purpose is for reading. But why double these elements of stereotypic knowledge by stipulating extra shift-ing-operations that express exactly the same information?

The third point of criticism is connected with a substantial trait of natural language processing systems. Motivated by the *combinatorial explosion puzzle*, recent work on underspecification and semantic interpretation (e.g. Alshawi & Crouch 1992, van Deemter & Peters 1996) has stressed the monotonicity prop-erty of language processing. The idea is to eliminate non-monotonic operations involving loss of information and destructive operations of semantic representa-tions and "to provide a model for semantic interpretation that is fully monotonic in both linguistic and contextual aspects of interpretation" (Alshawi & Crouch 1992: 32). The coercion view isn't in principle in conflict with this idea. How-ever, the insufficient restrictiveness of the coercion mechanism and the need to stipulate additional checking mechanisms diminishes the use of monotonic processing and makes it very difficult to generate the right things immediately.

Copestake & Briscoe (1995: 30 ff.) point out other problems with Pustejov-sky's analysis of "logical polysemy" stemming from the possibility of co-predication. Furthermore, Pustejovsky's account is problematic when it comes to deal with the phenomenona of blocking and deblocking considered in section 3.2 and 3.3.

Taken together, all these problems suggest that it is more promising to look for an alternative view. This alternative need not conform to the *sense enumera-tion view* (as Fodor & Lepore (1998) seem to suggest), but it may be another variant of the *selective generation view*. The main idea of the selective genera-tion view, I think, is basically correct: there are non-arbitrary, systematic con-nections between the different senses of polysemous expressions that we have to account for – simply enumerating the different senses is not enough. What is wrong with the particular approach to the selective generation view favored by Pustejovsky and others, I claim, is the idea to deviate from compositionality in a *minimal* way. This attitude is clearly reflected within the coercion view, which is summarized here.

(36)   *The Coercion View*

   a. Every lexical unit determines a primary conceptual variant which can be grasped as its (literal) meaning.
   b. The combinatorial system of language determines how the lexical units are combined into larger units (phrases, sentences).
   c. There is a system of type and sortal restrictions which determines whether the resulting structures are well-formed.
   d. There is a generative device (called type/sort coercion) that tries to overcome type or sortal conflicts that may arise by strict application of the combinatorial system of language. The coercion device is triggered (only) by type or sort violations.

5 Semantic underspecification and pragmatic strengthening

Unlike the other sections of this paper, the following contains more an intimation of new opportunities than a survey of completed research. What I will consider in this section is a variant of the *selective generation view* which may be called the *radical underspecification view*. This view sharply contrasts with the coercion view. It is more radically founded on underspecified representations, and makes use of a pragmatic mechanism of contextual enrichment.

(37)   *The Radical Underspecification View*

a. Every lexical unit determines an underspecified representation (i.e. a representation that may contain, for example, place holders and restrictions for individual and relational concepts)

b. The combinatorial system of language determines how lexical units are combined into larger units (phrases, sentences).

c. There is a system of type and sortal restrictions which determines whether structures of a certain degree of (under)specification are well-formed.

d. There is a mechanism of contextual enrichment (pragmatic strengthening based on contextual and encyclopedic knowledge).

This view of radical underspecification shares some ideas with the two-level semantics: (i) the distinction between lexicon and encyclopedia, i.e. between semantics and pragmatics is taken as an important one, (ii) the features of compositionality, monotonicity, and (perhaps) persistence of anomaly, are taken as crucial characteristics marking out the domain of semantics.

However, in contrast to Bierwisch's two-level semantics and Pustejovsky's generative lexicon, the present view disregards monotonic unification and type/sort coercion as mechanisms of contextual enrichment. Instead, it explores alternative proposals – proposals stressing open-ended default inference on real world knowledge. Here is a collection of candidates that may provide a suitable mechanism for the contextual enrichment of underspecified representations:

- Defaults as rules for filling in information gaps (see various papers in van Deemer & Peters 1995)
- Discourse interpretation based on a default conditional logic (e.g. Lascarides & Asher 1993)
- Persistent Default-Unification (Lascarides, Asher, Briscoe & Copestake 1995, Copestake & Briscoe 1995)
- Weighted abduction (Hobbs et al. 1993)
- Conversational implicature and lexical pragmatics (Blutner, Leßmöllmann, & van der Sandt 1995, Blutner 1998)

In the rest of this paper, I will refer to the last-mentioned account only, and I will outline how this account may solve some of the problems stated before. The details of the solutions are beyond the scope of this paper because it would require a detailed discussion of the proposed account to conversational implicature.

Using the idea of weighted abduction (Hobbs et al. 1993), the approach of *lexical pragmatics* has many similarities with Hobbs' account seeing conceptual interpretation as abduction, i.e. as "inference to the best explanation". The problem with Hobbs' account is that it can account neither for blocking nor for the non-persistence of anomaly (for details see Blutner, to appear). In the lexical pragmatics account abduction is only one component embedded in a more comprehensive architecture that seeks to explicate the notion of conversational implicature.

For Griceans, conversational implicatures are those non-truth-functional aspects of utterance interpretation which are conveyed by virtue of the assumption that the speaker and the hearer are obeying the *cooperative principle of conversation*, and, more specifically, various *conversational maxims*: *maxims of quantity, quality, relation* and *manner*. While the notion of conversational implicature doesn't seem hard to grasp intuitively, it has proven difficult to define precisely. An important step in reducing and explicating the Gricean framework has been made by Atlas and Levinson (1981) and Horn (1984). Taking Quantity as starting point they distinguish between two principles, the Q-principle and the I-principle (termed R-principle by Horn 1984). Simple but informal formulations of these principles are as follows:

Q-principle:
Say as much as you can (given I) (Horn 1984: 13).
Do not provide a statement that is informationally weaker than your knowledge of the world allows, unless providing a stronger statement would contravene the I-principle (Levinson 1987: 401).

I-principle:
Say no more than you must (given Q) (Horn 1984: 13).
Say as little as necessary, i.e. produce the minimal linguistic information sufficient to achieve your communicational ends (bearing the Q-principle in mind) (Levinson 1987: 402)

Obviously, the Q-principle corresponds to the first part of Grice's quantity maxim (*make your contribution as informative as required*), while it can be argued that the countervailing I-principle collects the second part of the quantity maxim (*do not make your contribution more informative than is required*), the maxim of relation and possibly all the manner maxims. As Horn (1984) seeks to demonstrate, the two principles can be seen as representing two competing forces, one force of *unification* minimizing the Speaker's effort (I-principle), and one force of *diversification* minimizing the Auditor's effort (Q-principle).

I guess that the proper treatment of conversational implicature crucially depends on the proper formulation of the Q- and the I-principle. The present explication rests on the assumption that the semantic description sem(α) of an utterance α is an underspecified representation determining a whole range of possible enrichments m, one of which covers the intended content m_{intend}. The idea of abductive specification may be used to define in which case m is a possible enrichment of sem(α): $<\alpha, m>$ is called a *possible enrichment pair* (short, *pep*) iff m is an abductive specification of sem(α) that can be generated by means of general world and discourse knowledge. Weighted abduction gives for each possible enrichment pair a cost value $\underline{c}(\alpha,m)$ that reflects the "proof" cost for deriving m from sem(α). Roughly, this cost is correlated with the *surprise* the particular enrichment m has for an agent confronted with the underspecified representation sem(α).

The Q- and the I-principle can be seen as conditions constraining possible enrichment pairs $<sem(\alpha), m>$:

(38)   a. $<\alpha, m>$ satisfies the Q-principle iff $<\alpha, m>$ is a pep and there is no other pep $<\alpha', m>$ [satisfying the I-principle] such that $\underline{c}(\alpha',m)<\underline{c}(\alpha,m)$.

   b. $<\alpha, m>$ satisfies the I-principle iff $<\alpha, m>$ is a pep and there is no other pep $<\alpha, m'>$ [satisfying the Q-principle] such that $\underline{c}(\alpha,m')<\underline{c}(\alpha,m)$.

In this (rather symmetrical) formulation, the Q- and the I-principle constrain the peps in two different ways. The I-principle constrains them by selecting the *minimal surprising* enrichments [provided Q has been satisfied], and the Q-principle constrains them by blocking those enrichments which can be grasped more economically by an alternative linguistic input α' [provided I has been satisfied].

It is not difficult to see that the Q-principle carries the main burden in explaining the blocking effects discussed in section 3.2. The additions put in brackets were introduced to explain the "division of pragmatic labor" (Horn 1984): the use of marked expressions – when a corresponding unmarked expression is available – tends to be interpreted as conveying a marked message. (Recall, for example, the case of productive causatives, as illustrated in (7)).[11]

Now I informally introduce the notion of *common ground*, an information state containing all the propositions shared by several participants, including general world and discourse knowledge. The important definitions now can be stated as follows:

(39)   a. A pep $<\alpha, m>$ is called *pragmatically licensed* (in a common ground cg) iff $<\alpha, m>$ satisfies the Q- and the I-principle and m is consistent with cg.

   b. An utterance α is called *pragmatically anomalous* (in cg) iff there is no pragmatically licensed pep $<\alpha, m>$.

   c. A proposition p is called a *conversational implicature* of α (in cg) iff p is a classical consequence of $cg \cup m$ for each m of a pragmatically licensed pep $<\alpha, m>$.

---

[11] For an extensive discussion of this point, see Blutner (1998).

What follows is a brief illustration how this framework can be used to solve two of Quine's puzzles concerning the pragmatics of adjectives (see section 3.1). The first one concerns the observation that the (preferred) interpretation of adjective noun combinations seems to affect different parts of the subject term in cases like (40a,b). The second puzzle has to do with the explanation of pragmatic anomalies in examples like (40c), where it is very difficult to get the interpretation (40d).

(40)   a. The apple is red [interpretation: its peel is red]
       b. The apple is sweet [interpretation: its pulp is sweet]
       c. ?The tractor is pumped up.
       d. The tires of the tractor are pumped up

In order to sketch how the mechanism solves the first puzzle let us concentrate on example (40a). Input of the analysis is an underspecified representation expressing that a certain part of the apple is red (roughly: $APPLE(d) \wedge PART(d,x)$-$\wedge COLOR(x,u) \wedge u=RED$). The specification of the relevant part(s) is guided by parameters of subjective probability (cue validity, diagnostic value). For example, it is plausible to assume that the color of the peel is more diagnostic for classifying apples than the color of other apple parts (such as the color of the pulp). From this assumption it can be derived that the *red peel*-enrichment is the cost minimal enrichment. Consequently, the I-principle selects the *red peel*-enrichment (and blocks the *red pulp*-interpretation). It follows the proposition expressing that the peel of the apple is red is a conversational implicature of (40a) (but not the proposition expressing that the pulp of the apple is red). In the case of (40b) analogous considerations give the *sweet pulp*-enrichment as the preferred interpretation.

Next, what about the pragmatic anomaly in cases like (40c), which contrast with examples like (40d) which are acceptable? Surely, the underspecified semantics of (40c) (saying that some part of the tractor is pumped up) isn't inconsistent with usual background knowledge. If it were, the sentence (40d) should be deviant in the same way. Consequently, the pragmatic anomaly of (40c) must be explained in another way. I think it follows from the fact that those parts of tractors that may be pumped on (the tires) are only marginally diagnostic for classifying tractors. if this is correct, then the *pumped up tires*-enrichment is blocked by enrichments that refer to more salient parts (such as the motor or the coachwork). However, the latter enrichments suffer from sort conflicts and therefore come out as not pragmatically licensed (cf. definition (39a)). In summary, a kind of garden path effect brings about that (40c) is pragmatically anomalous.

It is important to see that the present notion of anomaly isn't persistent in general. The anomaly can be canceled under special contextual conditions. For example, suppose the situation in a garage where we find tractors whose tires are pumped up and tractors whose tires are not. In this situation sentence (40c) sounds fine (explanation: the pressure state of the tires in this situation may be highly diagnostic for classifying tractors).

Let's content ourselves with these suggestions regarding the non-compositional aspects of conceptual interpretation, the phenomenon of blocking and the non-persistence of pragmatic anomaly. Blutner (1998) extends the approach to analyze the corresponding effects in case of systematic polysemy. Again, it is the pragmatic mechanism that carries the main burden in explaining restrictions on interpretation.

References

Alshawi, H. & Crouch, R (1992): "Monotonic semantic interpretation". In: Proceedings of ACL, Newark, Delaware, 32–39.

Aronoff, M. (1976): Word Formation in Generative Grammar. Cambridge, Mass.: MIT Press.

Atlas, J. & Levinson, S. (1981), "*It*-clefts, informativeness and logical form". In: P. Cole (ed.): Radical Pragmatics. New York: Academic Press, 1–61.

Bartsch, R. (1989): "Context-dependent interpretations of lexical items". In: R. Bartsch, J. van Benthem and P. van Emde-Boas (eds.): Semantics and Contextual Expressions. Dordrecht: Foris.

Bauer, L. (1983): English Word-Formation. Cambridge: Cambridge University Press.

Bierwisch, M. (1983): "Semantische und konzeptuelle Repräsentation lexikalischer Einheiten". In W. Motsch & R. Ruzicka (Hrsg.): Untersuchungen zur Semantik. Berlin: Akademie Verlag, 61–99.

   (1989): "The semantics of gradation". In: M. Bierwisch & E. Lang (eds.): Dimensional Adjectives. Berlin: Springer-Verlag, 71–261.

Blutner, R. (1995): "Ansätze zur Erzeugung und Beschränkung von Interpretationsvarianten". Arbeitspapiere des SFB 340, Bericht Nr. 71, University of Stuttgart, 33–67.

   (1998) : "Lexical pragmatics". Journal of Semantics 15, 115–162.

   & Leßmöllmann, A., and van der Sandt, R. (1996): "Conversational implicature and lexical pragmatics". In: Proceedings of the AAAI Spring Symposium on Conversational Implicature. Stanford, 1–9.

Bransford, J. D., Barclay, J.R. & Franks, J.J. (1972): "Sentence memory: a constructive versus interpretive approach". Cognitive Psychology 3, 193–209.

Carnap, R. (1936): "Testability and meaning". Philosophy of Science 3, 419–471.

Copestake, A. & Briscoe, T. (1995): "Semi-productive polysemy and sense extension". Journal of Semantics 12, 15–67.

Cruse, D.A. (1986): Lexical Semantics. Cambridge: Cambridge University Press.

Deane, P. D. (1988): "Polysemy and cognition". Lingua 75, 325–361.

Dowty, D. (1979): Word meaning and Montague grammar. Dordrecht: Kluwer.

Fabricius-Hansen, C. (1993): "Nominalphrasen mit Kompositum als Kern". Beiträge zur Geschichte der deutschen Sprache und Literatur 115, 193–243.

Fodor; J. A. & Lepore, E. (1998): The emptiness of the lexicon: Linguistic Inquiry 29, 269–288.

   & Pylyshyn Z. W. (1988): "Connectionism and cognitive architecture: a critical analysis". Cognition 28, 3–71.

Fodor, J. D. (1977): Semantics: theories of meaning in generative grammar. New York: Crowell.

Gärdenfors, P. (1993): "The emergence of meaning". Linguistics and Philosophy 16, 285–309.

– (2000): Conceptual spaces: The geometry of thought. Cambridge, Mass.: The MIT Press.

Hobbs, J. R., Stickel, M. E., Appelt, D. E., & Martin, P. (1993): "Interpretation as abduction". Artificial Intelligence 63, 69–142.

Horn, L. R. (1984): "Toward a new taxonomy for pragmatic inference: Q-based and R-based implicatures". In D. Schiffrin (ed.): Meaning, Form, and Use in Context. Washington: Georgetown University Press, 11–42.

Householder, F. W. (1971): Linguistic Speculations. London and New York: Cambridge University Press.

Jackendoff, R. (1983): Semantics and Cognition. Cambridge, Mass.: MIT Press.

Kamp, H. (1975): "Two theories about adjectives". In: E. L. Keenan (ed.): Formal Semantics for Natural Language. Cambridge: Cambridge University Press, 123–155.

Kaplan, D. (1978). "DTHAT". In: P. Cole (ed.): Syntax and Semantics 9: Pragmatics. New York: Academic Press, 221–243.

– (1979): "On the logic of demonstratives". Journal of Philosophical Logic 8, 81–89.

Katz, J. J. & Fodor, J. A. (1963): "The structure of semantic theory". Language 39, 170–210.

Keenan, E. L. (1974): "The functional principle: Generalizing the notion of Subject of". In: Papers from the Tenth Regional Meeting of the Chicago Linguistic Society. Chicago: Illinois, 298–310.

Kintsch, W. (1974): The representation of meaning in memory. Hillsdale: Erlbaum Associates.

Kiparsky, P. (1982), "Word-formation and the lexicon". In: F. Ingeman (ed.): Proceedings of the 1982 Mid-America Linguistic Conference.

Klein, E. & Sag, I. (1985): Type driven translation. Linguistics and Philosophy 8, 163–201.

Lahav, R. (1989): "Against compositionality: the case of adjectives". Philosophical Studies 55, 111–129.

– (1993): "The combinatorial-connectionist debate and the pragmatics of adjectives". Pragmatics and Cognition 1, 71–88.

Lakoff, R. (1987): Women, Fire, and Dangerous Things: What Categories Reveal About the Mind. Chicago: University of Chicago Press.

Lang, E. (1989): "The semantics of dimensional designation of spatial objects". In: M. Bierwisch and E. Lang (eds.): Dimensional Adjectives. Berlin: Springer-Verlag, 71–261.

Lascarides, A. & Asher, N. (1993): "Temporal interpretation, discourse relation, and common sense entailment". Linguistics and Philosophy 16, 437–494.

Lascarides, A., Briscoe, T., Asher, N., & Copestake, N. (1995): "Order independent and persistent typed default unification". Linguistics and Philosophy 19, 1–90.

Lehrer, A. (1978): "Structures of the lexicon and transfer of meaning". Lingua 45, 95–123.

Leßmöllmann, A. (1996): Das Problem der Modifikation polysemer Ausdrücke. Magister Artium, Humboldt University Berlin.

Levinson, S. (1987): "Pragmatics and the grammar of anaphora". Journal of Linguistics 23, 379–434.

McCawley, J. D. (1971): "Interpretive semantics meets Frankenstein". Foundations of Language 7, 285–296.

– (1978): "Conversational implicature and the lexicon". In: P. Cole (ed.): Syntax and Semantics 9: Pragmatics. New York: Academic Press, 245–259.

Meyer, R. (1993): Compound Comprehension in Isolation and in Context. Tübingen: Max Niemeyer Verlag.

– (1994): "Probleme von Zwei-Ebenen-Semantiken". Kognitionswissenschaft 4, 32–46.

Montague, R. (1970): "Universal Grammar". Theoria 36, 373–398.

Nunberg, G. (1979): "The non-uniqueness of semantic solutions: Polysemy". Linguistics and Philosophy 3, 143–184.

– (1995). "Transfers of meaning". Journal of Semantics 12, 109–132.

& Zaenen, A. (1992): "Systematic polysemy in lexicology and lexicography". In: K. Varantola, H. Tommola, T. Salmi-Tolonen and J. Schopp (eds.): Euralex II. Tampere: Finland.

Partee, B. (1984), "Compositionality". In: F. Landman and F. Veltman (eds): Varieties of Formal Semantics. Dordrecht: Foris, 281–311.

Partee, B. & Rooth, M. (1983): "Generalized conjunction and type ambiguity". In: R. Bäuerle, C. Schwarze, and A. von Stechow (eds.): Meaning, use and interpretation of language. Berlin: Walter de Gruyter, 361–383.

Pustejovsky, J. (1989): "Type coercion and selection". Paper presented at WCCFL VIII, April 1989, Vancouver, B.C.

(1991): "The generative lexicon". Computational Linguistics 17, 409–441.

(1993): "Type coercion and lexical selection". In: J. Pustejovsky (ed.): Semantics and the Lexicon. Dordrecht: Kluwer, 73–96.

(1995): The Generative Lexicon. Cambridge, Mass.: The MIT Press.

& Boguraev, B. (1993): "Lexical knowledge representation and natural language processing". Artificial Intelligence 63, 193–223.

Quine, W. V. O. (1960): Word and Object. Cambridge, Mass.: MIT Press.

Sag, I. (1981): Formal semantics and extralinguistic context. In: P. Cole (ed.): Radical Pragmatics. New York: Academic Press, 273–294.

Sweetser, E. E. (1990): From Etymology to Pragmatics. Cambridge: Cambridge University Press.

Taylor, J. R. (1994): "The two-level approach to meaning". Linguistische Berichte 149, 3–28.

van Deemter, K. & Peters, S. (1996): "Semantic Ambiguity and Underspecification". Stanford, California: CSLI Publications.

Wu, D. (1990), "Probabilistic unification-based intergration of syntactic and semantic preferences for nominal compounds". Proceedings of the 13th International Conference on Computational Linguistics (COLING 90), Helsinki, 413–418.

Zimmermann, T. E. (1991). "Kontextabhängigkeit". In: D. Wunderlich & A. von Stechow (Hrsg.): Semantik. Ein internationales Handbuch der zeitgenössischen Forschung Berlin: de Gruyter, 156–229.

Berlin   Reinhard Blutner

Institut für deutsche Sprache und Linguistik, Humboldt-Universität, Prenzlauer Promenade 149–152, D-13189 Berlin, blutner@german.hu-berlin.de

Genericity

Ariel Cohen

1 Introduction

We often express our knowledge about the world in sentences such as the following:

(1)   a. Ravens are black.
        b. Tigers have stripes.
        c. Mary jogs in the park.

We refer to such sentences as *generics*. They appear to express some sort of generalization: about ravens, about tigers, and about Mary, respectively. Yet it is far from clear exactly what they mean. What does it mean to say that some generalization holds?

It turns out that there are a great many theories trying to answer this question. This, in itself, is a fact that is in need of explanation. Why are generics so puzzling? What is it about them that forces researchers to come up with one theory after another, with no clear agreement on what the correct theory is? And, if they are so strange, why are generics so prevalent?

In this article we will consider some of the puzzles concerning generics, why they are so hard, and the various solutions proposed. Let me say at the outset that readers who expect to find definitive answers to these puzzles will unfortunately be disappointed. But if not the answers, I hope this article will at least convey the depth and significance of the problems.

2 Are generics quantificational?

Possibly the first interpretation that comes to mind is that generics express quantification of some sort. Perhaps a sentence such as (1a) is really just a different way to say something like

(2)   Every raven is black.

Things are not that simple, unfortunately. First, note that generics do not express universal quantification: while (1a) is true, (2) is false, because there are some albino ravens. Still, even if the quantifier is not the universal one, perhaps generics use some other quantifier. If this is the case, our role is to figure out what this quantifier is.

This, however, is far from an easy task. Consider the following examples of generics:

Linguistische Berichte Sonderheft 10 · © Helmut Buske Verlag 2002 · ISSN 0935-9249

(3)   a. Dogs are mammals.
        b. Birds fly.
        c. Mammals bear live young.
        d. The Frenchman eats horsemeat.
        e. Bulgarians are good weightlifters.
        f. The giant panda is an endangered species.
        g. Primary school teachers are female.
        h. People are over three years old.
        i. Members of this club help each other in emergencies.
        j. Supreme Court judges have a prime Social Security number.
        k. **A:** Nobody in India eats beef.
           B: That's not true! Indians do eat beef.

Sentences (3a)–(3f) are all presumably true, but what is it that makes them true? Sentence (3a) seems to hold for all dogs, (3b) for most birds, (3c) for most female mammals (presumably less than half the total number of mammals), (3d) for rather few Frenchmen, (3e) for very few Bulgarians, and (3f) for no individual giant panda. On the other hand, the majority of primary school teachers are female, and the majority of people are over three years old, and yet (3g) and (3h) are not true. Even if no emergencies ever occurred, (3i) may be true, and even if all Supreme Court judges happened to have a prime Social Security number, (3j) may be false. The truth of B's answer in (3k) requires only that *some* Indians eat beef.

The diversity of interpretations of generics, as exemplified by the sentences in (3), poses severe problems for any theory that attempts to relate the truth or falsity of a generic to properties of individual instances; e.g. any theory that relates the truth of (1a) to properties of individual ravens. Given this difficulty, there are two approaches one may take.

One, which Carlson (1995) calls the *rules and regulations* approach, is to deny that any semantic relation exists between generics and properties of individuals; generics, according to this view, are evaluated with respect to rules and regulations, which are basic, irreducible entities in the world. Each generic sentence denotes a rule; if the rule is *in effect,* in some sense (different theories construe differently what it means for a rule to be in effect), the sentence is true, otherwise it is false. The rule denoted by a generic may be physical, biological, social, moral, etc. The paradigmatic cases for which this view seems readily applicable are sentences that refer to conventions, i.e. man-made, explicit rules and regulations, such as the following example (Carlson 1995):

(4)   Bishops move diagonally.

According to the rules and regulations view, (4) is not about the properties of individual bishop moves, but refers directly to a rule of chess; it is true just in case one of the rules of chess is that bishops move diagonally. It is important to note that, according to the rules and regulations view, *all* generics are so analyzed: for example, (1a) is true not because of the properties of individual ravens, but because there is a rule in the world (presumably a rule of genetics) that states that ravens are black.

An alternative approach, which Carlson (1995) calls the *inductivist* view, is to accept the existence of a semantic relation between generics and properties of individuals. Theories that take this view attempt to define this relation in such a way that its nature (possibly in conjunction with facts about context, intonation and world knowledge) may account for the diversity of readings of generics, exemplified in (3).

The rules and regulation view and the inductivist view are each a cover term for a number of specific proposals. Let us briefly consider some of them.

2.1 Rules and regulations theories

Carlson (1977) proposes that a generic expresses simple predication of a property of a kind. Thus, (1a) has a very similar logical form to that of

(5)   Nevermore is black.

Both sentences express simple predication rather than quantification. The difference is only that whereas (5) predicates a property (being black) of an object (the individual raven Nevermore), (1a) predicates this property directly of the kind *raven*. Thus, Carlson's approach can, in principle, account for all the examples in (3). This, however, is done at a price: no explanation is given for why, say, eating horsemeat is a property of the kind *Frenchman,* or why being female is not a property of the kind *primary school teacher.* Moreover, Carlson's theory cannot account for scope ambiguities of generics, exemplified by the following sentences (from Schubert and Pelletier 1987):

(6)   a. Canadian academics are supported by a single granting agency.
         b. Storks have a favorite nesting area.
         c. Sheep are black or white.
         d. Whales are mammals or fish.

Krifka (1987) proposes that generics express a *default rule.* This is a type of inference rule that allows for exceptions. For example, we may assume that any raven, by default, is black, but we are ready to retract this conclusion if we learn more information about the raven – that it is an albino, that it fell into a bucket of whitewash, etc. According to Krifka, then, (1a) is true just in case every raven is black, unless its being black is not consistent with the facts assumed so far. One challenge that Krifka's approach has to face is to determine which rules are in effect and which are not. For example, a default rule that states that a primary school teacher is female is presumably a useful one, since, if we know that someone is a primary school teacher, we can reasonably assume that she is a woman, unless we learn something to the contrary. Yet this rule is not in effect, since (3g) is false. On the other hand, a default rule stating that a given Bulgarian is a good weightlifter is probably not very useful – if we know that someone is Bulgarian, we will be reluctant to conclude, solely on the basis of this information, that he or she is a good weightlifter. Yet this rule *is* in effect, since (3e) is true.

An alternative theory is that generics express not rules in the world, but rules of conversation (McCarthy 1986, Reiter 1987). Thus, the truth of (7a) implies that there is a convention of verbal behavior, according to which, whenever a speaker says (7b), the hearer is expected to infer (7c).

(7)   a. Birds fly.
        b. Tweety is a bird.
        c. Tweety flies.

This view can be cast in terms of *conversational implicature* (Grice 1975): (7a) is true just in case (7b) conversationally implicates (7c). Just like the case of conversational implicature, the inference from (7b) to (7c) is cancelable, e.g. by the additional information that Tweety is a penguin. Some sentences in (3) appear better suited for this approach than others. For example, it is hardly a language convention that if we hear that Charles is a Frenchman, we are supposed to infer that he eats horsemeat, and yet (3d) is true. On the other hand, there may very well be a convention that if we talk about a person, we may safely assume that he or she is over three years old; and yet (3h) is not true.

Rather than a verbal convention, other researchers (Geurts 1985, Declerk 1986) have suggested that a true generic sentence corresponds to a cultural convention, a stereotype. Thus (1a) is true because it corresponds to stereotypical beliefs about ravens in our culture – the stereotypical raven is black. Not all sentences are as amenable to the treatment proposed by this theory: for example, it may very well be that the stereotypical primary school teacher is female, and yet (3g) is not true. Another problem with this theory is that it takes a generic to be not a statement of fact about the world, but rather a statement about the stereotypical beliefs prevailing in one's culture. But it appears that this is not the way we interpret generics. For example, while (8a) (after Krifka *et al.* 1995) is a coherent sentence, (8b) is not:

(8)   a. Snakes are stereotypically believed to be slimy, but in fact they are not.
        b. *Snakes are slimy, but in fact they are not.

Working within the framework of Situation Semantics (Barwise and Perry 1983), several researchers (ter Meulen 1986, Cavedon and Glasbey 1994) have proposed that generic sentences express *constraints* an situations. Roughly speaking, (1a) expresses the constraint that every situation involving a raven involves a black raven.

Cavedon and Glasbey (1994) treat constraints as part of the natural order of the world; in particular, they are not reducible to properties of individual instances. This property of constraints enables them to tolerate exceptions, so that (1a) is true even if some ravens are not black. Crucial to Cavedon and Glasbey's account is the notion of a *channel* (Barwise and Seligman 1992). Roughly speaking, the role of channels is to relativize the interpretation of a generic sentence to a given context. For example, (9a) is evaluated relative to a channel which is concerned with female peacocks, and (9b), with respect to a channel which is concerned with male peacocks.

(9)   a. Peacocks lay eggs.
       b. Peacocks have brightly colored tail-feathers.

Just like other theories that follow the rules and regulations approach, both the strength and the weakness of Cavedon and Glasbey's account lie in this separation between the meaning of a generic and the properties of individual instances. The theory implies that the truth of a generic cannot be observed directly; as such, all the sentences in (3), as well as many others, can be accounted for: the true ones correspond to a constraint that is in effect, the false ones do not. However, this is also a weakness, since while the theory cannot be refuted, it is not clear what it would take to corroborate it – there is no clear prediction about the way things ought to be in the world for a generic sentence to be true or false. Some researchers have considered this to be an undesirable situation for a truth-conditional semantics, which defines the meaning of a sentence as the states of affairs that would make it true. Instead, they proposed versions of the inductivist view, in the hope of providing some relation between the facts obtaining in the world and the truth of a generic sentence. We will now turn to some of these theories.

2.2 Inductivist theories

The idea underlying the inductivist approach is rather simple. A generic sentence is true just in case sufficiently many relevant individuals in the domain of the generic satisfy the predicated property. This idea is, of course, vague on at least two issues: which instances count as "relevant," and how many is "sufficiently many"? Various inductivist approaches offer different answers to these questions. Let us briefly discuss some of them.

Farkas and Sugioka (1983) suggest that the quantifier is *significantly many*. For example, (1a) is true because significantly many ravens are black. *Significantly many* is, of course, a vague quantifier, so for many generic sentences it could be argued that this quantifier is applied correctly. It is not clear, however, that all generics can be accounted for in this way. For example, significantly many people are over three years old, and yet (3h) is not true.

Another possibility is that the appropriate quantifier is *most*. For example, (1a) is true because most ravens are black. This approach has not been explicitly proposed in any source of which I am aware, but it appears to be alluded to in Parsons (1970) and Nunberg and Pan (1975), as well as in many theories proposed within the Artificial Intelligence community, as discussed by Pelletier and

Asher (1997). The problem with this proposal is that in order for a generic to be true, it does not need to be the case that the majority of individuals satisfy the predicated property: sentences (3c) through (3e) are good counterexamples.

A more sophisticated version of this theory has been proposed by Schubert and Pelletier (1989). According to them, generics do not quantify over actual individuals, but possible ones. Thus, for example, if most, or even all actual Supreme Court judges had a prime Social Security number, (3j) would not be true: if we consider all possible judges, it is not true that most of them have a prime Social Security number. Schubert and Pelletier suggest that *most* is defined relative to a measure function on possible worlds, which favors worlds that are close to the real one in terms of the essential or inherent nature of things.

What is meant by terms such as "inherent" or "essential" is candidly left open by Schubert and Pelletier. Apparently, it is a modal notion, but it is clearly not the same as logical necessity: there is no logical necessity for birds to fly or for mammals to bear live young. The problematic nature of these notions becomes even more apparent when we consider sentences such as the following:

(10)   a. A cheetah outruns any other animal.
        b. Spices are affordable.
        c. Gold cubes are smaller than 10 cubic meters (after Koningsveld 1973).
        d. Dogs annoy Sam.

Perhaps running fast is an inherent property of cheetahs, but certainly not the property of running faster than any other animal, since some other animal could have been faster. Affordability is not a necessary property of spices; in fact, throughout much of history, spices were extremely expensive; yet (10b) is true nonetheless. Similarly, we would be hard-pressed to claim that gold cubes are inherently smaller than 10 cubic meters, or that annoying Sam is an essential property of dogs.

If *most* is problematic, perhaps the universal quantifier will work better. In fact, a number of scholars (e.g. Quine 1960, Bartsch 1972, Bacon 1974, Bennett 1974) have assumed that a generic sentence expresses universal quantification over actual individuals. It should be stressed, however, that these researchers do not propose a theory of generics as such; the researcher has some different goal in mind, and the precise interpretation of generics is not important for that goal. A moment's reflection, of course, shows that this suggestion cannot stand. If a counterexample is required, our well worn example, (1a), will suffice. This sentence is true, despite the fact that not all ravens are black.

Alternatively, we can take the quantifier to be a restricted universal (Declerk 1991, Chierchia 1995). Context, according to this view, provides a restriction for the domain of the quantifier. For example, (3c) says that all relevant mammals bear live young. Which are the relevant mammals? Declerk and Chierchia do not provide a principled account of how this restriction is obtained. Presumably, male mammals are irrelevant, as are females that are too young or too old to bear live young, etc. Strange mammals, such as the platypus, which lays eggs, are also somehow left outside the domain of the quantifier. The remaining mammals do lay eggs, hence the truth of (3c).

For Declerk, the universal quantifier ranges over actual individuals; for Chierchia, it ranges over possible individuals. Hence, Chierchia, unlike Declerk, can explain why (3j) is not true, but his account suffers from similar problems to those of Schubert and Pelletier (1989).

Schubert and Pelletier (1987) offer a more detailed discussion of how the restriction to relevant individuals is provided. It could be induced by the presupposition of the VP, as in (11), by focus, as in (12), by the linguistic context, as in (13), or by an explicit *when* clause, as in (14).

(11)   Cats land on their feet.
        = Cats that drop to the ground land an their feet.

(12) a. Leopards attack monkeys IN TREES.
         = Monkeys that are attacked by leopards are in trees.
      b. Leopards attack MONKEYS in trees.
         = Animals in trees that are attacked by leopards are monkeys.
      c. LEOPARDS attack monkeys in trees.
         = Animals that attack monkeys in trees are leopards.

(13)   Most monkeys flee when leopards approach. Baboons form a protective circle with males on the outside.
        = Baboons approached by a leopard form a protective circle with males on the outside.

(14)   When cats drop to the ground, they land on their feet.
        = Cats that drop to the ground land on their feet.

Later works (Partee 1991, Krifka 1995, Cohen 1996) combine this approach with theories of focus, claiming that generics are *associated* with focus, in the sense of Rooth (1985): focus provides a set of alternatives that restricts the domain of the generic quantifier.

For example, the following sentences have different truth conditions:

(15) a. In Saint Petersburg, ballerinas escorted OFFICERS.
      b. In Saint Petersburg, BALLERINAS escorted officers.

Sentence (15a) is true just in case, whenever a ballerina accompanied someone, it was generally an officer (but officers may have had other companions as well); sentence (15b), on the other hand, conveys the statement that, whenever someone escorted an officer, it was generally a ballerina (but ballerinas may have accompanied other people as well).

Rooth suggests that the union of the set of alternatives induced by focus determines the domain of the quantifier. With respect to (15a), this union is the set of ballerinas who escorted someone. The generic quantifier then quantifies over this set, conveying that such ballerinas generally escorted officers.

With respect to (15b), the union of the alternatives would be the set of officers escorted by somebody. Hence (15b) quantifies over such officers, stating that such companions were generally ballerinas.

This type of approach is quite powerful, in providing empirically testable predictions about the interpretations of many generics – see, for example, the effect of focus in (12). It can even be explained why, in cases such as (3k), generics get quasi-existential readings – the response only requires that some Indians eat beef. In such cases, it has been proposed (Cohen 1996), the role of the contrastive focus is to restrict the domain to only those Indians who eat beef; if this domain is not empty, the sentence is true.

Yet it is not clear that such approaches can account for the full range of readings of generics. For example, it is hard to see what sort of restriction of the domain of Frenchmen would yield the truth of (3d), when the sentence is not uttered in a contrastive context.

Yet another view of generics as expressions of universal quantification is that the quantifier quantifies over *normal* individuals (Delgrande 1987, Morreau 1992, Asher and Morreau 1995, Krifka 1995, Pelletier and Asher 1997, among others). Sentence (1a) is true, according to this view, because all normal ravens are black – albino ravens are abnormal ravens. Normality is taken to be a modal notion. Following Kratzer (1981), a partial ordering relation is assumed to be defined on possible worlds. This relation orders worlds according to their normality. Then, a generic sentence such as (1a) is true just in case in all worlds that are most normal, all ravens are black.

Thus, we can account for sentences such as (3g) and (3h): although male teachers are in the minority, they are still normal teachers; and although most people are over three years old, babies are still normal people. On the other hand, we can account for the truth of (3i) even when no emergencies occurred in the actual world, provided that in those most normal worlds where emergencies do occur, all members of the club help each other.

One problem with these approaches is that the ordering source of normality is not given an independent definition. Why is a black raven normal, and a white raven abnormal? Note that the interpretation of normality seems to change from sentence to sentence, as the following sentences (from Krifka *et al.* 1995) indicate:

(16)   a. Two and two equals four (normal = the rules of mathematics hold).
       b. A spinster is an old, never-married woman (normal = the rules of English hold).
       c. This machine crushes oranges (normal = machines perform as intended).
       d. Mary smokes cigarettes (normal = Mary shows her typical behavior).
       e. Bob jumps 8.90 meters (normal = Bob performs as well as he can).
       f. A lion has a mane (normal = stereotypical properties hold).
       g. Six apples cost one dollar (normal = the actual world).
       h. A turtle is long-lived (normal = ?).
       i. A pheasant lays speckled eggs (normal = ?).

There is some debate over what the standard of normality would be for (16b) and (16i), since worlds in which all turtles reach an old age (no predators?) or where all pheasants lay eggs (no males?) do not, on the face of it, appear to be normal. But perhaps this problem could be solved by adding a restriction to the domain of the generic quantifier (Krifka 1995, Pelletier and Asher 1997), thus, in a sense, combining the normality approach with a domain-restriction theory such as Schubert and Pelletier (1987).

Other than these skeptical doubts, quantification over normal individuals runs into some empirical problems as well. It is not clear how it would account for (3d) and (3e): it is hardly the case that all normal Frenchmen eat horsemeat or that all normal Bulgarians are good weightlifters. Moreover, sentences that express relations pose a particular problem for this approach. Sentence (17a), for example, clearly does not mean (17b).

(17)   a. Women live longer than men.
        b. Every normal woman lives longer than every normal man.

A somewhat similar idea is to regard generics as expressions of universal quantification over a set of *typical individuals*, rather than normal ones (Heyer 1985, 1990; see also Link 1995). Unlike normal individuals, typical individuals are usually not defined in terms of possible worlds. A distinction is drawn between characteristic and noncharacteristic properties of kinds; those individuals that possess the characteristic properties are considered to be typical representatives. A generic sentence is true, then, to the extent that it is true of all typical individuals: since all typical ravens are black, (1a) is true. This approach shares many of the strengths of the normality approach, but also its weaknesses. In particular, it provides no independent, non-circular definition of typicality.

Given the difficulty of deciding what the meaning of the generic quantifier is, some people have proposed that it is, in fact, ambiguous.

Strzalkowski (1988) takes a generic such as (18a) to be ambiguous between the senses paraphrased by (18b) and (18c).

(18)   a. Birds fly.
        b. All except for a negligible number of birds fly.
        c. A non-negligible number of flying animals are birds.

In this way he is able to account for sentences such as (3d) and (3e), assuming that a non-negligible number of horsemeat eaters are French, and that a non-negligible number of good weightlifters are Bulgarian. However, his theory predicts, wrongly, that (19) is true, since a non-negligible number of birds are grey.

(19)   Grey animals are birds.

It should be noted that under both readings of the generic quantifier, Strzalkowski takes it to quantify over actual individuals. Hence, his theory is subject to the problems with sentences such as (3j) and (3i).

In contrast, Dahl (1975) interprets the generic quantifier as quantifying over possible worlds. According to him, the quantifier is ambiguous between (re-stricted) universal and existential quantification over worlds, i.e. between the modal notions of necessity and possibility. Thus, (3a) states that all dogs are necessarily mammals. Dahl can account for (3d): it means that if we pick an arbitrary Frenchman, it is possible that he would eat horsemeat. This approach, however, would predict no difference between (3d) and (20), since it is also possible that an arbitrary American would eat horsemeat.

(20)   The American eats horsemeat.

Dahl's approach can handle with ease the cases that are difficult for Strzalkow-ski's theory, such as (3j) and (3i). However, just like Schubert and Pelletier's (1989) theory, it runs into difficulties with cases of contingent generics, such as those in (10).

Cohen (1996, 2000) has a different account of the ambiguity of generics. Generics, according to this proposal, express probability judgments. Thus, (3b) is about the probability that an arbitrarily chosen bird flies, and (3d) is about the probability that an arbitrarily chosen Frenchman eats horsemeat. However, ge-nerics are ambiguous with respect to the requirement that this probability needs to satisfy in order for the sentence to be true: the most plausible interpretation of (3b) is that the probability is higher than some constant (specifically, 0.5); the most plausible interpretation of (3d) is that the probability is greater than the probability that some arbitrary person eats horsemeat. Thus, (3d) is true just in case, if we pick an arbitrary Frenchman, however unlikely this person is to eat horsemeat, he would still be likelier to do so than a person of an arbitrary na-tionality.

2.3 Combining the two types of theory

It appears that there are some generics, e.g. (4) that are better explained by rules and regulations theories, and others, e.g. (1a), that are better explained by in-ductivist theories. One may wish to consider, then, whether the two types of theory can somehow be combined.

This possibility is rejected by Carlson (1995). He describes the two ap-proaches as a dichotomy: one has to choose one or the other, but not both. How can we decide which? One way is to consider a case where the behavior of ob-served instances conflicts with an explicit rule. For example, Carlson describes a supermarket where bananas sell for $.49/lb, so that (21a) is true. One day, the manager decides to raise the price to $1.00/lb. Immediately after the price has changed, claims Carlson, sentence (21a) becomes false and sentence (21b) be-comes true, although all sold bananas were sold for $.49/lb.

(21)   a. Bananas sell for $.49/lb.
        b. Bananas sell for $1.00/lb.

Consequently, Carlson reaches the conclusion that the rules and regulations approach is the superior one.

This conclusion has been challenged by Greenberg (1998) and Cohen (forthcoming). Suppose the price has, indeed, changed, but the supermarket employs incompetent cashiers who consistently use the old price by mistake, so that customers are still charged $.49/lb. In this case, there seems to be a reading of (21a) which is true, and a reading of (21b) which is false. These readings are more salient if the sentence is modified by expressions such as *actually* or *in fact:*

(22)   a. Bananas actually sell for $.49/lb.
         b. In fact, bananas sell for $1.00/lb.

Consequently, Greenberg and Cohen claim that generics are ambiguous: on one reading they express a descriptive generalization, stating the way things are. Under the other reading, they carry a normative force, and require that things be a certain way. When they are used in the former sense, they should be analyzed by some sort of inductivist account; when they are used in the latter sense, they ought to be analyzed as referring to a rule or a regulation. The respective logical forms of the two readings are different; whereas the former reading involves, in some form or another, quantification, the latter has a simple predicate-argument structure: the argument is the rule or regulation, and the predicate holds of it just in case the rule is "in effect."

A language that makes an explicit distinction between these two types of reading is French. In this language, generically interpreted plural nouns are preceded by the definite determiner *les,* whereas the indefinite determiner *des* usually induces existential readings. However, *des* may also be used to make a normative statement, i.e. to express some rule or regulation.

(23)   a. Des agents de police ne se comportent pas ainsi dans une Situation d'alarme.
            'INDEF-PL police officers do not behave like that in an emergency situation.'
         b. Les agents de police ne se comportent pas ainsi dans une Situation d'alarme.
            'DEF-PL police officers do not behave like that in an emergency situation.'

An observation which de Swart (1996) ascribes to Carlier (1989) is that (23a) "would be uttered to reproach a subordinate with his behavior. (23b) does not have the same normative value, but gives us a descriptive generalization which could possibly be refuted by providing a counterexample."

3 Lawlikeness and intensionality

3.1 Generics are lawlike

Perhaps one of the reasons why it is so hard to determine whether generics are quantificational, and, if so, what the quantifier is, is that generics are *lawlike*. The distinction between lawlike and nonlawlike statements is well known in philosophy, and is easily demonstrated using universally quantified sentences. For example, (24a) intuitively expresses a law of nature; (24b), in contrast, expresses an accidental fact.

(24)   a. All copper wires conduct electricity.
        b. All coins in my pocket are made of copper.

One way to characterize the difference between lawlike and nonlawlike statements is that only the former, not the latter, support counterfactuals. Thus, (24a) entails (25a), but (24b) does not entails (25b).

(25)   a. If this were a copper wire, it would conduct electricity.
        b. If this coin were in my pocket, it would be made of copper.

Note that we can turn (24a), but not (24b), to a felicitous generic; (26a) is fine (and true) but (26b), under its generic interpretation, is odd (cf. (3j) above).

(26)   a. Copper wires conduct electricity.
        b. Coins in my pocket are made of copper.

Generics, in general, support counterfactuals; the truth of (27a) entails (27b).

(27)   a. Birds fly.
        b. If Dumbo were a bird, he would probably fly.

It is tempting to think that rules and regulations theories are particularly well suited to handle this aspect of generics: it seems that all we need to require is that the rule or regulation a generic denotes be nonaccidental. Things are not that simple, however: rules and regulations approaches have difficulties accounting for the fact that generics support counterfactuals. If there is no relation between the truth of (27a) and the flying abilities of actual birds, why should there be such a relation between its truth and the flying abilities of hypothetical birds?

Inductivist theories face difficulties too. If generics involve a quantifier, it has rather special properties: this quantifier must be sensitive not only to the number of individuals satisfying a certain property, but also to whether the statement is lawlike or not. It is for this reason that, as we have seen above, many researchers proposed modal treatments of generics; the hope is that the notion of lawlikeness is similar enough to the notion of necessity to be formalizable within a possible worlds framework. If, indeed, generics can be captured by a theory that is based an possible worlds, it follows that they must be intensional. Let us now turn to the issue of intensionality.

3.2 Are generics intensional?

Suppose ψ_1 and ψ_2 are two extensionally equivalent properties, i.e. at this moment in time and in the actual world, the respective sets of individuals that satisfy ψ_1 and ψ_2 are equal. If generics behave extensionally, we would expect the following sentences to have the same truth conditions for every property ϕ:

(28)   a. ψ_1s are ϕ.
        b. ψ_2s are ϕ.

This does not hold in general. Consider (29), from Carlson (1989).

(29)   A computer computes the daily weather forecast.

Carlson observes that

"the daily weather forecast" requires an *intensional* interpretation, where its meaning cannot be taken as rigidly referring to the present weather forecast, e.g. the one appearing in today's copy of the *Times* predicting light rain and highs in the upper thirties (p. 179, emphasis added).

For example, if today's weather forecast predicts a blizzard, this may well be the main news item. Yet, (29) does not entail

(30)   A computer computes the main news item.

While a computer may have computed today something that turned out to be the main news item, this does not hold in general; on most days, the main news item will not be computed by a computer, hence (30) is false.

Intensionality, it is important to note, does not come in one form only. In particular, a construction may exhibit intensionality with respect to the time index, but not with respect to possible worlds, or vice versa. For example, Landman (1989), in his discussion of groups, draws the following distinction:

The intensionality that I am concerned with here concerns ... the fact that committees **at the same moment of time** can have the same members, without being the same committee. Another form of intensionality concerns the well known observation that ... in the course of time, they may change their members, while staying the same committee. I do not think that this kind of intensionality has the same source as the 'atemporal' intensionality that is the topic of this paper (pp. 726–727, original emphasis).

Generics and frequency statements, it turns out, behave intensionally with respect to the time index, but not with respect to possible worlds. Suppose that the weather report is Mary's favorite newspaper column. Then (31) would have the same truth conditions as (29), although there are any number of worlds where Mary has no interest in the daily weather forecast:

(31)   A computer computes Mary's favorite newspaper column.

To give other examples, it is true in the actual world that the whale is the largest animal an earth, and the quetzal is Guatemala's national bird, but there are any number of possible worlds where this is not the case. Yet (32a) and (33a) have the same respective truth conditions as (32b) and (33b).

(32)   a. The whale suckles its young.
       b. The largest animal on earth suckles its young.

(33)   a. The quetzal has a magnificent, golden-green tail.
       b. Guatemala's national bird has a magnificent, golden-green tail.

Generics, then, are parametric an time, but not on possible worlds; if two properties have the same extension throughout time, they can be freely interchanged in a generic sentence *salva veritate*. In other words, the truth conditions of the generic

(34) ψs are ϕ

do not depend on the extensions of ψ and ϕ in any other world but the actual one, though the truth conditions do depend an the extensions of these properties at different times.

How can a theory of generics account for this behavior? Clearly, a fully extensional theory, such as Declerk (1991) or Strzalkowski (1988), will not do justice to this phenomenon; according to such theories, generics ought not to be parametric on either time or possible worlds, which is not the case. On the other hand, a fully intensional theory would not do either, since it would predict that generics are parametric on possible worlds, which they are not.

Theories that make use of possible worlds, but restrict them to worlds that are normal, or that are close to the actual world in terms of its essential properties, fare better. They do, however, have to face the problem of defining normality or essence in such a way, that a world where Mary is not interested in the weather, or where the quetzal is not Guatemala's national bird, is somehow abnormal, or violates essential principles holding in the actual world.

An alternative way to explain the behavior of generics with respect to intensionality has been proposed by Cohen (1999), who uses a *branching* model of time. That is to say, for any given time there is more than one possible future: there is a future where it is going to rain tomorrow, and one where it is not. The generic (34) is evaluated with respect to all those futures where the frequency of ϕ among ψs is more or less the same as during an interval of time containing the reference time of the sentence. For example, (29) is true just in case in the extended present the daily weather forecast is computed by a computer, but (30) is false because in the extended present, the weather is rarely the main news item. On the other hand, (31) is true just in case (29) is true, given that in the extended present Mary's preference for the weather forecast remains unchanged.

4 Frequency adverbs

It is often pointed out that generics are similar to sentences involving an overt adverb of quantification. Consider the sentences in (1), when modified by an overt adverb.

(35) a. Ravens are usually black.
      b. Tigers always have stripes.
      c. Mary sometimes jogs in the park.

Just like the generics in (1), these sentences express some generalization about ravens, tigers, and Mary, respectively. The difference is that, unlike generics, which have no quantifier (according to the rules and regulations view), or an implicit quantifier with some special properties (according to the inductivist view), here we have an explicit quantifier. Thus, the sentences in (35) are also similar to overtly quantified sentence such as the following:

(36) a. Most ravens are black.
      b. All tigers have stripes.
      c. Some occasions of Mary's jogging are in the park.

Some researchers (de Swart 1991, Chierchia 1992) have proposed that frequency statements, are, in fact, equivalent to sentences such as (36); they express simple quantification. However, a problem with this approach is that frequency statements, like generics but unlike the sentences in (36), are lawlike. For example, the truth of (37), just like the generic (3j), requires more than simply that the current Supreme Court judges have a prime Social Security number.

(37)   Supreme Court judges always have a prime Social Security number.

Moreover, frequency statement, just like generics, support counterfactuals. The truth of (35b), for example, entails the counterfactual

(38)   If Simba were a tiger, he would have stripes.

An alternative is to treat frequency statements as just another kind of generic. As Carlson (1995) points out, this is problematic for the rules and regulations approach. While we may expect that there is a (genetic) rule making ravens black, it is hard to accept a rule that states that *most* of them are; while there may be a rule of Mary's behavior that makes her jog in the park, it is hard to imagine a rule that says, in effect: "Mary, jog in the park sometimes!"

Not all versions of the inductivist view fare better. As we have seen, some of them, being extensional, fail to account for the lawlike nature of generics, and hence cannot account for the lawlikeness of frequency adverbs either.

The normality approach, if applied to generics, faces a different problem. If frequency adverbs, just like generics, quantify over normal individuals only, (39) would be (wrongly) predicted false, since, by hypothesis, all normal ravens are black.

(39)   Ravens are sometimes white.

Other inductivist approaches, which take generics to express some quantification over possible individuals, appear to have better prospects for a uniform account of generics and frequency adverbs. The generic quantifier can be taken to be just another frequency adverb, with the semantics of *generally, usually,* or something of the sort.

The situation is more complicated, however. There is a difference between generics and frequency adverbs that needs to be commented upon. Sentences (3g) and (3h), although bad as generics, become perfectly fine (and true) if the frequency adverb *generally* (or *usually* and the like) is inserted:

(40)   a. Primary school teachers are generally female.
         b. People are generally over three years old.

Therefore, the interpretation of generics, though similar to that of some adverbs of quantification, cannot be identical to it.

Cohen (1999) proposes that generics presuppose their domain to be homogeneous, in the following sense. The generic (34) requires that the property ϕ hold not only for ψs, but over every psychologically salient subset of ψ. For example, assuming that it is salient to partition the domain of teachers according to sex, (3g) requires that both male and female teachers be female – a requirement that is clearly violated. Similarly, assuming that a partition of people according to age is salient, (3h) requires that people of all ages be over three years old, hence it is not true.

In contrast, frequency adverbs do not require homogeneity. Sentence (40a) only requires that the property of being female hold of the domain of teachers as a whole, which it does, since the vast majority of primary school teachers *are* female. Similarly, (40b) requires merely that the property of being over three years old hold, in general, of people as a whole, which it does.

5 Manifestations of generics

No known language contains a specific construction which is exclusively devoted to the expression of genericity (Dahl 1995). Yet there is no language that does not express genericity in some form or another. It follows that expressions used for generics have a double nature: they have generic as well as nongeneric uses. Of particular interest are the forms of noun phrases that may be given generic interpretation. In English, generic noun phrases may be bare plurals, definite singulars or indefinite singulars (and in some marked cases, definite plurals). It turns out that there are differences in the generic interpretations of these constructions; let us look at each one of them in turn.

5.1 Bare plurals

The most common way to express a generic sentence in English is with a bare plural, i.e. a plural noun preceded by no determiner. It is well known that bare plurals may receive not only a generic reading, but an existential one as well. Thus, while (41a) makes a generalization about plumbers in general, (41b) states that there are some plumbers who are available.

(41) a. Plumbers are intelligent.
      b. Plumbers are available.

There has been much research on the conditions that determine when a bare plural is interpreted generically, and when existentially (Carlson 1977, Diesing 1992, Chierchia 1995, Kratzer 1995, Dobrovie-Sorin and Laca 1996, Cohen and Erteschik-Shir 1997, de Smet 1997, Kiss 1998, McNally 1998, Jäger 1999, among others). In this section we will concentrate on the generic interpretation only.

What is the denotation of a generically interpreted bare plural? There are cases where the answer appears to be simple. Consider this typical example:

(42) Dinosaurs are extinct.

There is no individual dinosaur that is extinct; individual dinosaurs are just not the sort of thing that can be extinct – only the kind *dinosaur* can have this property. A natural account for (42) is that it predicates the property of being extinct directly of the kind *dinosaur.* It follows, then, that the bare plural *dinosaurs* denotes this kind in (42).

Krifka *et al.* (1995) refer to such sentences, which predicate a property directly of a kind, as cases of *direct kind predication.* They distinguish between them and sentences such as (1a), which predicate a property of instances of a kind, and not of the kind as a whole; these are named *characterizing generics.*

One test for cases of direct kind predication is to verify that it is impossible to modify the sentence by an overt adverb of quantification. For example, (43) is bad, confirming that (42) is a case of direct kind predication:

(43) *Dinosaurs are $\left\{ \begin{array}{l} \text{always} \\ \text{usually} \\ \text{sometimes} \\ \text{never} \end{array} \right\}$ extinct.

On the other hand, (44) is fine, indicating that (1a) is, indeed, a characterizing generic.

(44) Ravens are $\left\{ \begin{array}{l} \text{always} \\ \text{usually} \\ \text{sometimes} \\ \text{never} \end{array} \right\}$ black.

Another test involves scope: characterizing generics, but not direct kind predication, display scope ambiguities. For example, the characterizing generic (45a) may mean either that each stork has a (possibly different) favorite nesting area, or that there is one nesting area favored by storks. In contrast, (45b) can only mean that there is one predator endangering the species.

(45)   a. Storks have a favorite nesting area (Schubert and Pelletier 1987).
        b. Storks are in danger of being exterminated by a predator.

What is the denotation of a bare plural in a characterizing generic? Some researchers (e.g. Wilkinson 1991, Diesing 1992, Kratzer 1995) claim that bare plurals are ambiguous: they may denote kinds, in which case we get direct kind predication, or they may be interpreted as indefinites, i.e. as variables ready to be bound by the generic quantifier, resulting in characterizing generics.

There are, however, reasons to believe that generic bare plurals uniformly refer to kinds, in characterizing generics as well as in cases of direct kind predication. Consider the case of a bare plural that serves as the subject of two clauses: one a characterizing generic and one expressing direct kind predication:

(46)   a. Dodos lived in Mauritius and (they) became extinct in the 18th century
           (after Heyer 1990).
        b. Elephants are killed for their tusks and are therefore an endangered
           species.
        c. Dinosaurs, which are now extinct, were very large.

The most straightforward explanation for the phenomena exemplified by the sentences in (46) is that a generic bare plural unambiguously refers to kinds.

Moreover, Carlson (1977, 1982) points out that generic bare plurals behave in a way that is similar to referring expressions, rather than indefinites or quantifiers. His arguments apply equally well to characterizing generics and direct kind predication. For example, he notes that if the antecedent of a pronoun is a name, it can replace the pronoun without a change in meaning; not so, in general, when the antecedent is an indefinite. Generics seem to behave like names, rather than indefinites, in this regard:

(47)   a. Fred walked into the room. *He* smiled (= *Fred* smiled).
        b. A man walked into the room. *He* smiled (≠ A *man* smiled).
        c. Dogs are intelligent mammals. *They* are also man's best friend
           (= *Dogs* are man's best friend).

An additional observation, ascribed by Carlson to Postal (1969), is that names and generics, and only names and generics, can participate in *so-called* constructions:

(48)   a. Giorgione is so-called because of his size.
        b. Machine guns are so-called because they fire automatically.
        c. *A machine gun is so-called because it fires automatically.

Krifka *et al.* (1995) agree that bare plurals refer to kinds in characterizing generics too, but restrict this only to "well-established kinds." We will discuss this issue further in the next section.

If bare plurals in characterizing generics denote kinds, a natural question arises: how is a characterizing generic obtained from a kind-denoting bare plural? In order to answer this question, Carlson (1977) proposes a *realization* relation between an instance and a kind. Thus, for example, $R(x, \textbf{dog})$ indicates that x is an instance of the kind dog, i.e. x is a dog.

Ter Meulen (1995) proposes a type-shifting operator, which transforms a kind into the property of being an instance of the kind. The application of this type-shifting operator is optional. When it is applied, the result is a characterizing generic; when it is not – direct kind predication. Thus every generic sentence is ambiguous between characterizing and kind interpretations; but one of these readings is ruled out as semantically anomalous. For example, (1a) has a reading where the property of being black is predicated directly of the kind *raven*. But this reading is ruled out, because a kind is not the sort of thing that can have a color. Similarly, (42) has a reading where individual dinosaurs are extinct. This time, the characterizing interpretation will be ruled out, since individual dinosaurs cannot be extinct.

When interpreted generically, bare plurals may receive collective readings, e.g. they may be the arguments of predicates such as the intransitive *meet* and *gather*. Consider the following example (attributed by Krifka *et al.* to Gerstner 1979):

(49)   Lions gather near acacia trees when they are tired.

To account for this fact, Krifka *et al.* (1995) propose that groups of individuals are also individuals in their own right (see e.g. Link 1983, Ojeda 1993), and that, therefore, they can be instances of a kind just like single individuals can. Thus, (49) predicates the property of gathering on groups of lions, rather than individual lions. If sufficiently many such groups gather, (49) is true.

There is reason to believe, however, that groups of individuals are not always considered individuals. Consider generics with a distributive property, e.g.

(50)   Lions have a bushy tail.

According to Krifka *et* al. (1995), (50) is true just in case sufficiently many groups of lions have a bushy tail. The problem is that when a distributive property such as *have a bushy tail* is applied to a group, it needs to hold of all members of a group. For example, (51) means that each one of the lions in the cage has a bushy tail.

(51)   The lions in the cage have a bushy tail.

Now suppose that only two of all lions lack a bushy tail. Given that the number of lions is fairly large, sentence (50) ought to be true. However, it can be easily seen that only a quarter of all possible groups of lions contain neither of the

"deficient" lions. If we grant that a quarter of all groups of lions is not sufficiently many, (50) would be predicted false.

Sentence (50), for example, would cease to be a problem if we assume that
groups are simply not allowed as instances in this case, but only simple individuals are. And, in general, when the predicated property is distributive, group
instances are not considered in evaluating the truth of the generic sentence.

Mixed predicates, i.e. predicates that allow both distributive and collective
readings, pose a problem too. Consider the following example (from Krifka
1987):

(52)   The German customer bought 83,000 BMWs last year.

The most plausible interpretation of (52) is that the total number of BMWs
bought by Germans last year is 83,000; in other words, the number of BMWs
bought collectively by the group of all German customers is 83,000. No other
group of German customers bought 83,000 BMWs, yet it seems that only the
maximal group of German customers is relevant to the truth or falsity of (52).
Suppose the people living in the former West Germany bought 83,000 BMWs,
and the customers living in what used to be East Germany bought 83,000
BMWs too. In this case, there would be two groups of German customers, each
of which satisfies the predicate denoted by the VP, yet (52) would be false. It
seems, then, that not all possible individuals and groups of individuals should be
taken into account as instances of a kind. Moreover, what counts as an instance
of a kind may vary across sentences, and is probably affected by the context
(Cohen 1996).

5.2 Definite singulars

Just like bare plurals, definite singular generics may occur in cases of direct
kind predication as well as characterizing generics, as exemplified by the following:

(53)   a. The giant panda eats bamboo shoots.
         b. The giant panda is an endangered species.

Sentence (53a) is about individual pandas, whereas (53b) is about the kind *giant
panda* as a whole.

We therefore expect definite singulars to have collective readings, as the
following examples indicate:

(54)   a. The lion gathers near acacia trees when it is tired (Gerstner 1979,
            Krifka *et al.* 1995)
         b. The antelope gathers near water holes (Heyer 1990).

Are the sentences in (54) indeed acceptable, as the cited sources maintain?
Some informants agree, but others judge them to be marginal. This marginality,

however, may be due to other reasons, perhaps the number feature of the verb; intransitive *gather* is not normally used in the singular. When the collective verb is predicated of a conjunction of definite singular generics, so that the number of the verb is plural, the acceptability of the sentence improves markedly:

(55)   Two species of cats, the lion and the leopard, gather near acacia trees when they are tired.

A noncontrived, naturally occurring example is the following sentence, taken from the entry for *shark* in the American Academic Encyclopedia:

(56)   Some sharks, such as the tiger shark and the great white, are loners and seemingly swim at random, although they sometimes gather to feed.

We mentioned above that Krifka *et al.* (1995) claim that bare plurals may only refer to well established kinds. They reach this conclusion by comparing the distribution of generic definite singulars with that of bare plurals: they find that the distribution of the former is much more restricted. Compare the acceptability of (57a) with the oddness of (57b) (an example which Carlson 1977 ascribes to Barbara Partee).

(57)   a. The Coke bottle has a narrow neck.
       b. ?The green bottle has a narrow neck.

Krifka *et al.*'s account of this fact is as follows. Definite singulars must refer to a kind in order to be interpreted generically. The kind *Coke bottle* is well established in our culture, hence the reference succeeds and (57a) is interpreted generically. The kind *green bottle,* on the other hand, is not well established, hence the reference fails and (57b) cannot be interpreted generically (it is, of course, fine under the nongeneric reading). In contrast, both (58a) and (58b) are fine.

(58)   a. Coke bottles have narrow necks.
       b. Green bottles have narrow necks.

The acceptability of the sentences in (58) is explained by the claim that bare plurals do not always refer to kinds. The subject of (58a) denotes the kind *Coke bottle,* but the subject of (58b) does not refer to any kind – it is interpreted as a variable.

While the distribution of definite generics is, indeed, restricted, it is not clear that the facts about this distribution can be explained in terms of well established kinds. The acceptability of the definite generic seems to depend on a variety of factors (see Vendler 1971, Carlson 1977, Bolinger 1980, Dayal 1992, among others). For example, the definite generic is often more acceptable when the descriptive content of the common noun is richer. Contrast the oddness of (59a) (under the generic reading) with the acceptability of (59b).

(59)   a. ?The politician never misses a photo opportunity.
       b. The successful politician never misses a photo opportunity.

Yet one would be hard pressed to argue that *successful politician* is a well established kind, whereas *politician* is not.

There are additional, poorly understood factors affecting the productivity of the definite generic, which appear idiosyncratic and language dependent. Contrast (60a), which is fine, with (60b), which is odd (under the generic reading).

(60)   a. The tiger lives in the jungle.
       b. ?The dog barks.

Yet there is no reason to suppose that the kind *tiger* is better established than the kind *dog*. The distinction seems to be an idiosyncratic property of English; indeed, there are languages where the equivalent of (60b) is perfectly acceptable, e.g. German:

(61)   Der Hund bellt (Heyer 1990).

5.3 Indefinite singulars

Unlike bare plurals and definite singulars, indefinite singulars may not refer to kinds, as the unacceptability of the following examples indicate:

(62)   a. *A giant panda is an endangered species.
       b. *A dinosaur is extinct.

There is, in fact, a reading under which these sentences are acceptable, the *taxonomic* reading, according to which some subspecies of giant panda is endangered, or some species of dinosaurs is extinct. Under this reading, however, the subject is interpreted existentially, rather than generically, with the existential quantifier ranging over kinds. Therefore, this reading need not concern us here.

If indefinite singulars may not refer to kinds, we can predict that collective readings are impossible. This is, indeed, borne out:

(63)   *A lion gathers near acacia trees when it is tired.

The distribution of the indefinite singular is restricted compared with that of the bare plural, but in ways that are different from those of the definite singular. Consider the following pair (Lawler 1973):

(64)   a. A madrigal is polyphonic.
       b. *A madrigal is popular.

While (64a) receives a generic interpretation, (64b) cannot. In contrast, both (65a) and (65b) are fine.

(65)   a. Madrigals are polyphonic.
       b. Madrigals are popular.

Burton-Roberts (1977) provides a number of additional examples, among which are the following:

(66)   a. Kings are generous.
       b. *A king is generous.

(67)   a. Rooms are square.
       b. *A room is square.

(68)   a. Uncles are garrulous.
       b. *An uncle is garrulous.

Lawler (1973) claims that this difference between bare plural and indefinite singular generics is due to the fact that the latter are restricted to properties that are, in some sense, "necessary," "essential," "inherent," or "analytic." Thus, whereas polyphonicity is an essential property of madrigals, popularity is not, hence the unacceptability of (64b).

The problem with this approach is that it falls short of a complete explanation: why is it indefinite singulars, rather than bare plurals or definite singulars, that have this property? Moreover, it fails to account for sentences such as the following:

(69)   A madrigal is a popular song.

Although (69) seems to be saying exactly the same as (64b), it is perfectly acceptable.

Krifka et al. (1995) propose an account of this phenomenon, based on the fact that indefinite singulars may not refer to kinds. They suggest that all cases where the indefinite singular generic is disallowed are cases of direct kind predication. That is to say, just like (42) expresses a property directly of the kind dinosaur, and not of individual dinosaurs, (65b) expresses a property directly of the kind madrigal. Specifically, unlike (65a), the logical form of (65b) does not involve the generic quantifier. Since indefinite singulars cannot occur in cases of direct kind predication, (64b) is ruled out.

This approach amounts to disposing with the quantificational account of genericity except for a small number of cases such as (65a). It follows that characterizing generics are, in fact, the exception, rather than the rule.

However, it is not clear that the claim that (65b) is a case of direct kind predication can be maintained. If we apply the relevant tests, it appears that these are cases of characterizing generics rather than direct kind predication: the sentences in (70) are grammatical, and (71) exhibits a scope ambiguity.

(70)   a. Madrigals are always popular.
       b. Kings are usually generous.
       c. Rooms are sometimes square.
       d. Uncles are never garrulous.

(71)   Madrigals are popular with exactly one music fan.

Burton-Roberts (1977) proposes that indefinite singulars carry a normative force. He considers the following minimal pair:

(72)   a. Gentlemen open doors for Ladies.
        b. A gentleman opens doors for Ladies.

Burton-Roberts notes that (72b), but not (72a), expresses what he calls "moral necessity." Burton-Roberts observes that

If Emile does not as a rule open doors for ladies, his mother could utter (72b) and thereby successfully imply that Emile was not, or was not being, a gentleman. Notice that, if she were to utter... (72a) she might achieve the same effect (that of getting Emile to open doors for ladies) but would do so by different means... For (72a) merely makes a generalisation about gentlemen (p. 188).

Sentence (72b), then, unlike (72a), does not have a reading where it makes a generalization about gentlemen; it is, rather, a statement about some social norm. It is true just in case this norm is in effect, i.e. it is a member of a set of socially accepted rules and regulations.

    We have seen above (section 2.3) that Greenberg (1998) and Cohen (forthcoming) propose that generic bare plurals are ambiguous: they may express a characterizing generic, amenable to some sort of inductivist treatment, or they may express a rule, amenable to a treatment within the framework of the rules and regulations view. In contrast, indefinite singulars are not ambiguous: they only express rules. Thus, given the scenario with the supermarket described in section 2.3, only (73b) is true:

(73)   a. A banana sells for $.49/lb.
        b. A banana sells for $1.00/lb.

The rule may be a linguistic rule, i.e. a definition. Since polyphonicity forms a part of the definition of a madrigal, (64a) is fine. The acceptability of (69) stems from the fact that it has the classical *form* of a definition, even though it is not, in fact, the approved definition of a madrigal.

6 The use of generics

If generics are, indeed, so prevalent, a natural question arises: what are they good for? Why do we use them as often as we do? One possible answer is that generics are used to state default rules. Our beliefs about the world are almost never certain. In most cases, the conclusions we draw are plausible, but not guaranteed to be true. For example, when I turn the ignition key in my car, I expect it to start. I do not know for certain that it will; sometimes there is some malfunction, and the car fails to start. But it is a reasonable assumption that the car will start, an assumption I am ready to retract if I find out that this is not the case. It is not irrational to assume that the car will start although I do not have complete confidence in it; quite the reverse. The alternative would be to subject the car to a comprehensive inspection by a mechanic every time I am about to start it – clearly an impractical solution, and, in fact, an unnecessary one.

Rules of inference that allow us, for instance, to conclude that the car will start without actually establishing it conclusively, are usually referred to as *default rules*. The most important property that distinguishes them from classical logical rules of inference is that they are *nonmonotonic*: the conclusions may be retracted given additional information. For example, if I see that the car's battery has been stolen, I will no longer expect the car to start. Not so for classical logical rules: if we know that all men are mortal and that Socrates is a man, we conclude that Socrates is mortal, and no amount of additional information will invalidate this conclusion.

There is a sizeable body of research on nonmonotonic reasoning. See, for instance, Ginsberg (1987) for a classic collection of papers. Of particular relevance to our concern here is the fact that, when researchers discuss a default rule, they often characterize it, informally, in natural language; and they usually use a generic to do this. It is, therefore, an appealing idea that the use of generics is often to express default rules. We can say that one utters (1a) in order to express the following default rule: if we know that an individual is a raven, we should conclude, by default, that it is black.

We have seen above that Krifka (1987) proposes that the meaning of a generic is a default rule. But one need not be committed to the claim that the *meaning* is a default rule, to propose that the *use* is that of stating a default rule. What one does need to be committed to is that the meaning of generics supports the conclusions that follow from an appropriate system of default rules.

The problem is that there is little consensus on which inferences are sound and which ones are not. For example, ordinary (monotonic) entailment is transitive. If we believe that A entails B, and B entails C, we can conclude that A entails C. But what about nonmonotonic inference? Sometimes such a conclusion appears valid. Suppose we believe the following:

(74)   a. Tweety is a robin.
       b. Robins are birds.
       c. Birds fly.

We seem justified in concluding, on the basis of this, that Tweety flies.

But now suppose we believe the following:

(75)   a. Tweety is a penguin.
       b. Penguins are birds.
       c. Birds fly.

Are we justified in concluding that Tweety flies? Intuitively, the answer is no. This is because we also believe another rule:

(76)   Penguins don't fly.

Somehow, (76) ought to take precedence over (75c), and thus we should conclude that Tweety does not fly. In a sense, (76) is more specific than (75c), and it appears that this is the reason why it overrides it. There have been a number of

attempts to formalize this notion of specificity, and to give a semantics for generics that can support it (see, among others, Etherington and Reiter 1983,
Brewka 1991, Morreau 1992, Cohen 1997, Pelletier and Asher 1997).

Suppose we believe (77a) and (77b.). We are surely justified in concluding
(78) (Pearl 1988).

(77)   a. Red birds fly.
        b. Non-red birds fly.

(78)   Birds fly.

Any theory of the meaning of generics ought to be able to account for this trivial
inference.

But what about inference in the opposite direction? Can we conclude either
(77a) or (77b) from (78)? And, in general, can we conclude (79b) from (79a)?

(79)   a. ψs are ϕ.
        b. ψs that are χ are ϕ.

The general answer appears to be no. For example, we certainly do not conclude
(80) from (78).

(80)   Dead birds fly.

In order to account for this fact, Pearl (1988) proposes that we can conclude
(79b) from (79a) only if we have a rule stating

(81) ψs are χ.

For example, we can conclude (82b) from (78), because we also have the rule
(82a).

(82)   a. Birds lay eggs.
        b. Birds that lay eggs fly.

Thus (80) does not follow, because we do not have a rule saying

(83)   Birds are dead.

A problem with this requirement is that it appears to be too strong, blocking
desirable inferences. For example, the inference from (78) to (77a) is blocked,
whereas it appears that this is a conclusion worth having.

Pelletier and Asher (1997) go to the other extreme: they propose that concluding (79b) from (79a) is always licensed, unless we already have a rule stating

(84) ψs that are χ are not ϕ.

Thus, (80) does not follow, because we presumably have a rule stating

(85)   Dead birds don't fly.

In contrast with Pearl's approach, Pelletier and Asher's view appears too liberal, allowing inferences that appear not to be warranted. For example, we should not, intuitively, conclude either (86a) or (86b) from (78) – whether a sick bird flies or not depends an the type and severity of the disease.

(86)   a. Sick birds fly.
       b. Sick birds don't fly.

Yet, according to Pelletier and Asher, if we cannot conclude (86b), we should be able to conclude (86a).

An alternative approach is to allow the derivation of (79b) from (79a) only if the property ϕ is independent of the property χ. Thus, (77a) follows from (78), because the ability to fly is independent of one's color; but (86a) does not follow, because being able to fly is not independent of one's health. The problem with this approach is that it is not easy to specify an appropriate notion of independence; but see Shastri (1989), Bacchus (1990), Bacchus et al. (1993), Cohen (1997) for proposals.

Another question is how to treat exceptions to rules. In most work on default reasoning, being an exception to one rule does not affect the applicability of other rules. For example, suppose we have the following rules:

(87)   a. Mammals bear live young.
       b. Mammals have hair.

Suppose Pat is a platypus, so she violates (87a), by not bearing live young. Are we still justified in applying (87b) to conclude that she has hair? The answer appears to be yes.

There are cases, however, where this strategy leads to wrong conclusions. Suppose we have the following additional rule:

(88)   Mammals have an uterus.

Now it appears that we are not allowed to apply (88) and to conclude that Pat has an uterus.

Theories of generics that interpret them as expressions of quantification over normal individuals would block the conclusion that Pat has an uterus (see, in particular, Pelletier and Asher 1997). This is so because by failing to satisfy (87a), Pat has shown herself to be an abnormal mammal, and hence other rules should not apply to her either. The problem is that (87b) will not follow either. Pelletier and Asher propose to add such a conclusion as a special case, but a more general approach is probably desirable.

Theories that make use of the notion of independence, on the other hand, have better prospects of accounting for such cases. Rule (87b) is applicable, because the property of bearing live young is independent of the property of having hair. In contrast, bearing live young is not independent of the property of having an uterus, hence we are not justified in concluding that Pat has an uterus.

We have seen that the rules governing our default reasoning can be seen to hinge on a linguistic phenomenon – the meaning of generic sentences. While not necessarily subscribing to Barwise and Cooper's (1981) conclusion that "the traditional logical notions of validity and inference are a part of linguistics" (p. 203), we may safely conclude that when formalizing our common-sense intuitions, it is beneficial to look closely at the language we use to express them.

References

Asher, N. & Morreau, M. (1995): What some generic sentences mean. In: Carlson and Pelletier (1995) 300–338.

Bacchus, F. (1990): *Representing and Reasoning with Probabilistic Knowledge*. Cambridge, Massachusetts: MIT Press.

Bacchus, F., Grove, A. J., Halpern, J. Y. & Koller, D. (1993): Statistical foundations for default reasoning. In: *Proceedings of the International Joint Conference on Artificial Intelligence 1993 (IJCAI–93)* 563–569.

Bacon, J. (1974): Do generic descriptions denote? *Mind* 82. 331–347.

Bartsch, R. (1972): The semantics and syntax of number and numbers. In: *Syntax and Semantics*, ed. by J. Kimball volume 2 51–94. New York: Seminar Press.

Barwise, J. & Cooper, R. 1981. Generalized quantifiers and natural language. *Linguistics and Philosophy* 4. 159–219.

Barwise, J. & Perry, J. (1983): *Situations and Attitudes*. Cambridge, Massachusetts: MIT Press.

Barwise, J. & Seligman, J. (1992): The rights and wrongs of natural regularity. In: *Philosophical Perspectives*, ed. by J. Tomberlin.

Bennett, M. (1974): *Some Extensions of a Montague Fragment of English*. University of California at Los Angeles dissertation.

Bolinger, D. (1980): *Syntactic Diffusion and the Indefinite Article*. Bloomington: Indiana University Linguistics Club.

Brewka, G. (1991): Cumulative Default Logic: In defense of nonmonotonic inference rules. *Artificial Intelligence* 50. 183–205.

Burton-Roberts, N. (1977): Generic sentences and analyticity. *Studies in Language* 1. 155–196.

Carlier, A. (1989): Généricité du syntagme nominal sujet et modalités. *Travaux de Linguistique* 19. 33–56.

Carlson, G. (1977): *Reference to Kinds in English*. University of Massachusetts at Amherst dissertation. Also published 1980, New York: Garland.

(1982): Generic terms and generic sentences. *Journal of Philosophical Logic* 11. 145–181.

(1989): On the semantic composition of English generic sentences. In: Chierchia *et al.* (1989) 167–192.

(1995): Truth-conditions of generic sentences: two contrasting views. In: Carlson and Pelletier (1995) 224–237.

Carlson, G. & Pelletier, F. J. (eds.) (1995): *The Generic Book*. Chicago: University of Chicago Press.

Cavedon, L. & Glasbey, S. (1994): Outline of an information-flow model of generics. *Acta Linguistica Hungarica* 42.

Chierchia, G. (1992): Anaphora and dynamic binding. *Linguistics and Philosophy* 15. 111–183.

(1995): Individual-level predicates as inherent generics. In: Carlson and Pelletier (1995) 176–223.

Chierchia, G., Partee, B. H. & Turner, R. (eds.) (1989): *Properties, Types and Meaning*. Dordrecht: Kluwer.

Cohen, A. (1996): *Think Generic: The Meaning and Use of Generic Sentences*. Carnegie Mellon University dissertation. Also published 1999, Stanford: CSLI.

– (1997): Generics and default reasoning. *Computational Intelligence* 13. 506–533.

– (1999): Generics, frequency adverbs and probability. *Linguistics and Philosophy* 22. 221–253.

– (2000): Is there an unambiguous level of representation? In: *Interface Strategies*, ed. by M. Everaert, H. Bennis and E. Reuland. Amsterdam: Royal Netherlands Academy of Arts and Sciences.

– forthcoming. On the generic use of indefinite singulars. To appear in *Journal of Semantics*.

Cohen, A. & Erteschik-Shir, N. (1997): Topic, focus and the interpretation of bare plurals. In: *Proceedings of the 11th Amsterdam Colloquium*, ed. by P. Dekker, M. Stokhof & Y. Venema 31–36.

Dahl, O. (1975): On generics. In: *Formal Semantics of Natural Language*, ed. by E. L. Keenan 99–111. Cambridge: Cambridge University Press.

– (1995): The marking of the episodic/generic distinction in tense-aspect systems. In: Carlson and Pelletier (1995) 412–425.

Dayal, V. S. (1992): The singular-plural distinction in Hindi generics. In: *Proceedings of the Second Conference an Semantics and Linguistic Theory*, ed. by C. Barker & D. Dowty number 40 in Working Papers in Linguistics 39–57. Ohio State University.

Declerk, R. (1986): The manifold interpretations of generic sentences. *Lingua* 68. 149–188.

– 1991. The origins of genericity. *Linguistics 29*. 79–101.

Delgrande, J. P. (1987): A first-order conditional logic for prototypical properties. *Artificial Intelligence* 33. 105–130.

Diesing, M. (1992): *Indefinites*. Cambridge, Massachusetts: MIT Press.

Dobrovie-Sorin, C. & Laca, B. (1996): Generic bare NPs. Unpublished manuscript.

Etherington, D. W. & Reiter, R. (1983): On inheritance hierarchies with exceptions. In: *AAAI 83*.

Farkas, D. & Sugioka, Y. (1983): Restrictive if/when clauses. *Linguistics and Philosophy 6*. 225–258.

Gerstner, C. (1979): Über Generizität. Master's thesis. University of Munich.

Geurts, B. (1985): Generics. *Journal of Semantics 4*.

Ginsberg, M. L. (ed.) (1987): *Readings in Nonmonotonic Reasoning*. San Mateo, CA: Morgan Kaufmann.

Greenberg, Y. (1998): Temporally restricted generics. In: *Proceedings of SALT VIII*.

Grice, H. P. (1975): Logic and conversation. In: *Syntax and Semantics 3: Speech Acts*, ed. by P. Cole & J. L. Morgan. Academic Press.

Heyer, G. (1985): Generic descriptions, default reasoning, and typicality. *Theoretical Linguistics 12*. 33–72.

– (1990): Semantics and knowledge representation in the analysis of generic descriptions. *Journal of Semantics 7*. 93–110.

Jäger, G. (1999): Stage levels, states, and the semantics of the copula. In: *ZAS Papers in Linguistics* volume *191 65–94*. Zentrum für Allgemeine Sprachwissenschaft.

Kiss, K. É. (1998): On generic and existential bare plurals and the classification of predicates. In: Rothstein (1998) *145–162*.

Koningsveld, H. (1973): *Empirical Laws, Regularity and Necessity*. Wageningen, The Netherlands: H. Veenman & Zonen B.V.

Kratzer, A. (1981): The notional category of modality. In: *Words, Worlds, and Contexts: New Approaches to Word Semantics*, ed. by H. J. Eikmeyer and H. Rieser 38–74. Berlin: de Gruyter.

(1995): Stage-level and individual-level predicates. In: Carlson and Pelletier (1995) 125–175.

Krifka, M. (1987): An outline of genericity. Technical Report SNS-Bericht 87–25 Seminar für natürlich-sprachliche Systeme, Tübingen University Germany.

(1995): Focus and the interpretation of generic sentences. In: Carlson and Pelletier (1995) 238–264.

Krifka, M., Pelletier, J., Carlson, G., ter Meulen, A., Link, G. & Chierchia, G. (1995): Genericity: an introduction. In: Carlson and Pelletier (1995) 1–124.

Landman, F. (1989): Groups, II. *Linguistics and Philosophy* 12. 723–744.

Lawler, J. (1973): Studies in English generics. University of Michigan Papers in Linguistics 1:1.

Link, G. (1983): The logical analysis of plural and mass terms: A lattice-theoretical approach. In: *Meaning, Use and Interpretation of Language*, ed. by R. Bäuerle, C. Schwartze & A. von Stechow 302–323. Berlin: de Gruyter.

(1995): Generic information and dependent generics. In: Carlson and Pelletier (1995) 358–382.

McCarthy, J. (1986): Applications of circumscription to formalizing commonsense knowledge. *Artificial Intelligence* 28. 89–116.

McNally, L. (1998): Stativity and theticity. In: Rothstein (1998).

ter Meulen, A. (1986): Generic information, conditional contexts and constraints. In: *On Conditionals*, ed. by E. C. Traugott, A. ter Meulen, J. S. Reilly & C. A. Ferguson. Cambridge: Cambridge University Press.

(1995): Semantic constraints on type-shifting anaphora. In: Carlson and Pelletier (1995) 339–357.

Morreau, M. P. (1992): *Conditionals in Philosophy and Artificial Intelligence*. University of Amsterdam dissertation.

Nunberg, G. & Pan, C. (1975): Inferring quantification in generic sentences. In: *Papers from the Eleventh Regional Meeting of the Chicago Linguistic Society*.

Ojeda, A. (1993): *Linguistic Individuals*. Stanford: Center for the Study of Language and Information.

Parsons, T. (1970): An analysis of mass terms and amount terms. *Foundations of Language* 6. 363–388.

Partee, B. H. (1991): Topic, focus and quantification. In: *Proceedings of the First Conference on Semantics and Linguistic Theory*, ed. by S. Moore and A. Z. Wyner 159–187. Cornell University.

Pearl, J. (1988): *Probabilistic Reasoning in Intelligent Systems: Networks of Plausible Inference*. San Mateo: Morgan Kaufmann.

Pelletier, F. J. & Asher, N. 1997. Generics and defaults. In: *Handbook of Logic and Language*, ed. by J. van Benthem and A. ter Meulen 1125–1177. Amsterdam: Elsevier.

Postal, P. (1969): Anaphoric islands. In: *Papers from the Fifth Regional Meeting of the Chicago Linguistic Society* 205–239.

Quine, W. V. O. (1960): *Word and Object*. Cambridge, Massachusetts: MIT Press.

Reiter, R. (1987): Nonmonotonic reasoning. In: *Annual Review of Computer Science*, ed. by J. F. Traub, N. J. Nilsson & B. J. Grosz 147–186. Palo Alto: Annual Reviews Inc.

Rooth, M. E. (1985): *Association with Focus*. University of Massachusetts at Amherst dissertation.

Rothstein, S. (ed.) (1998): *Events and Grammar*. Dordrecht: Kluwer.

Schubert, L. K. & Pelletier, F. J. (1987): Problems in the representation of the logical form of generics, plurals, and mass nouns. In: *New Directions in Semantics*, ed. by E. LePore 385–451. London: Academic Press.

(1989): Generically speaking, or using discourse representation theory to interpret generics. In: Chierchia *et al.* (1989) 193–268.

Shastri, L. (1989): Default reasoning in semantic networks: a formalization of recognition and inheritance. *Artificial Intelligence* 39. 283–355.

de Smet, L. B. (1997): *On Mass and Plural Quantification*. University of Groningen dissertation.

Strzalkowski, T. (1988): A meaning representation for generic sentences. Technical Report 423 Courant Institute of Mathematical Sciences, New York University.

de Swart, H. (1991): *Adverbs of Quantification: A Generalized Quantifier Approach*. Groningen University dissertation. Also published 1993, New York: Garland.

-    (1996): (In)definites and genericity. In: *Quantifiers, Deduction and Context*, ed. by M. Kanazawa, C. Piñon & H. de Swart. Stanford: Center for the Study of Language and Information.

Vendler, Z. (1971): Singular terms. In: *Semantics: An Interdisciplinary Reader in Philosophy, Linguistics and Psychology*, ed. by D. D. Steinberg & L. A. Jakobovits. Cambridge: Cambridge University Press.

Wilkinson, K. (1991): *Studies in the Semantics of Generic Noun Phrases*. University of Massachusetts at Amherst dissertation.

Beer Sheva   Ariel Cohen

Department of Foreign Literatures and Linguistics, Ben Gurion University of the Negev, Israel, arikc@bgumail.bgu.ac.il

Event Semantics

Regine Eckardt

0 Introduction

The term "event semantics" seems to suggest that there is a special branch of semantics which deals with events. In fact, there should be no special kind of semantics for events, as little as there is a special branch of semantics for individuals. Any kind of formal semantics (of the kind the article is committed to) is based on models with individuals, and it is by now commonly accepted that the ontology's providing events goes without saying.

Nevertheless, it was less straightforward to adopt "events" in the ontological basis than it was for individuals. While one can't possibly think about semantics without reference to individuals, it was only through the study of some indicative phenomena that one got the conviction that some kind of spatio-temporal, "occurring" objects were needed. Among the issues in question, there are the representation of temporal and spatial modifiers, manner adverbs, nominalizations, the aspectual distinction between activity and accomplishment verbs, perception reports etc. Moreover, there is an interplay between our understanding of the nature of events, and our understanding of each of these topics.

Theories that use events are, for each of the phenomena listed above, part of a broader discussion which would be worth a survey in its own right. The present article can only provide selective bibliographic information in many cases. Apart from providing poor summaries of interesting topics, I have attempted to order the range of applications with respect to the notion of "event" which is used in the respective theories, starting with simple time intervals and ending up with the most fine-grained event notions. Certain ontological assumptions come along with each kind of application, hopefully growing into one coherent view of "events".

The paper is organized as follows: Section 1 repeats Davidson's classical argument in favour of the use of verbs with an event parameter. Section 2 will summarize those applications where events have mainly the function of time intervals. Section 3 will be devoted to the notion of events as spatio-temporal regions. Section 4 will cover those applications which rely on specific types of participance which can be defined for an event. The term "thematic roles" roughly describes the phenomenon in question. Section 5 will cover perception verbs, situated intervals and event negation. Section 6 finally treats questions of the syntax-semantics interface, where I will argue that sentences not only describe "small" events but also refer to certain macro objects which comprise more than one atomic event.

Linguistische Berichte Sonderheft 10 · © Helmut Buske Verlag 2002 · ISSN 0935-9249

The intermediate parts headed "Ontology I" to "Ontology III" summarize the formal requirements that restrict the domain of events, according to the applications discussed so far. An Appendix is devoted to those applications where the term "event" overlaps with what other authors might call "facts".

1 The polyadicity of verbs

The following observation by D. Davidson (Davidson 1967) provides one of the main points in favour of an event parameter of the verb: Verbs are usually taken to denote n-ary relations. The n arguments expected by the verb are introduced by noun phrases (or, occasionally, PPs) and identified by some kind of case marking. In addition, though, free modifiers can enter the sentence in many, if not infinitely many ways. This is illustrated in (1):

(1)   Alma buttered the toast *in the bathroom, at midnight, reluctantly, carefully, with a knife, for Sally, ...*

Do all these modifiers apply to further tacit parameters of the verb? Modifiers like "in the bathroom" or "at noon" can certainly be thought to specify a temporal or spatial argument of the verb. (This view will be elaborated in sections 2 and 3.) However, it is less clear what the nature of other parameters like the ones modified by "with a knife" or "carefully" should be. Apart from this conceptual vagueness, some of these parameters are optional. If we increased the arity of the verb according to the number of free modifiers that can be applied, we would have to conclude that each verb has several lexical representations of varying arity. Example (2) illustrates this point.

(2)   a. Alma put the letter into the fridge for Mary.
            Representation of "put": PUT(<agent>,<object>,<goal>,<beneficient>)
            ∃x,y(THE-LETTER=x & THE-FRIDGE=y &
            PUT(ALMA,x,y,MARY))

            b. Alma put the letter into the fridge. (She did it absent-mindedly, not for anyone else, not even for herself.)
            Representation of "put": PUT(<agent>,<object>,<goal>)
            ∃x,y(THE-LETTER=x & THE-FRIDGE=y & PUT(ALMA,x,y))

Without the representation in (2b) we would have to conclude that each time Alma put something somewhere, there also was someone who benefitted from this action. This is, however, not true.

It is not clear how such multiple ambiguities could be controlled (see Parsons 1990, McConnell-Ginet 1982 on this question). It is clear, though, that they will be inconvenient at least. Davidson suggested instead that all these modifiers apply to one and the same object, namely the *event* introduced by the verb. The event introduced by a verb can be related to a time or a place. It can happen in specific manners, and can optionally be related to instruments, beneficients, etc.

The event can also be referred to with anaphors and nominalizations. We will see how this project has been elaborated since, and what kinds of events have been developed in its course.

2 Events and time intervals

The simplest way to reconstruct events is this: Remember that verbs not only relate certain objects and individuals to one another, but that this relation moreover holds for a certain time. Verbs denote relations between objects and time intervals (see for instance Montague 1974, Taylor 1977). We can use this insight and simply call the respective intervals "events", and get a spellout of Davidson's suggestion which already will be useful for certain tasks.

2.1 Temporal modification

Modifications like "at noon", "on May 15th 1995", "from 2.00 to 4.00" exemplify a simple way in which an event can be further qualified. In order to analyse a sentence like (3), it is enough to know that the SLEEP relation holds between Alma and a time i and that i is a subset of, or equal to, the interval [2.00;4.00]. Sentence (4) will state that the marriage time j was during the day 15.5.1995.

(3)   Alma slept from 2.00 to 4.00.
       $\exists i$ (SLEEP(ALMA,i) & $i \subseteq$ [2.00;4.00])

(4)   Bertha and Clyde married on May 15th 1995.
       $\exists j$(MARRY(BERTHA$\oplus$CLYDE,j) & $j \subseteq$ 15.5.1995)

Eventually, i and j will refer to events with more than only temporal properties, but this is not yet necessary in order to explain (3) and (4).

Which are the intervals for which a sentence is true (the "overlapping intervals question")? Assume that i is an interval in time which starts while Alma is sleeping, but where she wakes up in the middle of i. Should SLEEP(ALMA,i) be true or false? If we perceive i as an event, the answer to this question is quite clear: There is a *subinterval* j of i for which SLEEP(ALMA,j) holds true. However, SLEEP(ALMA,i) is clearly false for the *overall* intervall i. (Remember that there is no event which is a sleeping of Alma and which has the running time i.) Generally, formulae like

   $R(x_1,...,x_n,e)$

will express that the relation R holds for participants x_1 to x_n for the overall time during which e goes on (see also the section ONTOLOGY III).

We have to relate this simple answer to the overlapping interval question to another observation which seems to indicate that the simple answer is wrong.

Imagine that Alma slept from 2.00 to 4.00 sharp. In this situation we would hesitate to accept the following dialogue as correct:

(5)   A: Did Alma sleep between 3.00 and 5.00? – B: No, she didn't.

B's answer is correct only if the question is uttered with a clear focus on "between 3.00 and 5.00". However, there also is a sense of A's question for which B's answer does not provide correct information. Should we conclude that the SLEEP relation still is true for Alma and the interval [3.00;5.00], in a certain sense? No, we should not. Examples like (5) indicate that more than one temporal object can be involved in an utterance. Sentences generally state the *existence* of certain events (or, events-as-intervals). The temporal dimension of these events (or, the events-as-intervals) are related to other *indexical* or *contextual* frames and reference points. If the question in (5) is interpreted as a question about the time frame [3.00;5.00], namely the question whether a sleeping of Alma took place somewhere during this time, then the answer should be "yes", because in fact there is a sleeping interval in this time. If the question is interpreted as a question about the nature of a sleeping event itself, namely the question if there was such an event with the property of "occuring from 3.00 to 5.00" then the correct answer is "no". It is important to keep reference times and times of occurrence apart. Tichy (1985) discusses some fatal consequences which arise if indefinite and indexical time parameters are falsely identified. We will shed more light on this distinction in the next section.

2.2 Reference time: past, present, future, and the progressive

The use of tenses in languages like German and English reflects the fact that no event may be left unrelated to the time of utterance, the "now". The past tense expresses that the event in its entirety took place before "now", while the future tense means that (ignoring modality) the event will take place in its entirety after "now". The simple present should then mean that an event is taking place. However, in order to express this fact, we have to use the progressive form[1]. This shows (after some reflection) that tenses not only involve the notions "before" and "after" but also a "peep hole" through which the event is perceived.

Reichenbach (1947) introduced the notion of reference time R, primarily in order to treat past perfect and future perfect. Today, a similar notion R is used by various authors in order to model progressivity. The existence of past perfect progressive demonstrates that Reichenbach's R and the reference point R of Hinrichs (1986), or topic time of Klein (1994) cannot be identified. Ignoring the past perfect for the moment, let me list some fruitful assumptions about the

---

[1] This is clearly visible in languages with a formal distinction of progressive and non-progressive form. Languages like German have verb forms which are ambiguous between simple and progressive aspect.

relation between reference time R and event e. (A more extended discussion of the interplay between states, events, and reference times can be found in Kamp & Reyle (1993), chapter 5.)

(T1)   There are (at least) three temporal objects involved in sentences: the event in question, the reference time R and the (indexical) time of utterance S. (Reichenbach 1947)

(T2)   Tense expresses a relation between S and R. Past tense states that R is before S.
        Present tense states that R is equal to S. Future tense expresses that S is before R. (Hinrichs 1986, Parsons 1990, Klein 1994)

(T3)   The time of utterance S is a point of time. (Klein 1994)

(T4)   Aspect expresses a relation between event time and R. The progressive expresses that R is within the running time of e. The simple tense expresses that e is inside R. (Hinrichs 1986, Klein 1994)

(T5)   The running time of an event always is an extended intervall, never just a point in time. (Parsons 1990, implicit in Hinrichs 1986)

(T1) to (T5) can be explored in various ways. (T2) and (T4) give an account for (the core cases of) uses of tense. (T3) and (T5) together explain why English sentences in the simple present normally do not express what German learners of English expect them to – i.e., why the progressive tense has to be used. Klein (1994) also sketches a distinction between R-modification and e-modification which explains example (5) above. Nevertheless, the reference parameter R may be felt to be too vague. As long as R can only be detected from the use of the progressive or the simple tense, and in turn does not explain anything but the use of these forms, the theory remains circular.

Hinrichs (1986) links the notion of reference time to another phenomenon. He develops a theory of the effects of simple past and past progressive *in narrative discourse*. Each sentence is evaluated relatively to the momentary point of reference R. Progressive tense and stative verbs mean that the event/state in question includes R. Eventive sentences in the simple tense mean that the event in question lies within R. (This corresponds to (T4) above.) Moreover, he enlarges the above list of assumptions by (T6):

(T6)   Eventive sentences have the effect to replace the old point of reference by a new one, which is after the previous point of reference. Stative and progressive sentences do not change R.

(T6) accounts for the observation that eventive sentences in narrative discourse are normally understood in the "...and then ... and then ... and then ..." mode. Hinrich's theory captures stories like the following:

(6)   Joe came in. He opened the fridge and took out a bottle of beer.
        (Sequence of events)

(7)   Joe came in. A woman was sitting in fron of the TV. She was blond.
        (Event, then overlapping states and events in progess)

Hinrichs suggest that process verbs ("run", "walk") pattern with stative and progressive sentences. However, if we count them among the eventive sentences, the theory can be extended to the present tense: According to Hinrichs, PAST means that R is before "now" (more precisely, that both the old and the new reference time in (T6) are before now) and Future means that R is after "now". If we claim that present tense means that R is equal to "now", and assume that "now" is a point of time, then we predict that no extended event can be introduced in the simple present tense, because a point is too short to contain an extended event. In contrast, progressive sentences and stative verbs (and therefore sentences like "John walks" in its habitual interpretation) are predicted to be acceptable in the present.

Sentences in the progressive do not only differ from simple sentences in their localization with respect to R. They can moreover refer to uncompleted events. This observation has been labelled the "progressive paradox" (Dowty 1979, Parsons 1990 among others). An illustrating example is given in (9):

(8)   Alma was running $\Rightarrow$ Alma ran

(9)   Theo was knitting a pullover $\not\Rightarrow$ Theo knit a pullover

The progressive sentence in (9) does not require completion of the pullover, which is expressed by the simple sentence in (9). The implication in (8) shows that events of running do not involve completion. Dowty (1979) treats this phenomenon without reference to events, using the notion of "intertia worlds": Theo is knitting a pullover in world w at time t iff there is a nearby "ideal" or "undisturbed" world w' like w up to t where t lies in an intervall I such that Theo knits a whole pullover in w' during I. Landman (1992) demonstrates that the notion of "undisturbedness" has to be formulated relatively to the event under debate. A world w' which is like w in all respects will also support all possible interrupting factors, like the interference of Theo's cat which destroyed the half-finished pullover. Thus, there are no "inertia worlds for w at t" but only "nearby worlds w' which contain continuation branches of an event e in w".

Landman's results suggest that although the *use* of the progressive tense only refers to temporal properties of the events in question, the *extension* of the progressive verb can only be formulated in terms of richer events. (World w' must be undisturbed for an event e, not only undisturbed for an interval I.) A different view on this problem is developed in Parsons (1990). Parsons rejects a modal treatment of the progressive puzzle. He argues that it is part of the speaker's competence to be able to identify parts of events of, say, Theo knitting a pullover - in the same way as s/he can identify whole knittings. Likewise one would know a part of an elephant (e.g. the tail) without making reference to counterfactual whole elephants. Parsons' view will be compatible with a temporal notion of events.

2.3 A–/Telicity: intervals in relation to plural objects

Surprisingly, there is one theory which makes use of events most explicitly but can nevertheless be reformulated in terms of time intervals: Krifka's (1989) theory of temporal modification of telic and atelic predicates. I will first outline the original aproach and afterwards give a purely temporal reformulation.

Krifka's starting point is the observation that examples (10) and (11) might be used to describe the same scene in the world, but nevertheless differ with respect to temporal modification. While (10) is compatible with an "in"-adverbial but not with a "for"-adverbial, (11) behaves the other way round. Sentence (10) is therefore called "telic", sentence (11) "atelic".

(10)   Alma drank two glasses of wine in an hour/ *for an hour.

(11)   Alma drank wine *in an hour / for an hour.

The respective aspectual tests originate from Vendler (Vendler 1967, 1969) although Vendler doesn't make clear statements whether he wants to characterize verbs, sentences or events.

Krifka suggests that the sentences "Alma drink- two glasses of wine" and "Alma drink- wine" denote sets of events A and B with different properties. The terms "telic" and "atelic" in fact characterize the sets A and B. Let us assume that events can have smaller events as parts (written as $e'<e$) and can be added up to yield bigger events (written as $e^*=e\oplus e'$). Intuitively, these operations are natural generalizations of set union and the subset relation on the domain of sets of times. Thus, they are in the spirit of the present section, although they will have to be studied in more detail.

The following properties of sets of events P are defined in the spirit of Krifka (1989: 194 ff.) and capture his essential intuitions. The optimal spellout of properties like SUM, QUA, etc. is still a matter of debate (see Krifka 1989, Krifka 1995, Eberle 1998, Egg 1993 and also section 2.3.1).

(12)   A set of events P is called
         summative: $SUM(P) \leftrightarrow \forall e \forall e'(P(e) \,\&\, P(e') \rightarrow P(e\oplus e'))$
         divisive: $DIV(P) \leftrightarrow \forall e \forall e'(P(e) \,\&\, e'<e \rightarrow P(e'))$
         quantized: $QUA(P) \leftrightarrow \forall e \forall e'(P(e) \,\&\, e'<e \rightarrow \neg P(e'))$

The combinatorial restrictions for "in"-PPs and "for"-PPs are then characterized as follows: A sentence S can be combined with an "in"-PP if it denotes a set of events which is quantized. A sentence S can be combined with a "for"-PP if it denotes a set of events which is divisive and summative (= homogeneous in Krifka's terms). These restrictions receive conceptual content on the basis of a theory of measure functions (see Krifka 1989, 1989a). Let us look at an example. Sentence (10) will denote the following set of events:

(13) $\lambda e(\exists x(WINE(x) \,\&\, SIZE(x,GLASSES) = 2 \,\&\, DRINK(A,x,e))$

If e is an event of this type, then it will have many parts where Alma drinks parts of the overall two glasses of wine: the first glass, the second glass, etc. These smaller events will not be in set (13), though, because the quantity consumed does not fit the description $SIZE(x,GLASSES)=2$ ("x is two glasses much"). Therefore set (13) is quantized. Sentence (11) on the other hand denotes the following set of events:

(14) $\lambda e(\exists x(\ WINE(x)\ \&\ DRINK(A,x,e)\ )$

All parts of an event of Alma drinking wine will again be events where Alma drinks wine. Therefore set (14) is divisive. If Alma drinks wine in e, and she drinks more wine in e', then she will drink wine in the sum $e \oplus e'$, which shows that set (14) is summative. Thus, (11) refers to a homogeneous set of events.

It is important to note which factors influence the properties of the set denoted by the overall sentence. Clearly, the referential properties of argument NPs have an impact. The verb itself determines how the objects refered to in the sentence are related to objects which participate in subevents and superevents. While "drink" states that Alma consumes the liquid incrementially, a verb like "push" behaves differently. The set

(15) $\lambda e(\exists x(\ CART(x)\ \&\ PUSH(A,x,e)\ )$

is homogeneous, because sub- and sum-events of an event of Alma pushing a cart are also events where Alma pushes a cart. Thus, sentence (16) is predicted to be atelic, which is correct.

(16)   Alma pushed a cart (for ten minutes/*in ten minutes)

I will use the term "incremental object of verb α" to refer to participants like the liquid consumed in a drinking, and the term "thematic object of verb α" for participants like the cart in a pushing. Note that these notions are not confined to grammatical objects. The subject "Alma" is a thematic object both of "push" and "drink", and parameters like "the distance covered" can be incremental objects of verbs like "run":

(17)   Bertha ran (for ten minutes/*in ten minutes)
             Bertha ran a mile (*for ten minutes/ in ten minutes)

Thus, the verb contributes the type of events involved. Other parts of the sentence can further narrow down the event descriptions. The overall sentence will finally be characterized as telic or atelic.

2.3.1 An interval-based reconstruction of Krifka's theory

Although Krifka's theory is developed in terms of events, we find examples which show that it is the temporal constitution of the sentence which counts. Look at the following sentence:

(18)   Bertha (simultaneously) pushed two carts (for ten minutes/ *in ten minutes).

Later sections will show that an event of Bertha pushing two carts has subevents of Bertha pushing only one cart. Thus, the set of events denoted by (18) is not divisive in the sense of DIV. Nevertheless, (18) is atelic. Atelicity seems to rely on a more temporal kind of divisivity. It is enough that Bertha pushes two carts *during all the subintervals of the time of the overall pushing*, no matter if there are subevents where she pushes less than two carts. This observation can be turned into a full reformulation of Krifka's theory in terms of intervals.

Let us assume that the verbal predicate relates participants with sets of times I, I', ... during which the action in question takes place. Like Krifka, we make use of the following kind of observations about verbs:

(19)   "eat"-type verb: $EAT(x,y,I)$ & $I' \subset I \to \neg EAT(x,y,I')$
$\quad\quad EAT(x,y,I)$ & $I' \subseteq I \to \exists y'(y'<y$ & $EAT(x,y',I'))$
$\quad$ "run"-type verb: x runs distance d during I
$\quad\quad RUN(x,d,I)$ & $I' \subset I \to \neg RUN(x,d,I')$
$\quad\quad RUN(x,d,I)$ & $d'<d \to \exists I'(I' \subseteq I$ & $RUN(x,d',I'))$
$\quad$ "push"-type verb: $PUSH(x,y,I)$ & $I' \subseteq I \to PUSH(x,y,I')$
$\quad$ "grow-up" type verb: $GROW\text{-}UP(x,I)$ & $I' \subset I \to \neg GROW\text{-}UP(x,I')$

For technical reasons, we have to assume that all incremental parameters are obligatory parameters of the verb. This means that we also have to be explicit about the instantiation of these parameters if they are not introduced in the sentence. Sentence (20) will have to be represented as either (20a) or (20b) – where (20b) can only arise in certain contexts, like a report of a 500m race (for a more detailed account of the factors which drive the choice between existential and definite interpretations, see Sæbø 1996).

(20)   Alma ran.

    a. There is some distance d such that Alma ran d.
    b. Alma ran the specific distance d (given in the context).

This leads us to the following three assumptions:

(21)   a. Incremental parameters are never conceptually optional.
        b. If left unmentioned, they are standardly bound existentially like in (20a). (This corresponds to Krifka's treatment.)
        c. They may be instantiated with a fixed value given in the context, as in (20b).

In fact, these assumptions generalize the observation that even grammatical argument NPs can be optional. The interpretations of unmentioned parameters that were suggested in (21b) and (21c) are common practice for sentences like (22):

(22)   Bertha ate (something; **for** 30 minutes)/(some fixed portion of food; **in** 30 minutes)

Having explicated these assumptions, we can now translate Krifka's criteria into properties of sets of points of time I:

(23)   temporal divisivity: $TDIV(Q) \leftrightarrow \forall I \forall I'(Q(I) \,\&\, I' \subseteq I \rightarrow Q(I'))$
          temporal summativity: $TSUM(Q) \leftrightarrow \forall I \forall I'(Q(I) \,\&\, Q(I') \rightarrow Q(I \cup I'))$
          temporal quantizedness: $TQUA(Q) \leftrightarrow \forall I \forall I'(Q(I) \,\&\, I' \subset I \rightarrow \neg Q(I'))$

The combination restrictions for "in"- and "for"-adverbials are the following:

(24)   S + "in"-PP $\Leftrightarrow$ S denotes Q and $TQUA(Q)$.

(25)   S + "for"-PP $\Leftrightarrow$ S denotes Q and $(TDIV(Q) \,\&\, TSUM(Q))$[2]

Observe that the initial example of this section, sentence (18), can be correctly treated on the basis of TDIV. This is comforting because example (18) was a first hint that temporal constitution was the relevant feature to characterize telicity and atelicity.

In view of the overall perspective of the article, it is interesting to relate this purely temporal characterization of telicity and atelicity to the event-based verb representation format which is aimed at in the end. (We eventually want to be able to analyse sentences like "Clara played the piano with a stick for two hours".) Let us assume that a sentence S leads to a set of events P. This set of events can be used to compute a corresponding set of sets of times $I(P)$ by the following definition:

$$I(P) := \{I \mid \text{there is an } e \text{ in } P \text{ such that e happens during } I \}[3]$$

By applying (23) to (25) to $I(P)$, we can combine a purely temporal theory of telicity and atelicity with an event-based representation of natural language.

2.4 Summary

Section 2 was devoted to localizing the role of events in temporal modifications. It was sufficient to perceive events as intervals in time. It is important, though, to make clear that these intervals in time have a different status in the interpretation of the sentence than indexical temporal parameters like reference points or frame intervals.

A review of Krifka's event-based theory of the telic/atelic distinction has shown that also these phenomena rely on the temporal constitution of events alone. It was Krifka's insight, though, that we can make use of subtle facts about

---

[2] There is some debate whether TSUM or TDIV alone suffice. Krifka favours SUM alone in later papers, because DIV requires him to be explicit about minimal parts of events. However, SUM requires to claim that there is a radical conceptual difference between "Clara ran twice" and "Clara read *Middlemarch* twice": while the former still must denote an event of Clara running, the latter may not describe an event of Clara reading *Middlemarch*.

[3] This definition will be part of a formal theory of events after the section ONTOLOGY II.

the way in which simple and group objects are involved while an event is going on.

The ontology of events inherits its mereological structure mainly from its temporal ancestors. The idea of an event having parts, and of events being summed up to get bigger events, generalizes set union and subset relations on sets of points of time. A first intermezzo on ontology will contain an axiomatic treatment of the underlying mereology.

ONTOLOGY I

The ontological sections will be devoted to describe logical languages L_E for models with events, to give axioms that restrict the use of these languages and to define further properties which are of use.

We assume that languages L_E are based on a two-sorted domain of entities, event entities and other individuals. I will use variables e, e', ... ranging over events and x, x', y, ... ranging over other individuals. L_E contains the following relations and operations:

$\leq$ (read: "part of")	– a binary relation symbol on events
$<$ (read: "nontrivial part of")	– a binary relation on events
o (read: "overlap")	– a binary relation on events
$\oplus$ (read: "sum")	– a binary operation on events

The following axioms guide the interpretation of $\leq$ and $\oplus$ (see Krifka 1989, Egg 1994):

(A1) $\forall e(\ e\oplus e = e\ )$ (idempotency)

(A2) $\forall e\forall e'\exists e''(\ e\oplus e' = e''\ )$ (totality of $\oplus$)

(A3) $\forall e\forall e'(\ e\oplus e' = e'\oplus e\ )$ (commutativity)

(A4) $\forall e\forall e'\forall e''(\ e\oplus(e'\oplus e'') = (e\oplus e')\oplus e''\ )$ (associativity)

(A5) $\forall e\forall e'(\ e\oplus e'=e' \leftrightarrow e\leq e'\ )$ (definition of $\leq$)

(A6) $\neg\exists e\forall e'(\ e\leq e'\ )$ (no bottom element)

(A7) $\forall e\forall e'(\ e\leq e'\ \&\ e\neq e' \leftrightarrow e<e'\ )$ (definition of $<$)

(A8) $\forall e\forall e'(\ e\ o\ e' \leftrightarrow \exists e''(\ e''\leq e\ \&\ e''\leq e'\ )$ (overlap)

(A9) $\forall e\forall e'\forall e''(\ e o(e'\oplus e'') \rightarrow e\ o\ e' \vee e\ o\ e''\ )$ (distributivity of o)

(A10) $\forall e\forall e'(\ e<e' \rightarrow \exists e''(\ \neg\ e''oe\ \&\ e''\oplus e = e'\ \&$
            $\forall e*(\ \neg e*\ o\ e\ \&\ e*\oplus e = e' \rightarrow e* = e''\ )))$
                (unique relative complements)

Requirements (A1) to (A10) ensure that the domain of events will be a boolean algebra without zero element (see Krifka 1989). The idea that events have parts and can be added up is of importance for temporal and other collective predications of which a survey is given in Eckardt (1996). The connection between the plural ontology of individuals and the event mereology is studied in Lasersohn (1994), Landman (1989). It is open whether requirement (A2) is too strong. In analogy to set union, we would like $\oplus$ to be total for systematic reasons. Some authors, however, favour a notion of summation which is restricted to "sensible" sums (like similar events, or temporally adjacent events; see Asher 1994).

Incremental Parameters

Axioms (A1) to (A10) are abstract requirements which are meant to capture general intuitions with respect to event mereology. In contrast, it is an empirical observation that certain verbs denote relations between individuals and events where the part-whole structure on the domain of individuals corresponds to the one on events.

Incrementality (Neo-Davidsonian format):

Let P be a predicate on events which is denoted by a verb α (of English, German, ...). Let R be a thematic relation defined for α such that the following holds true (empirically):

> Summation:
> $\forall e \forall x \forall e' \forall x'(P(e) \& R(e,x) \& P(e') \& R(e',x') \rightarrow P(e\oplus e') \&$
> $R(e\oplus e',x\oplus x')$
>
> Nontrivial parts:
> $\forall e \forall x \forall e'(P(e) \& R(e,x) \& e'<e \rightarrow \exists x'(x'<x \& P(e') \& R(e',x'))$

Then the R-participants of α are called *incremental parameters of the verb α*.

For example, the patient participant of "eat" is an incremental parameter. The distance participant of "run" is an incremental parameter. The agent-participants of "eat" and "walk" are not incremental parameters. The theme participant of "push" is not an incremental parameter.

In order to elaborate the claims of section 2.3.1, I add the definition of incrementality in a classical format, where the event parameter could in principle be understood as a set of times.

Incrementality (classical format):

Let the verb α (of English, German, ...) denote the n-place relation $R(x_1,...,$ $x_{n-1},e)$ between objects and events. The participant x_i is called an incremental parameter of α iff

$$\forall x_1...x_{n-1}\forall e\forall y_1...y_{n-1}\forall e' \,[\, R(x_1,...,x_{n-1},e)\ \&\ R(y_1,...,y_{n-1},e) \rightarrow$$
$$\exists z_1,...,z_{i-1},z_{i+1},...,z_{n-1}(\, R(z_1,...,x_i\oplus y_i,...,z_{n-1},e\oplus e')\,)\,) \text{ (summation)}$$
$$\forall x_1...x_{n-1}\forall e\forall e' \,[\, R(x_1,...,x_{n-1},e)\ \&\ e'<e \rightarrow$$
$$\exists z_1,...,z_i,...,z_{n-1}(\, z_i<x_i\ \&\ R(z_1,...,z_i,...,z_{n-1},e')\,)\,) \text{ (nontrivial parts)}$$

In adopting the classical format, we assume that the relation R denoted by verb α relates at least all those parameters which would be incremental in the neo-Davidsonian sense. We have to do this for technical reasons, but the assumption has conceptual content. The underlying generalization is this:

Incremental parameters are never semantically optional.

Those incremental parameters which are not explicated in a sentence are usually bound existentially before any other semantic combinations take place. Optionally they can be instantiated with a fixed value given in the context or by convention – having effects on the telicity of the sentence. The following is an example of this process which is common in Swabian conversations.

(26)   a. Der Karle hôt baut. ("Karle built", tacitly understood: a house)
        b. Der Karle hôt en anderdhalb jôhr baut. ("Karle built in a year and a half")

3 Events as spatio-temporal objects

In the case of temporal modifications, it was sufficient to think of events as a kind of temporal parameter of the verb. Yet, Davidson's original idea was that events should form a multi-purpose parameter, and it is easy to see that sets of times are too simple for this purpose. In particular, two events might take place at exactly the same time but in different places. This is illustrated by the following example.

(27)   Alma sang the Bavarian anthem in Munich.
        (Exactly at the same time) Otto prepared dinner in Augsburg.

        a. SING(A, BH, e_1) & LOCATION(e_1)=MUNICH
        b. PREP-DINNER(O,e_2) & LOCATION(e_2) = AUGSBURG
        c. running time of e_1 = running time of e_2

If $e1$ and $e2$ were time intervals, they would be identical. This would allow us to derive, for example, that Alma was also singing in Augsburg - which is wrong. Events need a spatial dimension apart from the temporal dimension. Sentences like (27) suggest that events have (at least) the following shape:

(28)   An event is a function f which maps a set of points of time into space.
        The domain of f consists of the running time of the event.
        For each point of time t, $f(t)$ is the place (in the world) where the event happens at t.

The time intervals of section 2 can easily be derived from these functional objects f by taking the domain dom(f). Thus, we lose none of the applications of section 2. On the other hand, mapping these times into space will also provide various kinds of local information.

Events e_1 and e_2 in (27a) and (27b) will be distinguished because they map the same time interval onto different places. Moreover, by looking at the image of f we find that it is inside the region called "Munich" for e_1, and inside the region called "Augsburg" for e_2, and can thus derive simple truth conditions for modifiers like "in Munich".

Due to the fact that the spatial dimension is functionally dependent of the temporal dimension, we can even do more: We will get a notion of direction. This is useful in cases like (29).

(29)   Alma went from Rosenheim to Munich.

Prepositional phrases which specify the local source or the local goal of an event can be evaluated by looking at the value $f(t)$ for the earliest time point t in dom(f), and the value $f(t')$ for the latest t' in dom(f).

Section 2.2 was devoted to the fact that the temporal information conveyed by a sentence depends on various contextual and indexical reference times. The same complications arise more severely for spatial information. We have to expect viewpoints (in front of/behind, come/leave), deixis, directions versus locations, vague notions like "nearby", the influence of conceptualization of objects ("im Stadion" = in the stadium, "auf dem Fussballplatz" = "on" the soccer field) etc. For further investigations see Lang (1989), Egg (1994), Buschbeck (1994).

While a reconstruction of events via time and space poses few ontological problems, it is not sufficiently fine-grained even for matters of spatial modification. We could treat example (29), but sentence (30) indicates that matters are not so simple. (30) does not state that the overall event (including Alma) ended up in the oven, but only the cake.

(30)   Alma carried the cake into the oven.

Evidently, we have to specify the MOVED OBJECT (MO) for an event. It is the location of the MO at the end of the event which is decisive for directional PPs like "to Munich" or "into the oven". The status of being an MO however does not depend on space and time alone. Compare (31) and (32):

(31)   Alma went to Bertha's house with a cake in her hand.

(32)   Alma carried a cake into Bertha's house.

Both events occupy the same space and time – yet we know that the verb "go" specifies the subject as MO, but the verb "carry" specifys the object. This brings us to the next section where we will systematically explore modes of participance in an event as an identification criterion.

For a modal refinement of the reconstruction of events via time and space, see the appendix.

4 Beyond space and time: participance

Two events may take place at exactly the same time and - naively looking at things - even at the same place, but still be different things to happen. Sentences (31) and (32) provided an example; another classical case is (33)/(34) (see Davidson 1969 and Lewis 1986).

(33)   The sphere rotated (quickly).

(34)   The sphere heated up (slowly).

We can assume that the heating up took place at the same time as the rotation and both occupy the entire of the sphere. Still, one may happen quickly and the other slowly. Note that this is not due to the comparative character of "quickly"/ "slowly". If it was, then we'd expect that rotations generally are slower than heatings. This is not only not the case, it even is a senseless statement. The parameters which are decisive for the speed of a heating up are different from those which determine the speed of a rotation.

Generally speaking, we know that two sentences talk about different events if we can independently apply further adverbial or other modifications. This can be done directly in the respective sentences or via nominalizations and anaphors which pick up the respective events, as in (35) and (36):

(35)   Bertha sold her car to Alma.
         (– hastily; she did it hastily; the hasty selling ...)

(36)   Alma bought the car from Bertha
         (– reluctantly; she did it reluctantly; the reluctant buying ...)

Thus we can conclude that not only the respective verbs, but also the respective nominalizations refer to different events. More interestingly, the possibility to apply further modifications via anaphoric reference and nominalization proves that the relevant distinctions should not be made on a merely grammatical basis, but on the basis of different events. It will not be enough to claim that the adverbs "hastily" and "reluctantly" in (35) and (36) have access to the grammatical subjects of the respective sentences and are interpreted with reference to those. These grammatical subjects are no longer there in nominalizations and thus have to be recoverable in semantic terms – for instance as AGENTS of the events.

I will use the term "participance" in a way which slightly differs from the notion "thematic role", although I will sometimes uncarefully adopt role labels like AGENT in order to name a mode of participance. The notion of thematic role is associated with attempts to derive grammatical processes like case marking from semantic constellations, like "who is the most active participant involved". It is not clear, though, to what extent the aim of the theory ("characterize indirect object") leads to relations ("beneficient") which have grammatical content ("... can appear as an indirect object"). An involuntary illustration of this kind of circularity is exhibited in Parsons's sample version of a theory of thematical roles (Parsons 1990). Parsons formulates the case assignment rule:

"GOAL participants are realized as indirect objects, or with a 'to'-PP" (p.73f.), and afterwards sketchily characterizes the role GOAL as: "GOAL is the usual term for indirect objects that are paraphrasable with 'to'." (p.75).

A thorough discussion of the problems of this kind of theory is given in Dowty (1992), for a more optimistic view see Levin/Rappaport (1995).

A mode of participance, in contrast, is a relation between an event and an object/individual which is essential for the treatment of further *semantic* phenomena. The relation MOVED-OBJECT proved to be of this type, the relations THEMATIC PARAMETER and INCREMENTIAL PARAMETER had semantic impact, the relation AGENT will prove to have semantic impact for adverbial modification. TIME and SPACE of events are parameters with semantic consequence. None of these notions, though, will be committed to any grammatical regularities. Generally, we can formulate the following non-identiy rule for events:

Two sentences are talking about different events if one can find a mode of participance which relates different objects to either event.
- According to the definition of "mode of participance", this will be testable by giving one further modification (relying on that participant) which behaves differently for the two sentences, due to their *different participants*.
- It is not sufficient, though, to find a modification which only behaves differently for the two sentences due to *different norms* made salient by different verbs.[4]

Section 4.1 will list some examples of adverbial and other manner modifications. After a short section on nominalizations, section 4.3 will discuss the phenomenon of adverb orientation and the links between syntax and participance in some more detail.

---

[4] For example, a drinking may also be a sipping, although "drinking carefully" is something different from "sipping carefully". This, however, is not due to any difference in participants, but due to the different standards for "drinking normally" and "sipping normally". The same phenomenon arises in the wellknown "big mouse ≠ big animal" example.

Manner adverbs like "carefully" and "shyly" essentially require the use of event parameters in order to receive a semantic representation. This may be surprising. At first sight, one might be tempted to claim that carefulness was a property of an individual during the time of a certain action, that is, a temporal property of individuals. However, example (37) shows that manners are exhibited by individuals with respect to certain events. Clara can at exactly the same time show carefulness with respect to the listening and absentmindedness with respect to the ironing.

(37)   Clara carefully listened to the news and (at the same time) ironed her shirt absent-mindedly.

Manner adverbs of the same kind are also restricted to events which have a VOLITIONAL participant in a sense close to the traditional term "agent". The minimal pair (38a.)/(38b.) shows that the verb "slide" denotes events that can be done "carefully" by human subjects, but not by inanimate subjects. The pair (39a.)/(39.b) proves that "being human" is not the crucial feature necessary for the possibility of showing care. Even human subjects can only be careful if they *control* the event in question, that is, if some kind of agency holds.

(38)   a. Mary carefully slid down the chute.
       b. *The cushion carefully slid down the chute.

(39)   a. Mary carefully listened to the news.
       b. *Mary carefully heard the news. (manner reading)

We know from previous investigations of thematic roles that properties like *volitional control* are more specific than what is expressed by an intuitive circumscription. The adverb can't apply to just anybody who exerts volitional control over an event, in an intuitive sense. The VOLITIONAL participant is a distinguished participant of the event in question.

In the light of these observations, it is possible to treat manner adverbs as predicates of events alone. It is part of the meaning of the adverb to know that it is the distinguished VOLITIONAL participant who has to exhibit the relevant behaviour in the event.

(40)   CAREFUL(e) iff the VOLITIONAL participant of e exhibits careful behaviour with respect to e.

A final observation which confirms the close link between manners and events concerns the non-opacity of adverbs. Briefly speaking, manner adverbs can't be operators on event-free verbal predicates. Operating on extensions of verbal predicates will produce unwelcome logical implications, and operating on intensions of verbal predicates will predict opacity effects which are not there. For more discussion see Eckardt (1998), Wyner (1994). Other main references on manner adverbs are Cresswell (1986), McConnell-Ginet (1982), Bartsch (1976) and Thomason & Stalnaker (1973).

Clearly, all these observations only apply to adverbs in their manner reading ("it was careful **how** ..."). Adverbs in an evaluative reading ("it was careful **that** ...") need a finer individuation of arguments than a sensible event level can provide. Wyner (1994) develops an event-based treatment, which however comes close to the "fact" level discussed in the Appendix.

Manner adverbs explore the VOLITIONAL role. Another mode of participance is the one labelled MOVED-OBJECT in section 4. I repeat the crucial examples below.

(41)   Alma went into the ice house.
         ⇒ Alma was in the ice house after *e*.

(42)   Bertha carried the cake into the ice house.
         ⇒ The cake was in the ice house after *e*.

(43)   Leo half dem Rentner in den Bus.
         Leo helped the(dat) pensioner into the bus
         = Leo helped the pensioner to get into the bus.
         ⇒ The pensioner was in the bus afterwards

The directional PP in each case gives the position of the MOVED-OBJECT (MO) at the end of the event. (42) and (43) show that no overt argument position can be identified as MO, and (43) casts doubt on the claim that the underlying direct object (in the sense of a theory of ergativity) uniformly provides the MO.

Note that it is not sufficient for the existence of a MO that the event in question accidentially has a manifestation which is a movement. An event of standing, for instance, might happen to be a standing by me in the IC train from Cologne to Stuttgart. Thus, one might expect that I am a MO of this event. This is however not the case[5].

(44)   *Regine stood to Stuttgart.

The role MOVED OBJECT is event determined like other traditional roles.

One of the rare cases of pure object orientation is exhibited by the adverb "fatally", as in

(45)   Brutus wounded Caesar fatally.

The example is too isolated, though, to elucidate this particular mode of participance.

Another optional parameter of events which is accessible for further modifcation are resultative states, as in example (46). Again, it is not a matter of world

---

[5] E. Zimmermann pointed out that the German sentence "Regine stand bis (nach) Stuttgart" (= "Regine stood until (to) Stuttgart") is acceptable. This seems to be an indirect temporal specification of the duration of the standing. On the other hand, directional local PPs like "nach Stuttgart", "in den Hauptbahnhof", "aus der Stadt" are uniformely unacceptable.

knowledge to know what kind of state might accidentally follow an event of a certain type. The RES-STATE is a parameter of the event like the VOLITIONAL participant or the MO. This can be demonstrated by contrasting (46) with (47).

(46)   Emily came to Munich for two days.

(47)   *Emily arrived at Munich for two days.

World knowledge would suggest that both a coming and an arrival are followed by a state of Emily being at Munich. Nevertheless, (46) is acceptable while (47) isn't. This proves that RES-STATES are not derivable from simpler conditions by world knowledge, confirming the idea that RES-STATE is similar to relations like VOLITIONAL PARTICIPANT, MOVED OBJECT etc. The nature of re-sultative states is discussed in Klein (1994).

   A final example of an optional event parameter I want to give are tacit scales. Certain verbs, like for instance "cry", do not only state that someone performed something, but moreover have access to a scale which measures the degree to which the action in question was performed. This becomes visible if we notice that apart from doing something to a normal degree ("cry"), one can do it to a larger or lesser degree ("cry much", "sehr weinen"). Systematically, high degrees are expressed with the comparative "very much", German "sehr".

(48)   Leopold hat sehr geweint.
         Leopold was crying very much/very hard.

(49)   Cecilie ist sehr gewachsen.
         Cecilie has grown very much/a lot.

We can also compare the degrees to which various individuals act.

(50)   Leopold cried harder than Bertha did.

Clearly, (50) does not necessarily refer to the duration of the cryings. It can be interpreted exclusively with respect to intensity. Thus, certain verbs behave in a way which was up to now only known for adjectives. In the same way as "big" refers to a size scale, "cry" seems to refer to a scale of intensity of crying. The SCALE parameter is still unexplored.

4.2 Nominalizations

Nominalized verbs provide a means for explicit reference to events, quantifica-tion and anaphoric resumption. This is exemplified in (51) to (53).

(51)   Alma sang the Bavarian anthem.
         ⇒ Alma's singing of the Bavarian anthem

(52)   There were many kissings and huggings going on.

(53)   Bertha read a poem to Alice. The recitation was slow and expressive.

An exhaustive discussion of English nominalizations in an event-based framework can be found in Zucchi (1995). He also discusses the intricacies of event nominals versus fact nominals, a distinction in English first described by Vendler (Vendler 1967).

Zucchi's theory should be applied with care, as his event ontology, being based on the situation theory of Kratzer (1989), does not obey certain desirable restrictions on event domains. These restrictions will be discussed in the section ONTOLOGY III (see also Eckardt 1998). However, the account can be transported into a purely Davidsonian framework without losses.

4.3 The passive: more manners, more events

This section is devoted to the observation that the close link between manner adverbs and events will enrich the underlying ontology of events in an unexpected way, namely by events of volitional consent. I will discuss the phenomenon for the "lassen"-construction in German, which is paralleled by the "let"-construction in English. Consider (54) to (56).

(54)   Clara rasierte Albert zögernd/gründlich
         Clara shaved Albert reluctantly/carefully

(55)   Albert ließ sich zögernd/aufmerksam von Clara rasieren.
         Albert let himself reluctantly/carefully by Clara shave

(56)   Albert ließ sich von Clara zögernd/aufmerksam rasieren.
         Albert let himself by Clara reluctantly/carefully shave

While the active sentence (54) is unambiguous, the two "lassen" sentences are potentially ambiguous. The adverbs in (55) and (56) can either describe the attitude of Albert or Clara. For reasons of content, "reluctantly" (zögernd) has the tendency to be understood as refering to Albert, while "carefully" (aufmerksam) is preferably interpreted with respect to Clara. Both orientations are possible in either of (55) and (56).

These observations can easily be accounted for if we assume that "lassen" (let) introduces an event of its own with a VOLITIONAL participant of its own. "Lassen" states the existence of an event of volitional consent of the subject to the event described by the embedded sentence. (55) will be represented as in (57).

(57) $\exists e \exists e'$(SHAVE(C,A,e') & CONSENT(A,e,e') & VOLITIONAL(C,e) &
         VOLITIONAL(A,e) & ... ! ...)
         ! for reading (1): RELUCTANT(e)
         ! for reading (2): RELUCTANT(e')

The verb "lassen" thus not only explicates the (classical) thematic role "theme", held by Albert in the shaving. (This suggestion was made in Higginbotham

1994.) On the contrary, it has the function to introduce a further event, the consentive nodding of Albert, so to speak, where Albert has volitional control. It is this event which provides the basis for the second reading of the complex sentences (55) and (56). Note that it's essential to have two events. If "lassen" could simply ascribe VOLITIONAL CONSENT to Albert in the shaving, then we could not explain why this volitional consent – *de facto* being the case – can not also yield two readings in the active case (54).

The account given here has its origin in the work of Wyner (1994) who develops a similar theory for passive "be" in English, arguing extensively against mixed syntax/semantic driven accounts for orientation pairs like the well-known

(58)   The doctor reluctantly examined Rose. (= 1 reading only)

(59)   Rose was reluctantly examined by the doctor. (= 2 readings)

The precise spellout of Wyner's account unfortunately also has the consequence of doubling the entire verb lexicon. (Why this is the case is shown in Eckardt 1998.) The account for "lassen" sketched here and Wyner's account for the passive are similar enough, though, to count as one basic approach in two variants.

The important insight with respect to the ontology of events of this approach is that there are "light events" which have the function to carry semantically effective roles, like VOLITIONAL participance. As this line of investigation is fairly recent, it is still too early to see through all consequences of this observation.

ONTOLOGY II: mapping to time and space

We argued that a reconstruction of events as regions in space and time was not fine-grained enough. Nevertheless, events can be related to the time and the place where they occur. Let us assume that each model of L_E contains a set of sets of points of times T (which could look like the power set over the reals $\wp(\Re)$) and a set of sets of points in space S (which could look like the power set over the three dimensional euclidian space $\Re^3$). We further assume that set union and intersection are defined on both T and S.

Let now f_{man} be a function symbol in L_E which is interpreted as the manifestation function from events into functions from T to S:

(60) $f_{man} : E \rightarrow S^T$
        $f_{man}(e)$ = the function which, for each point of time t during which e occurs, maps t onto the set of points where e occurs at t.

Technically speaking, $f_{man}(e)$ is an element of the four-dimensional euclidian space $\Re^4$. Knowing the spatio-temporal manifestation of an event e, we can derive the running time $\tau(e)$:

(61)   Let τ be the function which maps each event onto its running time:
$\tau(e) := \text{dom}(f_{man}(e))$

Remember that the domain of events comes with a mereological structure, and that we argued in the part "Ontology I" that this mereological structure was inspired by the temporal ancestors of events. This insight now turns into the assumption that f_{man} is a homomorphism between the respective structures: $f_{man}(e \oplus f) = f_{man}(e) \cup f_{man}(f)$. The same follows for the function τ.

$f_{man} : (E, \leq, \oplus) \rightarrow (\wp(\Re^4), \subseteq, \cup)$ is a homomorphism.
$\tau : (E, \leq, \oplus) \rightarrow (\wp(\Re), \subseteq, \cup)$ is a homomorphism.

The time axis underlying the sets of points in time T is modeled by the real numbers. Thus, we have the natural linear order $\leq_t$ on the reals to model notions like "before" and "after". In order to simplify formulae, we can lift this linear order to the set of events E. Keep in mind that the relation $\leq_t$ "temporal precedence" is different from $\leq$ "part of".

Let A, B be subsets of $\Re$. We say that A is *before* B
$A \leq_t B$ iff $\forall a \in A, \forall b \in B \; a \leq_t b$.
We say that A and B *overlap in time*
$A \; o_t \; B$ iff $A \cap B \neq \emptyset$.

Let e, e' be events. We say that e is before e'
$e \leq_t e'$ iff $\tau(e) \leq_t \tau(e')$
We say that e and e' *overlap in time*
$e \; o_t \; e'$ iff $\tau(e) \; o_t \; \tau(e')$

Temporal and mereological overlap interact, although they are not identical, of course. The following observation holds true due to the fact that τ is a homomorphism:

$e \; o \; e' \rightarrow e \; o_t \; e'$

The converse implication is false. Two events can partly occur at the same time without being related as parts or wholes.

The resulting structure does justice to the fact that events are a generalization of regions in time and space. Nevertheless, the spatio-temporal manifestation is not enough to individuate an event. This would be the case iff the manifestation function f_{man} was injective.

5 Perception: events, situated intervals, and negation

It may be taken as a strong point in favour of the existence of events that they can be used to account for data which they originally were not designed for. The data in question are bare infinitive perception reports like the one in (62).

(62)   Alma saw Bertha eat a *petit four*.

What kind of objects stand in the SEE relation to a perceiver? Barwise (1982) demonstrates that an analysis relating propositions to perceivers will make wrong predictions, and argues that *situations* are what perceivers perceive. This idea has been developed into an alternative semantic framework since, situation semantics. – Higginbotham objects to Barwise's claim that a new type of entity is necessary in order to treat sentences like (62). Higginbotham (1983) proposes an event-based treatment of sentences like (62) where the embedded infinitive clause introduces an event which is perceived by the subject of the main clause. Sentence (62) will be represented as in (63):

(63) $\exists e \exists e' \exists x ($ PETIT-FOUR(x) & EAT(B,x,e) & SEE$(A,e,e'))$

Higginbotham demonstrates that this kind of treatment not only remains within classical logic, but also supports a large number of empirical observations with respect to bare infinitive perception reports. The reader is refered to the original article for an extended discussion of examples.

The essential difference between the situation approach and the event approach concerns the treatment of negated embedded clauses like the following:

(64)   Alma saw Bertha not eat a *petit four*.

(65)   Alma saw nobody eat a *petit four* for an hour.

The event-based approach can give one straightforward representation for sentence like (64), namely the one in (66a).

(66a) $\neg \exists e \exists e' \exists x ($ PETIT-FOUR(x) & EAT(B,x,e) & SEE$(A,e,e'))$

(66a) lacks *factivity*, though: Bertha may have eaten a *petit four* while Alma wasn't watching. If one thinks that reading (66a) should be complemented by a factive reading, then we can propose two ways to get a strictly factive interpretation. First, we can claim that there is some kind of *contextual exhaustiveness* involved. If we are told (64) and know that Alma *was* watching Bertha the whole time, we will derive that no hidden eating events can have taken place. The weak point of this solution is that central steps of the analysis take place beyond formal semantic theory, in the contextual black box.

Higginbotham allows for a factive reading of (64), but instead of alluding to contextual exhausiveness, he strengthens the negation in (64). He claims that under the factive reading, Bertha does something antonymous to eating the *petit four* - for instance, she might have visibly struggled against the temptation to eat a *petit four*. He assumes that the word "not" in (64) denotes an operator which maps "eat" onto the set of distinct "non-eating-events".

(66b) $\exists e \exists e' ($ NOT$(\exists x($PETIT-FOUR(x) & EAT$(B,x)))(e)$ & SEE$(A,e,e'))$

Sentence (65) will not be tractable with Higginbotham's antonymous negation. It does not mean that Alma saw something happen which is antonymous to "someone eating a *petit four*", and neither does it imply that Alma saw everybody do something which was a "non-*petit-four*-eating". Alma may not even have seen all of the potential eaters. Alma simply observed the location surrounding the *petit-fours* over an hour, and no eating took place there.

A situation approach will supply this kind of "location plus information about the things going on there". Situations are thought to be exactly this kind of thing. Note, however, that we can make use of the same kind of object in order to save (65) with *contextual exhaustiveness*. The location surrounding the petit-fours is exactly what Alma must be watching in order to make sure that the tacitly understood "... and if anyone had eaten a petit four, Alma would have noted it ..." holds true. Can we explore the same temporal-spatial location in an event-based theory?

Interestingly, we find another kind of example where "events where something does not happen" play a role and where moreover no antonymy is involved. Krifka (1989) discusses examples of temporal modification like the following:

(67)   Olga did not sleep for an hour/*in an hour.

Krifka assumes that negated sentences refer to maximal events – events which have everything that happened during their running time as a part:

(68) $MAX(e) \leftrightarrow \forall e'(\tau(e')<\tau(e) \rightarrow e'<e)$

An event E of Olga not sleeping is a maximal event which has no sleeping event of Olga as part. If this holds true for E, then parts of E do not contain any sleepings by Olga either, and the same is true for sums. Thus Krifka explains the atelicity of (67)[6].

Can we adopt these maximal events in order to treat sentence (65) under a factive reading in an event-based theory? We can, but we have to make certain refinements. Assume that (65) is represented as in (69):

(69) $\exists e''\exists E(MAX(E)$ & $\forall x(BODY(x) \rightarrow \neg\exists e\exists y(EAT(x,y,e)$ & PETIT-
         FOUR(y) & $e<E))$ & $|E|=1$hour & $SEE(ALMA,E,e''))$

If Alma can see E, she sensibly should also have seen the bigger parts of E, like Clara sitting in the garden, Emily drinking Vodka, and what else might have happened during this one hour period. It is clear that sentence (65) does not mean this. Alma need not have seen Clara and Emily at all in order for (65) to be true.

However, if we restrict Krifka's maximality condition to the "location surrounding the *petit fours* during the relevant hour", we will exactly get the correct object for Alma to see. We may indeed conclude that Alma had exhausive perception of the *petit-four* location. Barwise's claim that situations are involved in bare infinitive perception sentences has thus been confirmed. But, while Bar-

---

[6] It makes sense to assume that the MAX condition is part of the sentence meaning. The reader may want to check, then, that $\lambda e(MAX(e)$ & $\neg\exists e'(SLEEP(O,e')$ & $e'<e))$ is not DIV in Krifka's original sense, but its temporal projection is TDIV in the sense of definition (23), section 2.

wise's account uses the situation in question as an object of perception itself, and the contextual exhaustiveness account alludes to this situation in the formulation of what the perceiver has seen such that he should have seen what in fact did not take place – a purely event-based approach can use this object in order to restrict the events among which the maximal one is perceived. Barwise was right in claiming that a situation concept is involved in perception sentences, but Higginbotham was right in remarking that this in and of itself does not force one to leave the realm of classical logic altogether.

Observe that representation (69) is distinct from all previous sentence meanings insofar as an extra level of events is involved: We have an event description introduced by the infinitive clause, existential quantification over these atomic events, negation, and a higher event E which is described in terms of smaller events. Representation (69) indicates that we will have to investigate the binding processes that take care of the event parameter of the verb. These might still be more complicated than suggested in Parsons (1990). For reasons of convenience, Parsons assumes that the event parameter is standardly existentially bound before any other semantic combination processes take place. After a last ontological intermezzo, Section 6 will be devoted to questions having to do with the scope of event quantification..

ONTOLOGY III: conjunction and negation

To what extent do the properties of simple events determine the properties of their sum? The assumptions with respect to incremental parameters in Sections 2.3 and Ontology I were one case where we made explicit statements with respect to this question. Do we know anything more general? Let us look at an example: What does the event described with "Anton had a nap and washed the dishes" look like?

(70)   From 2 to 4 o'clock, Anton had a nap and washed the dishes.

If we understand the PP "from 2 o'clock to 4 o'clock" as a precise measure of the length of the event, then we do not want (71) or (72) to follow from (70):

(71)   From 2 to 4 o'clock, Anton had a nap.

(72)   From 2 to 4 o'clock, Anton washed the dishes.

Various authors suggest that *persistence* should be the guiding principle for the flow of information in event structures (Lasersohn 1992, Kratzer 1989, Zucchi 1995). This means that sentence (70) should be represented by formula (73), where we can see that both descriptions of simple events hold for the summed event introduced in (70). The spellout of persistence in this example is given in (74).

(73) $\exists e(\text{NAP}(\text{ANTON},e) \,\&\, \text{WASH}(\text{ANTON}, D, e) \,\&\, \tau(e) = [2.00;4.00])$

(74)   NAP(ANTON,e_1) & WASH(ANTON, D, e_2) $\Rightarrow$
         NAP(ANTON,$e_1 \oplus e_2$) & WASH(ANTON, D, $e_1 \oplus e_2$)

This approach, however, fails to do justice to the first and original purpose for which events were introduced, namely, to handle optional information. Imagine that Alma crossed the street with crutches and then went to Oklahoma with a Porsche. We will thus be talking about events e_1,e_2 and their sum $e_1 \oplus e_2$. The sum event will make both sentences, (78) and (79), true. However, in the real world only (78) holds true.

(75)   CROSS(ALMA,S,e_1) & $\exists x$(CRUTCHES(x) & INSTR(x,e_1))

(76)   GO(ALMA,e_2) & GOAL(e_2)=OKLAHOMA & $\exists y$(PORSCHE(y) &
         INSTR(y,e_2))

(77)   CROSS(ALMA,S,$e_1 \oplus e_2$) & $\exists x$(CRUTCHES(x) & INSTR($x,e_1 \oplus e_2$))
         & GO(ALMA,$e_1 \oplus e_2$) & GOAL($e_1 \oplus e_2$)=OKLAHOMA
         & $\exists y$(PORSCHE(y) & INSTR($y,e_1 \oplus e_2$))

(78)   Alma crossed the street with crutches and went to Oklahoma with a Porsche.

(79)   Alma crossed the street with a Porsche and went to Oklahoma with crutches.

As long as we assume that independent properties can hold for one and the same event, this kind of false prediction can't be avoided under the persistence approach (for an extended discussion see Eckardt 1998).

The solution lies in interpreting the word "and" as summation instead of Boolean conjunction. We define a summation operation on sets of events which is the lift of event summation.

(80)   Let L_E contain a binary operation symbol $\oplus$ between sets of events
         which is interpreted according to the following axiom:
         $\forall P \forall Q \forall e(P \oplus Q(e) \leftrightarrow \exists e_1 \exists e_2(P(e_1)$ & $Q(e_2)$ & $e=e_1 \oplus e_2))$

The set $P \oplus Q$ thus contains all those events which consist of a P-part and a Q-part (see Krifka 1991, Eckardt 1996). Sentence (70), for example, is refering to an event of the following shape:

(81) $e \in \lambda e(NAP(ANTON,e)) \oplus \lambda e(WASH(ANTON, D, e))$

Refraining from the use of the persistence principle, we moreover avoid a further possible difficulty, namely, the clash of negative and non-negative information. The sum of an event where P and an event where $\neg P$ will not have any contradictory properties. We will assume classical negation on the domain of events, as on the domain of individuals.[7]

---

[7] Note that the natural language word "not" may sometimes refer to antonymic negation in certain examples, like the ones we saw in Section 5. This is an independent assumption.

Note that events are not situations. Situation theory involves partial logic, persistence, and possibly non-cassical negation (see Kratzer 1989, Muskens 1991). Section 5 has shown how the concepts "event" and "situation" can be linked without collapsing them.

6 Binding the event parameter

I will not be concerned with overt event quantification here as it can be found in sentences with nominalizations.

(82)   All examinations took place in the library.

(83)   Many kissings and huggings were going on.

The combination of overt determiners and event refering nouns should sensibly work the same way as it does for nouns refering to individuals. Verbs, on the other hand, do not standardly combine with determinerlike objects. Thus, it is formally interesting to know what happens to a parameter which is introduced by the verb but never overtly quantified over. It is this process that Section 6 is about.

6.1 Indefinite existential binding

We have tacitly assumed up to now that "normal" sentences which are based on an eventive verb will eventually state that an event of the respective shape exists. We share this assumption with the vast mayority of the literature on events.[8] A sentence like (84) is thus represented as in (85) (ignoring tense).

(84)   Alma ate a sausage.

(85) $\exists x \exists e(\text{SAUSAGE}(x) \ \& \ \text{EAT}(A,x,e))$

Note that both e and the variable introduced by the indefinite NP get bound existentially. Recent theories about discourse semantics have shown that the status of indefinite NPs with respect to quantification differs from that of other quantifying NPs: Indefinite NPs introduce a variable which only afterwards gets bound by independent processes: existential closure or unselective binding through adverbial or nominal quantifiers (see Kamp 1981, Heim 1982, see also Kracht [this volume]). It turns out that the same kind of unselective binding can also apply to the event argument. Examples (86)/(87) are parallels to the well-known donkey sentences (Heim 1982, Kamp 1981) and example (88) shows a

---

[8] The only exception is the Kratzer framework (Kratzer 1989a, Diesing 1992). Unnoted by the author, Diesing's theory predicts that the event should be definite. It is argued in Eckardt (1997) that Diesing in fact has to use a situation argument in addition to the Davidsonian event.

case of unselective adverbial quantification in a focus construction, as described in Rooth (1995), Krifka (1991).

(86)   Whenever Alma climbs the Matterhorn, she does it carefully.
        $\forall e(\ \text{CLIMB}(\text{ALMA},\text{M},e) \rightarrow \text{CAREFUL}(e)\ )$

(87)   All tourists who climb the Matterhorn do it carefully.
        $\forall x \forall e(\ \text{TOURIST}(x)\ \&\ \text{CLIMB}(x,\text{M},e) \rightarrow \text{CAREFUL}(e)\ )$

(88)   Alma always climbs the Matterhorn *carefully*$_f$
        $\forall e(\ \text{CLIMB}(\text{ALMA},\text{M},e) \rightarrow \text{CAREFUL}(e)\ )$

This observation suggests that the event gets bound by the same process which takes care of indefinite noun phrases, and if this is to happen at a specific place, then it will be reasonable to assume that the event is bound at the same place. This is welcome as it spares us to postulate any silent non-visible event quantifiers at LF. Nevertheless it makes sense to investigate the potential scope of events.

6.2 The scope of events

I will look at three kinds of scope bearing operations and their scope relative to the event: Negation, quantificational NPs, and temporal PPs. Among these, we expect the following list of scope effects:

(S1)   If a temporal PP is to modify a parameter, then the parameter must still be free when the PP applies. Otherwise, it would not be accessible for the operator.

(S2)   We get clear scope relations between quantificational NPs and temporal PPs which can be diagnosed by simply looking at what the sentence means (see (104)/(105) below).

(S3)   We get a more unobtrusive kind of scope effect between PPs and NPs which arises with respect to the telicity/atelicity distinction. Remember that the influence of nominal arguments on *aktionsart* was investigated in section 2.3. Within the theory of Krifka (1989) of section 2.3 we could in principle give two analyses for sentence (89), the ones in (90) and (91). Empirically speaking, analysis (90) is the correct one. (89) does not have the telic reading (91). But, looking at scope effects, we must keep in mind that (91) is a combinatorial possibility. If it doesn't correspond to any actual reading, we will have to explain why.

(89)   Sally ate pudding for 30 minutes.

(90) $[[\ \text{for 30 minutes}\ ]] + (\ \lambda e \exists x(\ \text{PUDDING}(x)\ \&\ \text{EAT}(S,x,e))$
        $\Rightarrow$ PP combines with a homogeneous predicate

(91)   [[Pudding]] + ([[for 30 minutes]] + $\lambda e.\text{EAT}(S,x,e)$) for fixed variable x,
        $\Rightarrow$ PP combines with a quantized predicate

The distinction between (90) and (91) was never discussed by Krifka.

(S4)   Usually all examples in the literature which involve a quantified NP can sensibly be represented by giving the NP scope over the event argument. There is no direct evidence in favour of event quantifiers having scope over the quantificational NP. Thus, it is unclear whether we need representations like (94) for sentence (92), and if yes, what they mean.

(92)   Sally opened each door with a key.

(93) $\forall x(\text{DOOR}(x) \rightarrow \exists y \exists e(\text{KEY}(y) \ \& \ \text{OPEN}(S,x,e) \ \& \ \text{INSTR}(y,e)))$

(94) $\exists e \forall x(\text{DOOR}(x) \rightarrow \exists y(\text{KEY}(y) \ \& \ \text{OPEN}(S,x,y) \ \& \ \text{INSTR}(y,e)))$

(S5)   The same question as (S4) arises for the relative scopes of event and negation.

(S6)   We expect indirect evidence with respect to (S4) and (S5) by looking at modifiers which have visible scope over NP or negation, and apply to an event, thus proving that the event has scope over NP or negation.

Using the scope effects listed in (S1) to (S6), we get the following set of empirical observations about the scopes of NP, PP, negations and events.

(A) Bare plurals and mass terms (BP/MT in the following) almost always make a sentence in which they occur atelic. This means that they standardly should have scope below temporal PPs. However there are verbs in German which do not seem to allow a combination with BP/MT at all. Sentences like (95) are only marginally acceptable, and if they are, they are telic.

(95)   ??Bertha aß Pudding auf.
        "Bertha ate up pudding"
(96)   Bertha aß Pudding ?in 5 Minuten / *5 Minuten lang auf.
        "Bertha ate pudding in 5 minutes/ for 5 minutes up"

If the hearer is willing to accept (95), she will understand "Pudding" roughly like "there was this food there, pudding, and ... ". In an intuitive sense, the mass term has to establish the existence of pudding on its own account (I will suggest later what this means in formal terms). The speaker, however, would more appropriately do this using "etwas Pudding" (some pudding) or "den Pudding" (the pudding).

Once the hearer has become aware of this interpretive possibility for BP/MT like "Pudding", she will also accept sentences like (97)/(98) as telic sentences, and moreover to the same degree of marginality as (96).

(97)   ?Alma aß Müsli in zehn Minuten.
         Alma ate muesli in ten minutes

(98)   Clara las Broschüren in 10 Minuten.
         Clara read brochures in ten minutes[9]

The respective readings of (95) to (98) can easily be captured by an analysis as in (91) where the MT/BP has wide scope over the temporal PP. We only have to explain in what sense these wide scope readings are marginal, and why the narrow scope readings are not available for certain verbs.

   (B) NPs other than BP/MT never have the homogenizing effect which is predicted by Krifka's theory. Even NPs which clearly refer homogenously, like those in (99), only give rise to telic sentences, like (100). This observation is discussed by Zucchi & White (1996).

(99)   a quantity of milk, some pudding, a line, ...

(100)   Alma drank a quantity of milk in/*for ten minutes.
         ("Alma trank in 10 Minuten/ 10 Minuten lang etwas Milch")

I will adopt Zucchi & White's conclusion that singular indefinite NPs get bound by existential closure above the temporal PP (and thus have scope higher than the PP).

   (C) There are sentences which involve both "small" and "large" events. Example (65)/(69) in Section 5 was of that kind. Another example involving temporal modification is given in (101):

(101)   In one hour, Alma hit each boxer with a (different) picket.

(102)   In one hour, Alma stored each pigeon into a cage.

The temporal PP measures the duration of the overall event of hitting all boxers, storing all pigeons, etc. On the other hand, we have to refer to single events of hitting or storing in order to ensure that there is a different cage for each pigeon, or a different picket for each boxer. Following Parsons, I suggest that as soon as the event e introduced by the verb gets existentially bound, we may add the condition that this e is part of a more global object I which is available for further qualification. (101) will be represented as in (103) (for details see the next section).

(103) $[[$ in one hour $]]$ +
         $\lambda I [\forall x(BOXER(x) \rightarrow \exists y \exists e (PICKET(y) \& HIT(A,x,e) \& INSTR(e,y)$
         $\& e < I))]$

---

[9] In fact, there are two readings: Clara read certain brochures in ten minutes each, and: Clara read certain brochures all within ten minutes. Note that I am *not* concerned with generic readings which arise due to the BP/MT's position to the left of the temporal PP and which are much better than those which we are discussing here.

The I in (103) ranges over time intervals, or, if we also want to account for the perception data of the previous section, over *situated maximal events*. The free variable is accessible in the further computation of the sentence, and we can in particular lambda abstract over it. Thus we can combine temporal PPs with a set of time intervals. It was discussed in section 2.3.1 that Krifka's theory of combinatorial restrictions for PPs and sentences does not need anything richer than time intervals. Therefore we know that we can apply it without loss in cases like (103).

It is moreover important to stress that this situated interval I does not correspond to any kind of "contextual frame interval" or "reference time". Reference time intervals are thought to be indexical objects, to which sentences refer definitely. If sentences refer definitely to these objects then we can't explain straightforwardly why these objects are sometimes telic and sometimes atelic, depending on the description. It is one of the great merits of Krifka's theory to have shown that there are no telic *objects in the world* but only telic *descriptions* of objects. Forming sets of macro intervals, we can lift this insight to a higher level[10].

(D) The same mechanism can also account for negation data like (65)/(69), Section 5. I will assume that negation has always scope over the first event quantifier. Higher temporal modifications and perception predicates always apply to macro intervals I like the ones in (C). This is exemplified in (104).

(104)   Bertha did not sleep for an hour.
        [[for an hour]] + λI [$\neg \exists e($ SLEEP(B,e) & $e{<}I)$]

(105)   Alma saw Bertha not sleep for an hour.
        $\exists I($ SEE(A,I) & $|I|$ = 1 hour & $\neg \exists e($ SLEEP(B,e) & $e{<}I)$)

Sentence (105) suggests that I ranges over situated rather than full world-wide intervals. It does not make sense, though, to assume that I is just *any* sum of events. Else, the non-existence conditions in (104) and (105) could always be made trivially true.

(E) There is independent evidence from the literature on predication and the stage level/individual level distinction, that events and indefinite NPs should be existentially bound at the same place, below negation, and per default below quantificational NPs. This insight is implicit or explicitly stated in the following papers, among others: Ladusaw (1994), Kiss (1993), Diesing (1992), Kratzer (1989a). I will not go into the stage level/individual level discussion at this point. It is interesting, though, to see that the above data are confirmed by independent considerations.

---

[10] I will not exclude the possibility that properties like the one in (103) are afterwards predicated of a contextually given interval. However the step via sets of intervals is necessary in order to account for *aktionsart* phenomena.

6.3 A shell model of scope

The following shell model of scope summarizes the empirical results of the previous section.

Step 1: The verb introduces an event parameter in the Davidsonian sense. Note that I do not make a statement about stative predicates. These behave differently in the shell model.

Step 2: Mass terms and bare plurals denote properties. Taking up an idea of van Geenhoven (1996), I assume that verbs can come in two versions: One normal version, and a version which combines with a property and states that an object with this property exists and stands in the verbal relation to the other arguments. "eat pudding" will for instance be analyzed as in (107):

(107) $\lambda x \text{PUDDING}(x) + \lambda P \lambda x \lambda e \exists y (P(y) \ \& \ \text{EAT}(x,y,e))$
         $= \lambda x \lambda e \exists y (\text{PUDDING}(y) \ \& \ \text{EAT}(x,y,e))$

This mechanism guarantees lowest scope for all mass terms and bare plurals. Moreover it can explain why some verbs "do not allow MT/BP": It has become the verb's job to provide the quantifier for the BP/MT NP. Some verbs simply do not come in a version which can combine with a property. In that case, the BP/MT can marginally be interpreted as being accesible to existential closure like other indefinites. This however is not the standard way to interpret MT/BP and for that reason, the respective sentences sound marginal.

Step 3: The descriptive content of other indefinites will be computed (according to word order), but existential closure will only take place later.

Step 4: Temporal modifications take place, following the restrictions spelled out in Section 2.3. Note that both the event variable and indefinites are still unbound and thus have scope over the temporal PP[11].

Step 5: Existential binding of indefinites and of the verbal event variable takes place. Optionally the frame variable I is introduced with the condition $e{<}I$.

Step 6: Quantifying NPs and negations are combined with the representation reached so far. It seems also possible that further indefinite NPs arrive at this point. An example of the relevant type is (108):

(108)   For one hour, a girl welcomed each guest with a rose.

Step 7: Further predicates may apply to the situated frame interval I: We have seen examples involving temporal modifications ((101), (106), ...) and perception predicates (see (65), (105)).

The restrictions for the combination of sets of intervals with temporal PPs are exactly the same as those for sets of events. We know from Section 2.3 that the theory in question can be applied to both events and intervals.

---

[11] Technically speaking, we will have to lambda-bind the event parameter, apply the temporal modification, and finally apply the resulting predicate of events to a standard event variable, again.

Step 8. Final existential closure takes place. I will leave it open to what extent the introduction of further frame intervals is a recursive process which might again take place here. In principle it makes sense to assume that the binding of a simpler type of eventive argument leads to an introduction of a further frame parameter, because we do not want to claim that we are grammatically limited to talk only about temporal objects of a certain complexity. Sentences like (109) show that we can even think of rather complex temporal objects.

(109)   For several years, Clara weekly knocked out all members of her karate club with a stick in an hour.

Figure 1 summarizes the relations and operations of steps 1 to 8. I do not want to commit myself to any syntactic labelling of the structure. The node labelled "VP?" corresponds to a position which has been called the "VP boundary" in a certain type of theory (see 6.2. (D).) Essentially, the relations are to be read as a hierarchy which is suggested by semantic observations and which can be integrated into any syntactic framework. (We match syntax, though, in that the structure respects overt word orders. We didn't assume hidden movements at any stage.)

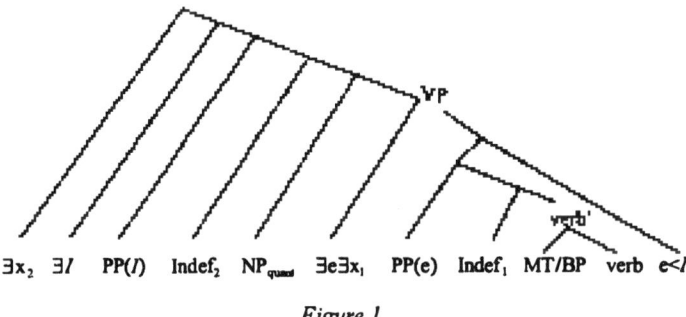

$\exists x_2$ $\exists I$ PP(I)   Indef$_2$ NP$_{quad}$ $\exists e\exists x_1$ PP(e)   Indef$_1$ MT/BP   verb   e<I

Figure 1

Appendix: Fact-like events

Let me mention two other kinds of applications for events where the concept of "event" undergoes a substantial change in comparison to what we have seen so far: Evaluative adverbs, and causation. Up to now we fruitfully assumed that an event e can have more than one property. For example, e can be an opening, have tongs as instrument, happen within a certain time, be done in a careful manner etc. In contrast to this view, the two abovementioned applications require that we distinguish an opening e from an opening done with tongs, or from a careful opening – where we previously have assumed that these are simply different descriptions of one and the same event. Sentences (110) and (111) give an example with the adverb "carefully" used in an evaluative sense, that is, in a sense paraphrasable with "it was careful **that** ...".

(110)   Bertha carefully opened the fridge with tongs.
         (reading: It was careful **that** Bertha opened the fridge with tongs.)

(111)   Bertha carefully opened the fridge.
         (reading: It was careful **that** Bertha opened the fridge.)

Wyner (1994) argues that "carefully" in its evaluative reading (let me write "carefully$_1$" in distinction to "carefully$_0$", the manner adverb) shows the crucial non-opacity effects which prove that it doesn't embed a proposition (see section 4). He concludes that "carefully$_1$" must be an event predicate. He then observes that sentence (110) does not imply sentence (111) and vice versa. Therefore, the event e of Bertha opening the fridge with tongs can't be the same event as the event f of Bertha opening the fridge. Wyner suggests a subatomic fine structure of the event mereology, splitting up each traditional events into parts which bear single properties. Taking adverbs as a starting point, he demonstrates that manners are not sensitive for this subatomic fine structure but evaluative adverbs are. The applications we have listed so far would also not be sensitive to the subatomic structure. A more thorough critique of Wyner's treatment of evaluative adverbs, and a suggestion for an alternative treatment based on traditional events, can be found in Eckardt (1998).

A similar process shows in causation sentences. Again, it seems to depend on the event description (i.e. subatomic events in Wyner's sense) whether certain causation statements are true.

(112)   The train's leaving early caused Clara's delayed arrival. (She missed the train and had to wait for the next one.)

(113)   The train's leaving caused Clara's arrival. (False in the scenario above.)

The discussion on causation in the philosophical literature has brought up a notion of event which is close to Wyner's subatomic level. The authors did not care for any of the linguistic applications listed in Sections 1 to 5. An extensive survey of the difficulties that arose due to mixing up "events" and "facts" can be found in Bennett (1990); classical authors in causation theory are Davidson (1969), Lewis (1983, 1986) and Kim (1969, 1980).

I want to sketch a reconstruction of events in terms of space, time, and possible worlds which was suggested in theories which require fine-grained individuation (see for example Montague 1974, Lewis 1986, Cresswell 1985).

(114)   An event F is a function which maps each possible world onto a function from a set of points of time into space.
         $F: w \rightarrow (F(w): T \rightarrow R^3)$

The objects $F(w)$ are the same as the functions f we saw in Section 2.2. The reasoning is this: The reconstruction in Section 2.2 was too coarse grained, because there might be events which are different, but accidentally occur at the same time and space. In other worlds, however, they will happen independently and therefore correspond to two different functions F and F' of the shape characterized in (114).

This kind of event reconstruction however requires thorough knowledge about possible ways in which an event might have happened elsewhere. Assume that Alma forcefully hit Joe with a stick. Talking about this (these?) event(s?) F, we know $F(w)$ in the real world w_0. However we have no idea how many functions F of the shape in (114) crystalize out in w_0 at the same time and place. There might be F_1, with F_1 being manifested as a hitting of Joe by Alma in all worlds, there might be F_2, with F_2 being a hitting by Alma in all worlds, but with different patients, there might be F_3, a forceful hitting in all worlds but with arbitrary participants, etc. Cresswell (1985) offers a spellout of this idea where an F_4 might even be Alma driving a car in other worlds. Thus, we would predict that not only *one* or *finitely* many, but an *infinity* of events is taking place here and now. Note that, due to the results of Section 2.2, we can't say that $F_i(w)$ is what counts for "linguistic" applications while the finer F_1, F_2, F_3 objects are good for causation. We argued in Section 2.2 that spatio-temporal manifestations like $F(w)$ were exactly *not* the appropriate kind of event object. The reconstruction of events in terms of times, space and worlds appears to offer the advantage of being defined in terms of objects which we already had available. However, they provide too many objects, and it is not clear what kind of equivalence relation provides the basis for coming down to a realistic number of linguistically relevant events.

Acknowledgements

I would like to thank all those who were willing to discuss the above issues with me, and helped me to get a better understanding of what events are: Fritz Hamm, Ede Zimmermann, Kurt Eberle, Willi Geuder, Manfred Krifka, Manfred Kupffer, Sebastian Löbner, Chris Piñón, Henriette de Swart, Adam Z. Wyner, the audiences of the Povo Workshop on Events and Facts 1995 and the *Sinn und Bedeutung* Conference Tübingen 1997, and most importantly, the participants of my seminar "Sprache und Ereignis", Düsseldorf 1996/97 and ESSLLI 1997, Prague.

Bibliography

Asher, N. (1993): *Reference to Abstract Objects in Discourse*. Kluwer Academic Publishers, Dordrecht, Holland.

Bartsch, R. (1976): The Grammar of Adverbials. North Holland Publishing Company, Amsterdam.

Barwise, J. (1982): "Scenes and other Situations". *The Journal of Philosophy* LXVIII 11, 668–691.

Barwise, J. & Perry, J. (1983): *Situations and Attitudes*. MIT Press, Cambridge, Massachusetts.

Bennet, J. (1988): *Events and their names*. Hackett Publishing Company, Indianapolis/Cambridge.

Buschbeck, B. (1994): *Konzeptuelle Interpretation und interlinguabasierte Übersetzung räumlicher Präpositionen*. Ph.D. Diss., university of Stuttgart. Appeared as Working Papers of the Institute of Logic and Linguistics 15, IBM Heidelberg.

Cresswell, M. (1985): *Adverbial Modification*. Reidel, Dordrecht.

Davidson,D. (1967): "The logical form of action sentences". Reprinted in: Davidson, D.: *Essays on Actions and Events*, Oxford University Press (1980).

Davidson, D. (1969): "Event individuation". Reprinted in: Davidson, D.: *Essays on Actions and Events*, Oxford University Press (1980).

Davidson, D. (1980): *Essays on Actions and Events*. Oxford University Press, Oxford.

Dekker, P. (1993): *Transsentential Meditations*. Ph.D. dissertation, University of Amsterdam. ILLC dissertation series, 1993, No.1.

Diesing, M. (1992): *Indefinites*. Cambridge, Mass., MIT press.

Dowty, D. (1979): *Word Meaning and Montague Grammar*. Dordrecht, Kluwer.

Dowty, D. (1992): "Thematic Proto Roles and Argument Selection". *Language* 67, 547–619.

Eberle, K. (1998): "The influence of Plural NPs on Aktionsart in DRT". In: Hamm, F., Hinrichs, E. (eds.): *Plurality and Quantification*. Kluwer Academic Publishers, Dordrecht (1998).

Eckardt, R. (1996): *Events, Adverbs, and Oher Things*. Ph.D. diss., Stuttgart university.

Eckardt, R. (1997): "Judgement Structure, Focus, and the Interpretation of Indefinites". Proceedings of the 1996 IATL conference, University of Jerusalem.

Eckardt, R. (1998): *Adverbs, Events, and other Things*. Tübingen, Niemeyer.

Egg, M. (1993): *Aktionsart und Kompositionalität*. Studia Academica, Berlin.

van Geenhoven, V. (1996): *Semantic Incorporation and Indefinite Descriptions* Ph.D. dissertation, Tübingen university. Appeared as SfS Report 03-96.

Heim, I. (1982) "The Semantics of Definite and Indefinite Noun Phrases." Ph.D. dissertation, University of Massachusetts, Amherst.

Higginbotham, J. (1983): "The Logic of Perceptual Reports: an Extensional Alternative to Situation Semantics", *The Journal of Philosophy*, LXXX 2: 100–127.

Higginbotham, J. (1994): Course material, ESSLLI 1994, Copenhagen.

Hinrichs, E. (1986): "Temporal Anaphors in Discouse". *Linguistics and Philosophy* 9, 63–82.

Kamp, J. A. W. (1981) "A Theory of Truth and Semantic Representation." In: J. Groenendijk, T. Janssen & M. Stokhof (eds.) *Formal Methods in the Study of Language*, 277–321. Amsterdam: Mathematical Centre.

Kamp, H. & Reyle, U. (1993): *From Discourse to Logic*. Kluwer Academic Publishers, Dordrecht.

Kim, J. (1969): "Events and their descriptions: Some Considerations". In: Rescher, N. (ed.): *Essays in Honour of C.G.Hempel*, Reidel, Dordrecht, 198–215.

Kim, J. (1980): "Events as Property Exemplifications". In: Brand, M. & Walton, D. (eds.): *Action Theory*. Reidel, Dordrecht: 159–77.

Kiss, K.E. (1993): "On generic and existential bare plurals and the classification of predicates." Presentation at the Workshop "Events and Grammar", Bar Ilan University, Israel.

Klein, W. (1994): *Time in Language*. Oxford, Routledge.

Kratzer, A. (1989): "An investigation of the lumps of thought", *Linguistics and Philosophy* 12 (5): 607–53.

Kratzer, A. (1989a): "Stage-Level and Individual-Level Predicates", in: Krifka, M.: *Genericity in Natural Language – Proceedings of the 1988 Tübingen Conference*. SNS-Bericht Nr. 42, Tübingen University.

Krifka, M. (1989): *Nominalreferenz und Zeitkonstitution*. München, Wilhelm Fink Verlag.

Krifka, M. (1990a): "Boolean and Non-Boolean *And*". In: L. Kálmán & L. Pólos (eds.): *Papers from the Second Symposium on Logic and Language*. Akadémiai Kiadó, Budapest.

Krifka, M. (1992): "Thematic Roles as Links between Nominal Reference and Temporal Constitution". In: Sag, I. & Szabolsci, A.: *Lexical Matters*. CSLI Lecture Notes, Stanford University.

Krifka, M. (1995): "Telicity in Movement", in: Amsili, P. et al (eds.): *Time, Space, and Movement*. Notes of the 5th international workshop on TSM 1995, Toulouse.

Ladusaw, W. (1994): "Thetic and Categorical, Stage and Individual, Weak and strong". Proceedings of SALT IV conference.

Landman, F. (1992): "The Progressive" *Natural Language Semantics* 1, 1–32.

Landman, F. (1989): "Groups I", *Linguistics and Philosophy* 12, 607–653.

Lang, E. (1989): "The Semantics of Dimensional Designation of Spatial Objects". In: Bierwisch, M. & Lang, E. (eds.): *Dimensional Adjectives: Grammatical Structure and Conceptual Interpretation*. Springer Verlag, Berlin.

Lasersohn, P. (1992): "Generalized Conjunction and Temporal Modification", *Linguistics and Philosophy* 15, 381–410.

Lasersohn, P. (1995): *Plurality, Conjunction and Events*. Kluwer Academic Publishers, Dordrecht.

Levin, B. & Rappaport Hovav, M. (1995): *Ergativity*. MIT press, Boston.

Lewis, D. (1973): "Causation". In: *Journal of Philosophy* 70 (1973). Reprinted with postscripts in Lewis (1986); 556–567.

Lewis, D. (1986): "Events". In: Lewis, D.: *Philosophical Papers* vol II. Oxford University Press, New York.

Lewis, D. (1986): *Philosophical Papers*. Vol.II, Oxford University Press, New York.

McConnell-Ginet, S. (1982): "Adverbials and Logical Form: A Linguistically Realistic Theory". In: *Language* 58 (1982).

Montague, R. (1974): "On the Nature of Certain Philosophical Entities". In: Thomason, R. (ed.), *Formal Philosophy*, New Haven, CT: Yale University Press, pp. 148–187.

Muskens, R. (1990): *Meaning and Partiality*. Ph.D. dissertation, University of Amsterdam.

Parsons, T. (1990): *Events in the Semantics of English*. MIT Press, Boston.

Reichenbach, H. (1947): *Elements of Symbolic Logic*. Macmillan, New York.

Rooth, M. (1995): "Indefinites, Adverbs of Quantification and Focus Semantics". In: Carlson, G. & Pelletier, J.: *The Generic Book*. University of Cambridge Press, Cambridge, 265–300.

Sæbø, K.J. (1996): "Anaphoric Presuppositions and Zero Anaphora". In: *Linguistics and Philosophy* 19 (1996): 187–209

Taylor, B. (1977): "Tense and Continuity". *Linguistics and Philosophy* 1, 199–220.

Thomason, R. & Stalnaker, R. (1973): "A Semantic Theory of Adverbs". In: *Linguistic Inquiry* 4 (1973), 195–220.

Tichy, P. (1985): "Do we need Interval Semantics?" *Linguistics and Philosophy* 8, 263–282.

Vendler, Z. (1967): *Linguistics in Philosophy*. Cornell University Press, Ithaca.

Wyner, A.Z. (1994): *Syntactic and Semantic Issues in Adverbial Semantics*. Ph.D. diss., Cornell university.

Zucchi, A. (1993): *The language of Propositions and Events*. Kluwer Academic Publishers, Dordrecht.

Zucchi, A. & White, M. (1996): "Twigs, Sequences, and the Temporal Constitution of Predicates". Proceedings of the SALT VI Conference, 329–346.

Konstanz   Regine Eckardt

Universität Konstanz, FB Sprachwissenschaft/SFB 471, Universitätsstr. 10, 78457 Konstanz, regine.eckardt@uni-konstanz.de

Compositionality: A Global Perspective

Sean A. Fulop / Edward L. Keenan

Recent work, from diverse points of view – Lakoff (1987), Keenan (1993), Keenan and Stabler (1996), Kalman (1995), Zadrozny (1994) among others, has called into question the empirical force of *Compositionality* as a constraint on the interpretation of natural languages. There is even perhaps something of a consensus that Compositionality as standardly formulated is too weak, allowing too great a range of possible interpretations. But, as is clear from the detailed presentation in Janssen (1997), there is considerable difference as to precisely where the problems lie and precisely what modifications should be imposed.

Here we propose a modest strengthening of Compositionality, one that is, we feel, often assumed though not consciously intended. We call this strengthening Global Compositionality (GC). In §1 below we provide a formal statement of Standard Compositionality (SC). In §2 we review an extension to Compositionality proposed by Keenan and Stabler (1996), *Strong* Compositionality. We show precisely what kinds of semantic interpretations it rules out which nonetheless satisfy SC, and show that it properly generalizes SC, i.e. it entails but is not entailed by SC. In §3 we define GC and prove that GC properly generalizes Strong C. We exhibit semantic interpretations which satisfy Strong C but fail GC, thereby illustrating the sort of phenomena that GC excludes over and above what Strong C excludes.

1 Standard compositionality

Compositionality is usually formulated as follows:

Preliminary Definition 1. *The (semantic) interpretation of a derived expression is a function of the interpretations of the expressions it is derived from plus how it is derived.*

Assumed here is that the language is given by a grammar; i.e. some expressions are derived from others, and some are *basic* (not derived). Preliminary Definition 1 imposes no conditions on underived expressions.

Let us spell out our preliminary definition more explicitly, making clear the sense in which Standard Compositionality is a "local" constraint. We shall, noncommittedly, think of a language as determined by a grammar G, where G consists essentially of a set Lex_G of basic (i.e. non-derived) expressions, sorted into categories, and a set F_G of *generating (structure building)* functions. An f in F_G maps tuples of expressions in specified categories to an expression of a specified

Linguistische Berichte Sonderheft 10 · © Helmut Buske Verlag 2002 · ISSN 0935-9249

category. L_G, *the language generated by* G, is the closure of Lex (subscripts are omitted when no confusion results) under the structure building functions F. That is, L_G is the set of (categorized) expressions that can be built from Lex by applying the structure building functions finitely many times. We illustrate these notions, as well as the notion of semantic interpretation, with a minimal language L. Our considerations apply to extensions of L to full type theoretic languages.

The basic symbols of L are some *individual constants* (ICs) *john, andy, ...,* some 1-place predicate symbols (P1's) *walks, talks, ...,* and the symbols & and ¬. The generating functions are PA, AND, and NOT. PA maps pairs $\langle p, c \rangle$, p of category P1 and c of category IC, to $c \frown p$ of category S (Sentence). AND maps pairs $\langle s, t \rangle$ of category S to $(s \frown and \frown t)$ of category S. NOT takes unary sequences $\langle s \rangle$ of category S to ¬s of category S.

Now consider the standard extensional interpretations for L. The type of object an expression denotes depends on its category. ICs denote objects in the universe of objects under discussion. P1's denote subsets of that universe. Different interpretations may differ both with regard to the choice of universe and, even holding the universe fixed, with regard to the objects denoted by the ICs and the subsets denoted by the P1's. Let us say then that a *model* for L is a pair (E, m_E), with E a universe and m_E an *interpretation* of L relative to E. Then m_E is a function with domain L satisfying:

Definition 1.

1. *for all sentences s, $m_E(s) \in \{0,1\}$*
2. *for all individual constants c, $m_E(c) \in E$*
3. *for all P1's p, $m_E(p) \subseteq E$*
4. *for all P1's p and all ICs c,*
   $m_E(PA(p, c)) = 1$ *iff* $m_E(c) \in m_E(p)$
5. *for all s, t of category S,*
   $m_{,E}(AND(s,t)) = m_E(s) \wedge m_E(t)$ and $m_E(NOT(s)) = \neg (m_E(s))$

We think of '$\wedge$' here as a binary function on $\{0,1\}$ given by the standard truth table for conjunction; a comparable claim connects the use of '¬' to the truth table for negation. We note that m_E may be required to map specific basic expressions to specific denotations. For example, if *exists* of category P1 is in Lex we may require that $m_E(exists) = E$.

We turn now to a proper characterization of Compositionality, illustrating both how interpretations of L above satisfy it and how variations on those interpretations fail it. We use the following notational simplification: if t is a sequence $\langle t_1, ..., t_n \rangle$ and m is a function with each t_i in its domain we write $m(t)$ for $\langle m(t_1), ..., m(t_n) \rangle$. Also if K is a subset of Dom m then by $m(K)$ is meant $\{m(x) \mid x \in K\}$.

Definition 2 (Standard Compositionality). *Consider a grammar* G *with generating functions* F_G.

For all models (E, m_E), *the interpretation* m_E is compositional *iff*

$$\forall f \in F_G, \{\langle m_E(t), m_E(f(t))\rangle \mid t \in \text{Dom } f\} \text{ is a function.}$$

Given f, we can identify this set of pairs as the function f* so that

$$m_E(f(t)) = f^*(m_E(t)) \qquad \text{for all } t \in \text{Dom } f.$$

It is easy to see that the interpretations of our minimal L above are compositional. For example, given a universe E and an interpretation m_E relative to E, the set of pairs in (1) is clearly a function.

(1) $\{\langle\langle m_E(p), m_E(c)\rangle, m_E(\text{PA}(p, c))\rangle \mid p \text{ a P1}, c \text{ an individual constant}\}$

(1) contains tuples like those in (2):

(2) $\langle\langle m_E(\text{walks}), m_E(\text{john})\rangle, m_E(\text{john walks})\rangle$
             $\langle\langle m_E(\text{talks}), m_E(\text{andy})\rangle, m_E(\text{andy talks})\rangle$

Now if it happens that m_E maps *walks* and *talks* to the same subset of E and it maps *john* and *andy* to the same element of E then it must map the S *john walks* to the same truth value it maps *andy talks* to. This follows directly from the conditions we imposed on each m_E.

   To see what non-compositional interpretations might look like, imagine the following:

Condition 1 (pathological). *We require interpretations* m_E *of* L *to satisfy the conditions that are like those in Definition 1 except that line 1.4 is replaced by (3):*

(3) $m_E(\text{PA}(p, c)) = \begin{cases} 1 & \text{if } c \text{ begins with a consonant,} \\ 0 & \text{if } c \text{ begins with a vowel.} \end{cases}$

Then in an interpretation m (omitting subscripts) in which $m(\text{john}) = m(\text{andy})$ the set of pairs in (1) would contain ones like $\langle\langle m(\text{walks}), m(\text{john})\rangle, 1\rangle$ and $\langle\langle m(\text{walks}), m(\text{andy})\rangle, 0\rangle$ which fails to be a function since the left hand sides $\langle m(\text{walks}), m(\text{john})\rangle = \langle m(\text{walks}), m(\text{andy})\rangle$ are equal but the right hand sides are not. Observe, then, that given a grammar, SC is non-trivial; it admits some functions and not others.

2 Strong compositionality

Standard compositionality rules out pathological cases of the sort just illustrated. But it does not block certain others we feel should be blocked. One reason is that it doesn't insist that the *class* of interpretations available for a given universe has a uniform character. Consider the following scenario:

Condition 2 (pathological). *Let* M_1 *be the class of models* (E, m_E) *given as in Definition 1. Let* M_2 *be the class of models* (E, m_E) *such that for each* E, *the interpretation* m_E *is as in Definition 1 except that line 1.4 is replaced by:*

$$m_E(PA(p, c)) = 0 \ iff \ m(c) \in m(p).$$

Now, consider the class of models $M = M_1 \cup M_2$.

M has, in effect, contradictory members. Observe that for any particular model (E, m_E) in M, m_E is a compositional function just as before. But this time, the nature of the interpretation for a particular universe is allowed to vary, with the result that an expression's truth value could change from one interpretation to another. This, we contend, is an odd situation which does not correspond to the generally conceived notion of compositionality.

A stronger form of compositionality which constrains the variation of interpretations for a particular universe was formulated by Keenan and Stabler (1996). We recast it here for uniformity:

Definition 3 (Strong Compositionality). *Consider a grammar* G *with generating functions* F_G. *For all universes* E, $\forall f \in F_G$,

$$\{\langle m(t), m(f(t)) \rangle \mid (E, m) \ a \ model \ for \ L_G \ \& \ t \in Dom \ f\} \ is \ a \ function.$$

This formulation effectively constrains the class of models available; it is no longer a purely local condition on a single model, though it obviously does entail Standard Compositionality.

Moreover, we find that Strong Compositionality rules out the pathological scenario in Condition 2. Let us use the models of M above for our language, and consider two models $(E, m_1) \in M_1$ and $(E, m_2) \in M_2$. Let $m_1(john) \in m_1(walks)$ and $m_2(john) \in m_2(walks)$ and $m_1(john) = m_2(john)$ and $m_1(walks) = m_2(walks)$. Then $m_1(john, \ walks) = m_2(john, \ walks)$ but $m_1(john \frown walks) = 1$ while $m_2(john \frown walks) = 0$. This result contradicts Strong Compositionality. In consequence:

Proposition 1. *Strong Compositionality entails but is not entailed by SC.*

3 Global compositionality

Is Strong Compositionality sufficient? We think not. While it does constrain the variation of interpretations for a particular universe, Strong Compositionality says nothing against making the interpretation dependent on properties of the universe in its model – any properties. This can have unfortunate consequences:

Condition 3 (pathological). *We require that for each* E, *interpretations* m_E *of* L *are as in Definition 1 except that line 1.4 is replaced by:*

$$if \ 5 \in E \ then \ m_E(PA(p, c)) = 1 \ iff \ m(c) \in m(p) \ and$$
$$if \ 5 \notin E \ then \ m_E(PA(p, c)) = 0 \ iff \ m(c) \in m(p)$$

We observe that for any given E, either 5 is in E or it isn't. Thus for each E, m_E is provably a compositional function. Moreover, the entire class of functions available to a particular E obeys Strong Compositionality. But clearly whether *john walks* is true under a given interpretation depends on more than just the denotation of *john* and of *walks*; it also depends on whether 5 is an element of the universe. Thus let E be a non-empty set $\{a, b, \ldots\}$ which lacks 5 and set E' = $E \cup \{5\}$. Let m_E(john) = $m_{E'}$(andy) = b and let m_E(walks) = $m_{E'}$(talks) = $\{a, b\}$. But clearly m_E(john walks) $\neq$ $m_{E'}$(andy talks), even though m_E interprets the constituents of this sentence exactly the same as $m_{E'}$.

Variations on this pathological case are easy to come by. We might, for example, condition how m_E interprets a derived expression according as E was finite or not, or had an even number of elements or not, rather than according to whether a given object was an element of E. It is pathological conditions like these that we rule out with Global Compositionality.

Definition 4 (Global Compositionality). *Consider a grammar G with generating functions F_G and model class M_G.*

$$\forall f \in F_G, \ \{\langle m(t), m(f(t)) \rangle \mid (E, m) \in M_G \ \& \ t \in \text{Dom} f\} \ \text{is a function.}$$

That GC does entail Strong C is immediate from the comparison of Definition 4 with Definition 3. GC also blocks the pathological Condition 3, whereas Strong C does not; this shows:

Proposition 2. *Global Compositionality entails but is not entailed by Strong Compositionality.*

A problem for GC is posed, however, by shifting to a framework in which predicates are defined to be characteristic functions rather than subsets of the universe. Consider what can happen when Definitions 1.3 and 1.4 are replaced by the appropriate counterparts which use characteristic functions:

1. for all Pl's p, $m_E(p) = \Phi_p : E \rightarrow \mathbf{2}$
2. for all Pl's p and all ICs c,

$$m_E(PA(p, c)) = 1 \quad \text{iff} \quad m_E(p)(m_E(c)) = 1$$

Now it would be possible to push through the various effects of an unwanted pathological condition such as Condition 3 by making a condition not on the way $m_E(PA(p, c))$ is defined, but rather solely on the definition of the characteristic function interpretation of p. For example, it is possible to obtain the very same unfortunate set of interpretations for *john walks* as above by stipulating that one of the cases in a definition of m_E(walks) reads:

(4) $m_E(\text{walks})(m_E(\text{john})) = \begin{cases} 1 & \text{if } 5 \in E \\ 0 & \text{if } 5 \notin E \end{cases}$

In this situation, GC still restricts the truth value of *john walks* to depend only on the denotations of *john* and *walks*, with the trick being accomplished entirely within the definition of the denotation of *walks*. The easy way out here is to simply say that in order to be delivered the desired assurance by the Global Compositionality condition, the user must either define predicate denotations to be subsets of E rather than characteristic functions, or he should agree to use only such characteristic functions that can be defined in pure casewise fashion without the use of any conditions. Such a restriction on the allowed characteristic functions for predicate denotations captures the spirit of the subset denotation; for any element c, either it is in a subset or it isn't, and this can always be determined without reference to other conditions.

Note that GC does not prevent us from making the interpretation of an expression dependent on the universe of the model. As we have noted, it would be natural to require of the P1 *exists* that each m_E interpret it as E. Equally, enriching our minimal L with P2's in the obvious way, it would be natural to require that for all E, $m_E(is) = \{\langle a, a \rangle \mid a \in E\}$. Similarly, as van Benthem (1986) notes, a P1-level negation such as *non-* in *non-student* is universe-dependent; we might have two universes with the same students but different non-students.

4 Concluding reflections

It is explicit in our definition of Compositionality that it is a relation between semantic interpretation and syntactic derivation. A given set of expressions, or even categorized expressions, may be generated by many different grammars and a fixed semantic interpretation may be compositional with respect to some of these but not others. Hence on our view the question of whether a given interpretation of a set of (categorized) expressions is compositional is not well-defined. We can only ask this relative to a grammar which generates these expressions, and different choices of grammars will give rise to different results (c.f. Janssen's 1997 example involving nonarithmetic versus arithmetic interpretations of digit sequences like '007').

Of course we may ask a different question: Does a given set of expressions have a grammar that can be compositionally interpreted? But here the answer is a trivial "yes." (To construct a compositional interpretation of the expressions L_{G1}, define a grammar G_2 where $Lex_{G2} = L_{G1}$ and $F_{G2} = \emptyset$; interpret the expressions in any fashion whatsoever.) Whether a given interpreted grammar (G, m) is compositional is a non-trivial question; more interestingly, whether a given G admits of a compositional interpretation is also non-trivial (Janssen, as we have shown above).

In linguistic practice the syntactic functions are given in partial independence from semantic interpretation. In accord with this, a grammar G with generating functions F_G has no semantics built in. A semantic interpretation provides each syntactic f with a corresponding f^*, and it is of these "semantic generating functions" that questions of compositionality should be raised.

References

Janssen, T. (1997): Compositionality. In: J. van Benthem & A. ter Meulen (eds.), *Handbook of Logic and Language*. Elsevier, Amsterdam, pp. 417–473.

Kálmán, L. (1995): 'Strong Compositionality'.

Keenan, E. (1993): Anaphor-antecedent asymmetry: A conceptual necessity?. In: U. Lahiri & Z. Wyner (eds.), *Proceedings of Semantics and Linguistic Theory 3*. Department of Modern Languages and Linguistics, Cornell University.

Keenan, E. & E. Stabler (1996): Abstract Syntax. In: A. Di Sciullo (ed.), *Configurations*. Cascadilla Press, pp. 329–344.

Lakoff, G. (1987): *Women, Fire and Dangerous Things*. University of Chicago Press, Chicago.

van Benthem, J. (1986): *Essays in Logical Semantics: Chapter 3*. Reidel, Dordrecht.

Zadrozny, W. (1994): 'From Compositional to Systematic Semantics', *Linguistics and Philosophy* 17, 391–428.

Chicago / Los Angeles   Sean A. Fulop / Edward L. Keenan

Dept. of Linguistics, UCLA, Los Angeles, Ca., USA, ekeenan@ucla.edu
Dept. of Linguistics, University of Chicago, Chicago, IL, USA, sfulop@uchicago.edu

Quantifiers and Anaphora

Fritz Hamm / Thomas Ede Zimmermann

1 Introduction

The purpose of this paper is twofold. Our first aim is to introduce some basic
quantifier theory and give some easy linguistic application of the most important
notions of generalized quantifier theory. This theory was fashionable during the
eighties but has since then lost its influence an semantic theorising. One of the
reasons for the lack of interest for quantifier theory certainly was the *dynamic*
turn in semantics. It was commonly held that the theory of quantifiers didn't
offer a theoretically insightful analysis of cross-sentential anaphora resolution.

This leads to the second aim of our paper. In van der Does 1996 Jaap van der
Does has shown that this folklore opinion is plainly false. The paper contains
two important results concerning dynamic theories of meaning. The first answers the question which quantifiers give rise to the proportion problem (about
which section 3 below). The somewhat surprising answer is that the proportion
problem exists for all quantifiers except those in the Aristotelian square of op-
position.

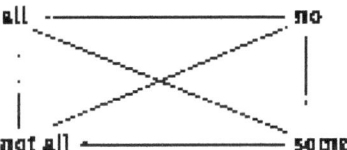

This gives a theoretical justification to the solution of the proportion problem
proposed in Kamp & Reyle 1993. We will not explain this theorem but concentrate on van der Does's second result. Roughly put, in the second part of his
paper he develops a formal characterization of those quantifiers which allow
their scope to be extended in the way familiar from the treatment of the existential quantifier in *Dynamic Predicate Logic* (DPL). The existential quantifier in
combination with the definition of conjunction given in DPL satisfies the
equivalence in (1).

(1) $(\exists x \phi \wedge \psi) \leftrightarrow \exists x (\phi \wedge \psi)$.

Van der Does abstracts away from the existential quantifier in the above scheme
and characterizes the quantifiers for which the resulting modification of scheme
(1) is valid. He then investigates whether this class of quantifiers is rich enough
for natural language anaphora resolution. The answer is that the method of
scope extension is adequate for anaphora with singular antecedents but fails for

some plural cases. This provides a significant insight into the working of one branch of dynamic theories. As an alternative van der Does proposes to analyse anaphora as contextually restricted quantification. This is a generalisation of Evans's E-type approach[1]. We will show in some detail how the results in the second part of van der Does's paper are achieved.

2 Quantifiers

Aristotle thought of quantifiers such as *all, some, no* as two-place relations between properties. So, for instance, a sentence like *All men are mortal* is true if the property of *being a man* is a part of the property of *being mortal*. Let us presume that we are able to express the *extension* of properties in terms of sets. We can then rephrase the above example in modern set-theoretical terminology by saying that *All men are mortal* is true just in case the set of men is a subset of the set of mortal individuals. The determiner *all* therefore denotes a two-place relation between sets, the subset-relation. Likewise we can fix the denotations of other determiners[2].

(2)   Let M be a non-empty set (the domain of discourse):

a. $\textbf{All}_M = \{<X,Y>: X,Y \subseteq M \wedge X \subseteq Y\}$.
b. $\textbf{Some}_M = \{<X, Y>: X, Y \subseteq M \wedge X \cap Y \neq \emptyset\}$.
c. $\textbf{No}_M = \{<X, Y>: X, Y \subseteq M \wedge X \cap Y = \emptyset\}$.

Following Westerståhl 1989 we call the denotation of a *determiner* a *quantifier*. Determiners are therefore the objects of natural language syntax corresponding to quantifiers. The denotation of a full noun phrase will be called a *generalized quantifier*. Since we will assume in the following that X, Y are subsets of the domain of discourse M, we can simplify the clauses for the denotations of the quantifiers in (2). For example (2a) now reads:

$$\textbf{All}_M = \{<X, Y>: X \subseteq Y\}.$$

Other examples of natural language quantifiers are:

(3)   a. $\textbf{Most}_M = \{<X, Y>: |X \cap Y| > |X \setminus Y|\}$.
b. $\textbf{Both}_M = \{<X, Y>: X \subseteq Y \wedge |X| = 2 \}$.
      Therefore $\textbf{Both}_M = \textbf{All}_M$ plus the cardinality-restriction on the first argument.
c. $\textbf{Neither}_M = \textbf{No}_M$ plus $|X| = 2$.
d. $\textbf{Two}_M = \{<X, Y>: |X \cap Y| \geq 2\}$.

---

[1] For another argument in favour of the E-type approach see Lasersohn 1992; and for further discussion Kadmon 1990.

[2] In the examples we use boldface notation for the denotation of a linguistic expression; thus **All** is short for the semantic value of the determiner *All*.

For a more comprehensive list of simple natural language quantifiers see Keenan & Stavi 1986.

Abstracting away from a particular universe M we arrive at the following definition of a quantifier:

(4)   A quantifier $\mathbf{Q}$ is a functor which assigns to each set M a subset $\mathbf{Q}_M$ of $\wp(M) \times \wp(M)$; i.e. a binary relation on $\wp(M)$.

Alternatively we can think of a quantifier on a set M as a function from the powerset of M to the powerset of the powerset of M. Thus **Every** on M is the function $\mathbf{Every}_M : \wp(M) \to \wp(\wp(M))$ which assigns to every subset X of M the set $\{Y \mid X \subseteq Y\}$. We will switch between these two conceptions of quantifiers freely, using whichever is more convenient. For example, if we want to talk about the denotations of NPs the functional approach is more appropriate than the relational.

As an illustration consider sentence (5):

(5)   Some teacher knows every student.

We know what **Some** does: it relates the set of teachers to the set of individuals who know every student. But what is the semantic contribution of the object-NP *every student* to the denotation of the VP *knows every student? Every student* denotes the set of sets Y such that **student** is a subset of Y; i.e. $\{Y : \mathbf{student} \subseteq Y\}$. Furthermore **knows every student** should be the set of individuals who know every student.

If R is a binary relation let $R_x = \{b : xRb\}$. For example $\mathbf{knows}_x = \{b : x$ knows $b\}$ and therefore **knows every student** is $\{x : \mathbf{known}_x \in \mathbf{every\ student}\}$.

Is definition (4) general enough? Consider the following examples.

(6)   a. *More* philosophers *than* linguists attended the meeting.
        b. *Fewer* linguists *than* philosophers were surprised by the talk.
        c. *Exactly as many* teachers *as* students went to the party.

These examples are most straightforwardly analyzed as follows:

(7)   a. | **philosopher** $\cap$ **attend the meeting** | $>$
           | **linguist** $\cap$ **attend the meeting** |.
        b. | **linguist** $\cap$ **surprised by the talk** | $<$
           | **philosopher** $\cap$ **surprised by the talk** |.
        c. | **teacher** $\cap$ **went to the party** | $=$
           | **student** $\cap$ **went to the party** |.

The denotations of the determiners *more ... than, fewer ... than* and *exactly as many ... . as* seem to be sensitive to two arguments; in (7a) for example to the sets of philosophers and linguists. If this is correct the determiner *more ... than* corresponds to a three-place relation between sets on a universe M.

(8) $\mathbf{More...than}_M = \{ <X, Y, Z> : \mid X \cap Z \mid > \mid Y \cap Z \mid \}$.

Other examples of three-place quantifiers include those studied in Beghelli 1994 in which the VP-denotation contributes two arguments to the quantifier.

(9)   More students came early than left late.

To cover cases such as (6) and (9) we would have to rephrase definition (4) in order to allow for quantifiers which have three arguments. But even such a revised definition may turn out to be too restrictive for natural language quantifiers. Keenan 1992, for instance, analyzes the quantificational structure in examples like (10) as involving quantifiers which take three arguments, two sets and one binary relation.

(10)   Every student read a different book.

The denotation of *Every ... a different* according to Keenan is as follows:

(11)   **(Every, a different)** =
          $\{<X, Y, R>: \forall x, y \in X (x \neq y \rightarrow Y \cap R_x \neq Y \cap R_y) \land \forall x \in X \mid Y \cap R_x \mid = 1\}$

The crucial part of the defining condition is the one before $\land$. Applied to example (10) it says that for every two distinct members x, y of the student set, the set of books x read is not equal to the set of books y read.

Since we don't know *a priori* which quantifiers are realized in natural language we choose to give the most general definition of quantifier, which has been worked out by now[3]. Let us classify quantifiers by assigning them a type. The type of a quantifier is a tuple of natural numbers which gives us information about the number and the kind of the arguments of the quantifier. For example the type of the quantifier in (11) is $< 1, 1, 2 >$, which means that this quantifier takes three arguments, two of which are sets (1) and the third one is a binary relation (2). The simple quantifiers in (2) are all of type $< 1,1 >$. Generalizing we arrive at the following definition:

Definition 1. *A quantifier type is a sequence $< n_1 ... n_k >$ of natural numbers.*

The quantifiers which correspond to type $< n_1 ... n_k >$ are:

Definition 2. *A quantifier Q of type $< n_1 ... n_k >$ is a functor which assigns to each set M a subset Q_M of $\wp(Mn_1) \times ... \times \wp(Mn_k)$.*

Of course definition 2 covers also cases of quantifiers which are of mathematical interest only. For example the Rescher Quantifier (12a) and the Härtig Quantifier (12b) are extremely unlikely to occur as natural language determiners[4]. We will show in chapter 2.1, that there are principles valid for natural language quantifiers, which prohibit the relations in (12) as possible denotations for natural language determiners.

---

[3] See Mostowski 1957 and Lindström 1966.
[4] For more information about quantifiers in mathematical logic see Barwise & Feferman 1985, especially Mundici 1985.

(12) a. $\mathbf{R}_M XY \Leftrightarrow |X| > |Y|$.
      b. $\mathbf{H}_M XY \Leftrightarrow |X| = |Y|$.

The abstract notion of quantifier given in Definition 2 however allows to ask the following question of specific linguistic interest: Which types of quantifiers are realized in natural languages? In this paper we won't address this question, but refer the interested reader to the relevant literature: Keenan 1987*b*, Keenan 1992, Hella, Väänänen & Westerståhl 1997, Väänänen 1997, van Benthem 1989, Westerståhl 1995, Keenan & Westerståhl 1997.

Most natural-language quantifiers of type $< 1, 1 >$ satisfy a restriction which roughly says that only the quantity of the argument sets is of importance for their behaviour with respect to truth conditions. Examples are: *every, no, most, two* etc. If we add this requirement to definition 2 for quantifiers of any type $<n_1 ... n_k >$ we get Lindström's general definition (Lindström 1966) of the notion *quantifier*. Stated more formally this restriction says that quantifiers are isomorphism invariant.

Restriction 1 (ISOM).
$\mathbf{Q}_M R^{n_1} ... R^{n_k} \Leftrightarrow \mathbf{Q}_{M'} \pi(R^{n_1}) ... \pi(R^{n_k})$ *for every bijection* $\pi: M' \to M;$
with $\pi(R^n) := \{ < \pi(d_1),... , \pi(d_n) >:$

$< d_1,... , d_n > \in R^n\}$

A special case often considered is:

Restriction 2 (PERM).
$\mathbf{Q}_M R^{n_1} ... R^{n_k} \Leftrightarrow \mathbf{Q}_M \pi(R^{n_1}) ... \pi(R^{n_k})$ *for every bijection* $\pi: M \to M;$
where $\pi(R^n) := \{ < \pi(d_1),... , \pi(d_n) >: < d_1,... , d_n > \in R^n\}$

If we decide to consider the denotations of expressions like *some red, every liberal* and *John's* or *some student's* as quantifiers of type $< 1, 1 >$, we get counterexamples in type $< 1,1 >$ to ISOM and PERM. This is shown by the following argument: Assume that *Some student's book is yellow* is true. Define a permutation π on the universe which permutes the set of books and, say, the set of CDs and is the identity map on the rest. Then it certainly does not follow that *Some student's CD is yellow* is true as well. The reason is that the denotation of a Det like *some student's* involves a particular set (the set of students)[5], whereas in *Some students are lazy* the sets **students** and **being lazy** are fixed but arguments of **some**. This also destroys the permutation invariance for almost all quantifiers of type $< 1 >$ or NP-denotations, since they too involve particular N-denotations: **every ⟨teacher⟩, three ⟨apples⟩, four of ten books.**

In the following sections we will only consider quantifiers of type $< 1, 1 >$ which satisfy PERM or ISOM.

---

[5] A subset X of M is permutation invariant iff $X = M$ or $X = \emptyset$. Therefore most subsets of M are not permutation invariant.

2.1 Quantifier constraints

Given a fixed universe M, quantifiers of type $< 1, 1 >$ denote in $\wp(\wp(M) \times \wp(M))$. How many quantifiers exist on M? Consider the following picture:

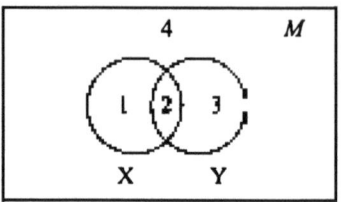

It is clear that the behaviour of a quantifier is completely determined by the sets $X \setminus Y$ (1), $X \cap Y$ (2), $Y \setminus X$ (3) and $M \setminus X \cup Y$ (4). Moreover if we assume the constraints ISOM or PERM only the cardinalities of these sets matter. To be more precise if $|X \setminus Y| = |X' \setminus Y'|$, $|X \cap Y| = |X' \cap Y'|$, $|Y \setminus X| = |Y' \setminus X'|$, and $|M \setminus X \cup Y| = |M' \setminus X' \cup Y'|$, then $Q_M XY$ iff $Q_{M'} X'Y'$[6].

The following argument, attributed to Johan van Benthem in Thijsse 1984, answers the above question. A quantifier is a set of pairs of subsets of M. Let us first determine the number of pairs (X, Y) of subsets of M. Observe first that a pair (X, Y) of subsets of M can be identified with a function $f_{(X,Y)}$ from M into $\{1,2,3,4\}$ in the following way:

$$a \in X \text{ and } b \in Y \text{ iff}$$
$$(f_{(X,Y)}(a) = 1 \vee f_{(X,Y)}(a) = 2) \text{ and } (f_{(X,Y)}(b) = 2 \vee f_{(X,Y)}(b) = 3)[7]$$

If we assume that the cardinality of M is n, we get 4^n such functions and therefore that there are 4^n pairs of subsets of M. Since a quantifier is a set of pairs of sets it follows that the number of quantifiers on a universe with n elements is 2^{4^n}. This means that on a universe with two elements there are $2^{4^2} = 2^{16} = 65536$ quantifiers.

Conservativity is a constraint which rules out the majority of possible quantifier denotations.

Restriction 3 (CONS).
$$Q_M XY \Leftrightarrow Q_M XX \cap Y$$

This restriction says that the left argument of Q_M is more prominent than the right argument; it rules out the set $Y \setminus X$ from the list $X \setminus Y$, $X \cap Y$, $Y \setminus X$, $M \setminus X \cup Y$. Therefore the picture is now as follows:

---

[6] For the more general case of arbitrary monadic quantifiers, i.e. those that don't have relations as arguments, see Westerståhl 1989.

[7] $f_{(X,Y)}$ is just a generalization of the concept of *characteristic function*.

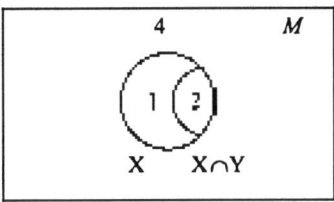

Hence under CONS the number of quantifiers on a universe with n elements reduces to 2^{3^n}. Therefore if $n = 2$ there are only $2^9 = 512$ quantifiers left. This shows that CONS is a rather drastic constraint[8].

Empirically CONS seems to be a rather trivial constraint. It just says that (13a) and (13b) are equivalent for instance.

(13)   a. Every book is expensive.
       b. Every book is a book and expensive.

Since only extensional determiner constructions are considered in this paper, counterexamples to CONS are marginal. The standard example violating CONS is *only*, defined as in (14).

(14) $\mathbf{Only}_M XY \leftrightarrow Y \subseteq X$

$\mathbf{Only}_M$ is not conservative, because $\mathbf{Only}_M X\ X\cap Y$ is equivalent to $X \cap Y \subseteq X$ hence always true, but $Y \subseteq X$ is not.

However it is rather doubtful, whether *only* in examples like *Only books were bought* should be analyzed as a determiner at all.

A less trivial counterexample to CONS is one reading of *many* given by:

$$\mathbf{Many}_M XY \Leftrightarrow | X\cap Y | > \frac{|X|\cdot|Y|}{|M|}$$

But there are arguments which at least strongly suggest excluding *many* from the class of extensional determiners[9]. Further note that many quantifiers discussed in logic or mathematics are not conservative. For example the Rescher and Härtig quantifier defined in (12) are not conservative.

Up to now no constraint excludes the following empirically implausible situation. The determiner *some* means **some** on a universe with ten elements and **most** on a universe with ninety elements. The constraint called *Extension* excludes such cases. It roughly says that determiner denotations are constant across universes.

Restriction 4 (EXT).
If X, $Y \subseteq M \subseteq M'$, *then* $\mathbf{Q}_M XY \Leftrightarrow \mathbf{Q}_{M'} XY$

---

[8] Of course ISOM also reduces the number of quantifiers. Thijsse 1984 shows that under ISOM there are $2^{\binom{n+1}{2}}$ quantifiers on a universe with n elements. The combined force of CONS and ISOM reduces the number of quantifiers to $2^{\frac{1}{2}(n+1)(n+2)}$.

[9] See Keenan & Stavi 1986 for a discussion.

EXT excludes the set $M \setminus X \cup Y$ from the list $X \setminus Y, X \cap Y, Y \setminus X, M \setminus X \cup Y$. In graphical terms this means that EXT erases the frame in the above picture.

The above reading of *many* also constitutes a counterexample to EXT.

The combined force of CONS and EXT is given by:

Restriction 5 (UNIV).

If $X, Y \subseteq M$, *then* $\mathbf{Q}_M XY \Leftrightarrow \mathbf{Q}_X X X \cap Y$

The picture is now reduced to:

$$X \quad X \cap Y$$

Quantifiers satisfying UNIV and ISOM or PERM are called *logical*.

For the representation of quantifiers via van Benthem trees one additional constraint will be used[10].

Restriction 6 (FIN). *The universe is finite.*

A logical quantifier is completely determined by the cardinality of the sets $X \setminus Y$ and $X \cap Y$. Assuming FIN these cardinalities are just natural numbers. We therefore can associate with every logical quantifier $\mathbf{Q}$ on a universe M a relation $\mathbf{q}$ between natural numbers, with the property:

(15) $\mathbf{Q}_M XY \Leftrightarrow \mathbf{q} \, | \, X \setminus Y |, | \, X \cap Y |$

This allows a quantifier to be represented as a region in the following tree of numbers.

$\|X\| = 0$						0,0					
$\|X\| = 1$					1,0		0,1				
$\|X\| = 2$				2,0		1,1		0,2			
$\|X\| = 3$			3,0		2,1		1,2		0,3		
$\|X\| = 4$		4,0		3,1		2,2		1,3		0,4	
$\|X\| = 5$	5,0		4,1		3,2		2,3		1,4		0,5

Let us mark a pair of natural numbers with + if it is an element of a given quantifier and with − if it is not an element of a given quantifier in the tree of numbers. Then **All** as defined in (2a) corresponds to the following region:

---

[10] Every quantifier which is isomorphism invariant can be represented by a tree of numbers; see Väänänen 1997 and van Deemter 1984.

$|X| = 0$ +
$|X| = 1$.   +
$|X| = 2$ −   −   +
$|X| = 3$ ..   −   +
$|X| = 4$ − .   −   −   +
$|X| = 5$ ..   −   +

Thus **All**XY iff $|X \setminus Y| = 0$. In the trees to follow we will omit the cardinality information for the set X. Then the quantifiers **no, at least three**, and **most** are graphically represented as follows:

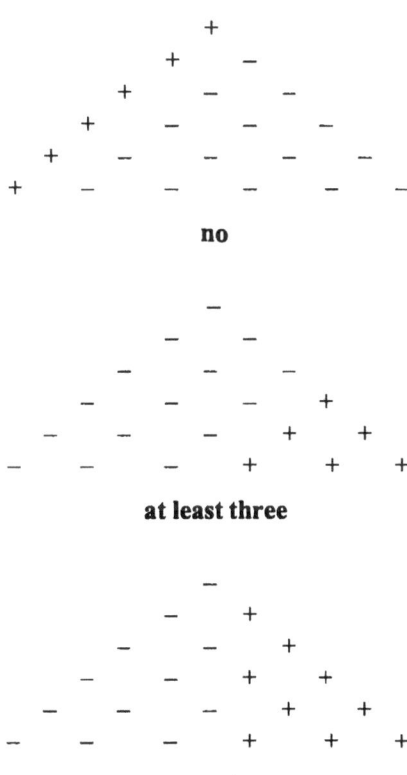

The tree representation will be used for one of the main results of Section 4.

2.2 Two applications

2.2.1 *There-are* sentences

Barwise & Cooper 1981 try to give a semantic explanation for the facts in (16) by distinguishing strong and weak quantifiers.

(16)   a. There are no cigars.
         b. *There are all cigars.
         c. There are many philosophers who know N. Chomsky.
         d. *There are not all philosophers who know N. Chomsky.
         e. There are some bottles on the table.
         f. *There are most bottles on the table.

The linguistic question is: Which quantifiers don't lead to ungrammaticality in the structure (17)?

(17)   There are QX.

If we exclude the analysis of the informative effect of tautologies and contradictions from semantics proper, thereby shifting it to pragmatics, then the following argumentation gives an explanation for the facts in (16).

Let the structure in (17) be interpreted by QXM, where M is the domain of discourse.

Definition 3. *A binary quantifier* **Q** *is strong if it is either reflexive or irreflexive for nonempty arguments, i.e. for all $X \neq \emptyset$ QXX or for all $X \neq \emptyset$ $\neg QXX$. All other quantifiers are weak.*

The following lemma shows that strong quantifiers always lead to tautologies or contradictions in structure (17).

Lemma 1. *Let* **Q** *be a strong quantifier. Then* QXM *is either a tautology or a contradiction.*

Proof: We only have to show that QXM is equivalent to QXX. The result then follows from the assumption that **Q** is strong. By conservativity: QXM iff $QXX \cap M$ iff QXX.

It is easy to see that the quantifiers in (16) which lead to ungrammaticality are all strong. For example: Most XX iff $|X \cap X| > |X \setminus X|$ iff $|X| > 0$, which is true for nonempty X.

Therefore the above question is answered: The weak quantifiers don't lead to ungrammaticality in *there-are* constructions. But what about examples like (18)?

(18)   *There is the philosopher who knows N. Chomsky.

The as defined in (19)

(19)   **The** $_M = \{< X, Y >: |X| = 1 \wedge X \subseteq Y\}$

is not a strong quantifier, but (18) is ungrammatical. This is not a serious problem, because we can slightly change the semantic definition of **The** to the one in (20):

(20)   **The** $XY = \begin{cases} \textbf{All } XY, \textit{ if } |X| = 1 \\ \textit{undefined, otherwise} \end{cases}$

and consider the weak/strong distinction only for those arguments for which the domain is defined. Then **The** is strong because it coincides with **All** on its domain.

More serious problems are posed by the proportional quantifiers as defined in (21).

(21)   ***n* percent of the** $XY \Leftrightarrow |X \cap Y| \geq \frac{n}{100} \times |X|$

Nearly all determiners defined by this scheme are weak, but (22) is ungrammatical.

(22)   *There are ten percent of the philosophers who know N. Chomsky.

Examples like (22) suggest redefining the weak quantifiers as the symmetric ones, i.e. those quantifiers which satisfy scheme (23).

(23) $\forall X \forall Y (\mathbf{Q} XY \rightarrow \mathbf{Q} YX)$.

The only strong (in the sense of Barwise/Cooper) symmetric quantifiers are the trivial quantifiers which are the empty set and $\wp(M) \times \wp(M)$[11]. Therefore non-trivial symmetric determiners are weak.

The following argument shows that this new notion of weakness leads to an interesting generalization. Observe first that three-place determiners like *More ... than* (see (8) above), *as many ... as, fewer ... than* can all occur in There-are sentences.

(24)   There are more linguists than philosophers who know N. Chomsky.

Keenan 1987a defines indefinite or weak quantifiers as the intersective ones.

Definition 4. *An n-place conservative quantifier* **Q** *is intersective iff*

$$\mathbf{Q} X_1 ... X_n Y \Leftrightarrow \mathbf{Q} X_1 \cap Y ... X_n \cap YY$$

It is easily seen that the determiner denotations of *More ... than, As many ... as,* and *fewer ... than* are all intersective and that the denotations of the proportional determiners are not intersective. The prototypical example in the binary case is **Some.**

---

[11] For a proof of this claim see van der Does & van Eijck 1996.

(25)   **Some** $XY \Leftrightarrow X \cap Y \neq \emptyset \Leftrightarrow (X \cap Y) \cap Y \neq \emptyset \Leftrightarrow$ **Some** $X \cap YY$

Therefore the intersection property is taken as the formal correlate of indefiniteness by Keenan[12].

The following lemma shows that in the binary case the intersective quantifiers and the symmetric quantifiers are the same class. This shows that the notion of intersection generalizes the notion of symmetry to the n-ary case.

Lemma 2. *A binary conservative quantifier is intersective iff it is symmetric.*

Proof: Assume **Q** intersective. We have to show that **Q** is symmetric. **Q**XY iff (intersectivity) **Q**$X \cap Y$ Y iff (conservativity) **Q**$X \cap Y$ $X \cap Y$ iff (intersectivity) **Q**Y $X \cap Y$ iff (conservativity) **Q**YX. This shows that **Q** is symmetric.

Assume now that **Q** is symmetric. **Q**XY iff (conservativity) **Q**X $X \cap Y$ iff (symmetry) **Q**$X \cap Y$ X iff (conservativity) **Q**$X \cap Y$ $X \cap Y$ iff (conservativity) **Q**$X \cap Y$ Y. Therefore **Q** is intersective.

For a critical discussion of analyses of *there-are* constructions based on generalized quantifier theory and an alternative approach the reader is advised to consult Zucchi 1992.

2.2.2 Negative Polarity Items

Consider the distribution of the negative polarity item *any* in (26):

(26)   a. John didn't see any birds in the garden.
        b. *John saw any birds in the garden.

Klima 1964 observed that the distribution of expressions like *any* or *ever is* restricted to contexts with negative expressions such as *not*. Unfortunately this observation is not general enough.

(27)   a. No student answered any question correctly.
        b. * Some student answered any question correctly.
        c. Neither John nor Mary have ever been to Italy.
        d. *Either John or Mary have ever been to Italy.
        e. Fewer than six students answered any question correctly.
        f. *More than six students answered any question correctly.
        g. At most six students have ever been to Italy.
        h. *At least six students have ever been to Italy.

Although one could account for the distribution of *any* and *ever* in examples (27a)–(27d) by reducing *No student* to *Not a student* and *Neither John nor Mary* to *Not either John or Mary*, the examples (27e) – (27h) clearly show that such a strategy is insufficient.

---

[12] See Keenan 1996 for a thorough discussion.

Keenan & Westerståhl 1997 state the linguistic problem posed by negative polarity items (npis) as follows:

Define the class of NPs which license the npis, and state what, if anything, those NPs have in common with *n 't/not*.

Observe first that the NPs which license npis satisfy the following scheme of inference:

(28)   All students work hard.
        X work hard.
        ∴ *X* is a student (are students).

Quantifiers which satisfy scheme (28) are called monotone decreasing. More formally:

Definition 5

a. A quantifier **Q** of type < 1 > is monotone decreasing iff whenever $X \in$ **Q** and $Y \subseteq X$, then $Y \in$ **Q**.

b. *A quantifier* **Q** *of type < 1 > is monotone increasing iff whenever $X \in$* **Q** *and $X \subseteq Y$, then $Y \in$* **Q**.

Examples of monotone increasing quantifiers are: **Every student, someone, John**, and **most teachers.** They satisfy scheme (29):

(29)   All students work hard.
        X is a student.
        ∴ *X* works hard.

An example of a quantifier which is neither decreasing nor increasing is **Exactly ten students**.

The following empirical generalization is based on the work of Ladusaw and Fauconnier (Ladusaw 1979, Ladusaw 1983, Fauconnier 1979). In order to simplify the comparison of monotone decreasing quantifiers with negation we use the functional approach to quantification in the statement of the generalization.

> *The Ladusaw-Fauconnier Generalization (LFG)*
> Negative polarity items occur within arguments of monotone decreasing functions but not within arguments of monotone increasing functions.

Keenan 1996 and Keenan & Westerståhl 1997 note that the LFG also gives the correct prediction for cases not considered by Ladusaw and Fauconnier.

(30)   a. No player's agent should ever act without his consent.
        b. *Every player's agent should ever act without his consent.

(31)   None of the teachers and not more than three of the students have ever been to Moscow.

In order to isolate the common feature of decreasing quantifiers and negation responsible for licensing negative polarity items, we have to give a more general definition.

Definition 6

a. *A partial order is a pair $< M, \leq >$, where M is a set and $\leq$ is a binary relation M which is reflexive ($\forall x(x \leq x)$), antisymmetric ($\forall x, y (x \leq y \wedge y \leq x \Rightarrow x = y)$) and transitive ($\forall x, y, z (x \leq y \wedge y \leq z \Rightarrow x \leq z)$).*

b. *If M and N are the domains of partial orders and $\phi : M \rightarrow N$ then*
   i. ϕ is increasing iff for all x, y $\in$ M, if x $\leq$ y, then $\phi(x) \leq \phi(y)$.
   ii. ϕ is decreasing iff for all x, y $\in$ M, if x $\leq$ y, then $\phi(y) \leq \phi(x)$.

It is easily seen that VP-negation as well as classical sentential negation are decreasing functions. For example *didn't cry* is interpreted as $M \setminus$ **cry**. Therefore **not** maps a set X to $M \setminus X$ and if $X \subseteq Y$, then **not**$(Y) = M \setminus Y \subseteq M \setminus X =$ **not**(X).

The partial order an the set of truth values $\{1, 0\}$ is given by: $1 \leq 1$, $0 \leq 1$, and $0 \leq 0$. Since classical negation maps 1 to 0 and 0 to 1 it is clearly a decreasing function. Therefore the LFG correctly predicts the facts in (26) too.

For refinements of this method and for observations about negative polarity items in other languages than English the reader is referred to Nam 1994, van der Wouden 1994 and Zwarts 1998.

Since the quantifiers in the following paragraphs will be of Type $< 1, 1 >$ we have to distinguish between quantifiers monotone increasing or decreasing in the first argument and monotone increasing in the second argument. For example **every** is right monotone increasing but left monotone decreasing and **no** is left and right monotone decreasing. If, in the following explanations, the argument, in which the quantifier is increasing or decreasing is not explicitly mentioned, then it will always be the right argument which is under discussion.

3 E-type pronouns and plural

It is is well known that the interpretation of indefinites as (generalized) existential quantifiers faces serious problems when it comes to analyzing so-called donkey sentences:

(32)   a. Every farmer who owns a donkey beats it.
        b. If a farmer owns a donkey, he beats it.

Given its intuitive truth-conditions, the correct formalisation of (32a) appears to be:

(33) $(\forall x)[Fx \rightarrow (\forall y)[Dx \wedge xOy] \rightarrow xBy]]$

However, the formalisations available to Generalized Quantifier Theory (GQT) are (34a) and (34b):

(34) a. $(\forall x)[Fx \rightarrow (\exists z)[Dz \wedge xOz]] \rightarrow xBy$
     b. $(\exists z)[Dz \wedge (\forall x)[Fx \rightarrow [Dx \wedge xOz]]]$

Although these formulae do represent certain possible 'specific' construals of (32a), they do not cover its most straightforward reading, viz. (33). Moreover, the formalisation suggests that, on that missing reading, the indefinite noun phrases do not express existential but, rather, universal quantifiers. Similar observations can be made concerning the conditional version (32b) of the donkey sentence. Here too it appears that, on its most prominent reading, the indefinites do not express existential quantifiers. In fact, a common analysis has it that indefinites never denote quantifiers but rather properties that get quantified by whichever grammatical construction they appear in.

Slightly less dramatic – and possibly related – problems have been known to arise with *discourse anaphora*, i.e. third-person pronouns that relate back to an indefinite in a previous sentence of the same text:

(35) a. A farmer owns a donkey. He beats it.
     b. $(\exists x)[Fx \wedge (\exists z)[Dz \wedge [xOz \wedge xBz]]$

Though in order to obtain the intended formalization (35b), the indefinites may be construed as existential quantifiers, they would have to take scope over the whole discourse, leading to a rather bad case of non-compositionality.

An assumption underlying the above formalizations is that *anaphoric links correspond to bindings of pronouns*. Maybe this assumption is an illusion. After all, (35a) could be roughly paraphrased by:

(36) A farmer owns a donkey. The farmer beats the donkey.

where the pronouns have been replaced by functionally equivalent definite descriptions, which can in turn be interpreted as quantifiers. In particular, analysing these descriptions as 'Russellian' quantifiers takes us to (37) where uniqueness is symbolized by $\exists^1$:[13]

(37) $(\exists x)[Fx \wedge (\exists z)[Dz \wedge xOz]] \wedge$
     $[(\exists^1 x)Fx \wedge (\exists^1 z)Dz \wedge (\exists x)[Fx \wedge (\exists z)[Dz \wedge xBz]]]$

However, (35b) and (37) are not equivalent: the former does not imply that there is a unique farmer-donkey pair, whereas the latter obviously does. Since (35a) may be appropriately – and truthfully – uttered even if there is more than one farmer, (37) cannot be the correct formalisation.

Why, then, does (36) easily pass as a paraphrase of (35a)? One reason could be that (37) is not a correct formalisation of (36). In fact, it has often been observed that definite descriptions do not always imply uniqueness as applied to

---

[13] In other words, '$(\exists^1 x)\phi$' means that the formula ϕ is satisfied by exactly one object (in *lieu* of x). It is important to realize that the bound variables appearing in these (and other) formulae do not refer to any specific individuals. This fact is brought out more clearly if we switch to set theoretic notation and write (37) as: $[(\mathbf{F} \times \mathbf{D}) \cap \mathbf{O} \neq \emptyset \wedge |\mathbf{F}| = 1 \wedge (\mathbf{F} \times \mathbf{D}) \cap \mathbf{B} \neq \emptyset]$

the predicate expressed by their head noun, but rather with respect to some further restricted property. For instance, someone who utters (38) usually does not mean to imply that there is only one teacher, but only presupposes that there is just one contextually relevant teacher:

(38)   The teacher is on her way.

This uniqueness presupposition appeals to the background knowledge shared by the participants in the conversation. If no particular teacher is commonly agreed to be the only contextually relevant one, an utterance of (38) would be inappropriate. Something similar may be felt about the definite descriptions in the second sentence in (36). Given the first sentence (and taking it that it has not been disputed), it may be natural to assume that there be only one *farmer who owns a donkey* and only one *donkey owned by a farmer.* This contextual restriction could be made explicit by the paraphrase (39a) and formalised along Russellian lines, as in (39b):

(39)   a. A farmer owns a donkey. The farmer who owns a donkey beats the donkey owned by a farmer.

   b. $(\exists x)[Fx \wedge (\exists z)[Dz \wedge xOz]] \wedge (\exists^1 x)[Fx \wedge (\exists z)[Dz \wedge xOz]] \wedge (\exists^1 z)[Dz \wedge (\exists x)[Fx \wedge xOz]] \wedge (\exists x)[Fx \wedge (\exists z)[Dz \wedge xOz \wedge xBz]]$

If we now take (35a) as a pronominal version of (39a), we arrive at a *descriptive* construal of anaphoric pronouns, i.e. one that does not equate anaphora with variable binding. According to this contrual, the pronoun is interpreted as a definite description whose restrictor consists of the restrictor and the (conjoined) scope of its antecedent. This interpretation of (certain) anaphoric pronouns is known as the *E-type* approach[14].

The E-type approach naturally covers certain cases of plural anaphora as in (40), which can be paraphrased by (41):

(40)   John sold most of his donkeys to Mary. They did not fit in her truck.

(41)   John sold most of his donkeys to Mary.
          The donkeys of John's that John sold to Mary did not fit in Mary's truck.

The important thing to notice about this pronoun-free paraphrase is that the underlined plural description can be analyzed in a straightforward way, i.e. as a quantifier over groups, selecting the maximal group with the (plural) property expressed by the noun. Using capital X, Y, ... to range over groups we could thus give the following formalisation[15]:

---

[14] Nobody seems to know why. The term E-type pronoun made its first appearance in Evans 1977. A precise account of plural E-type anaphora can be found in Kamp & Reyle 1993: 307ff.

[15] The notation '$(\sigma x)\phi$' is supposed to express plural abstraction, i.e. the largest group containing only individuals satisfying ϕ (in *lieu* of x). If we think of groups as sets, this boils down to the class abstraction $\{x \mid \phi\}$.

(42) a. $(MOSTx) (JD(x), S(j, x, m)) \wedge$
      b. $(\exists^1 X)[X = \sigma x(JD(x) \wedge S(j, x, m))] \wedge (\exists X)[X = \sigma x(JD(x) \wedge S(j, X, m)) \wedge \neg F(X, mt)]$

It should be noted that (42b) is quite parallel to (39b) in that the descriptive content of the anaphoric noun *(donkey of John's)* is enriched by the content of the scope of the antecedent quantifier.

Judging from these examples, one may suspect that, somewhat surprisingly, discourse anaphora are not bound variables, but quantifiers – to wit contextually restricted definite descriptions. Unfortunately, things are not that simple, as a variation of a famous (cf. Heim 1990) example reveals:

(43)   Irene bought a sage-plant and, because they were so cheap, she bought eight others along with it.

The problem the E-type approach has with (43) lies in its built-in uniqueness condition: obviously, the *it* in (43) cannot be paraphrased as *the (unique) sage-plant that Irene bought*. And more dramatic cases can be found when we turn to donkey sentences[16]:

(44)   When a donkey scents an animal, it runs away from it.

Again, there is no way to construe the anaphoric pronouns as definite descriptions – not even if the latter are relativised to the scenes implicitly quantified over by the *when*-clause. For such descriptions would be empty in scenes involving two donkeys scenting each other, so that the E-type approach would predict that (44) remains silent on them. But then (44) does say something about the two donkeys scenting each other, viz. that they start running. Indeed, it is hard to avoid the impression that (44) expresses quantification over pairs of animals – just as the dynamic approach to donkey anaphora would have it[17]. This connection is further investigated in Dekker 2001.

The above counter-examples turn on the uniqueness condition built into the E-type approach. What happens if we lift that constraint on descriptive pronouns, thus taking them as short for *indefinite descriptions?* After all, in the simplest cases (46) the corresponding existentially quantified description (47) come out as redundant, but truth-conditionally equivalent to existentially bound variables (48):

(45)   A farmer has just arrived. He is rich.

(46)   A farmer has just arrived. A farmer who has just arrived is rich.

(47) $(\exists x) [Fx \wedge Ax] \wedge (\exists x) [Fx \wedge Ax \wedge Rx]$

---

[16] This type of example has been brought up by Hans Kamp; cf. Heim 1990: 147f.

[17] Note that this quantification need not be universal in the sense that every donkey is said to run away from every animal it scents. A more natural reading might be that every donkey runs away from at least one donkey. We will return to this observation at the end of this section.

(48) $(\exists x)\,[Fx \wedge Ax \wedge Rx]$

However, in slightly more involved cases, the pronouns cannot be paraphrased by existential quantifiers. If we try to paraphrase both pronouns in (49) by indefinites (50) and analyze the latter as existential quantifiers (51), the result will not be adequate:

(49)   A farmer owns a donkey. He beats it.

(50)   A farmer owns a donkey.
          A farmer who owns a donkey beats a donkey owned by a farmer.

(51) $(\exists x)\,[Fx \wedge (\exists z)\,[Dz \wedge xOz]] \wedge (\exists x)\,[Fx \wedge (\exists z)\,[Dz \wedge xOz] \wedge$
          $(\exists z')\,[Dz' \wedge (\exists x')[Fx' \wedge x'Oz'] \wedge xBz']]$

As a paraphrase and analysis of (49), (50) and (51) are obviously too weak – they could, e.g., be true if all farmers only beat their neighbour's donkey. To be sure, there is an adequate way of paraphrasing the pronouns in (49) by indefinites:

(52)   A farmer who owns a donkey ($\sim$ he) beats a donkey he owns ($\sim$ it).

However, in order for this to come out correctly, the underlined pronoun cannot be interpreted in the same descriptive way as the other occurrence of *he*, but rather corresponds to a bound variable:

(53) $(\exists x)\,[Fx \wedge (\exists z)\,[Dz \wedge xOz]] \wedge (\exists x)[Fx \wedge (\exists z)\,[Dz \wedge \underline{x}Oz \wedge xBz]]$

(53) can even be derived in an orderly, compositional fashion[18]. However, on such an approach, bound pronouns play a role that is strikingly similar to that of discourse referents in dynamic semantics. This is as close as one can get to an adequate treatment of discourse anaphora in terms of descriptive pronouns.

Examples like (43) and (44) invite the conclusion that E-type pronominalisation is merely an epiphenomenon produced by the interaction between discourse anaphora and contextual background. However, as has been noted by (van Rooy 1997: 79ff.), there are problem cases for dynamic semantics that an E-type approach can handle rather naturally:

(54)   a. It is not true that there is a bus stop in this village. It is near the post office.
          b. It is not true that there is no bus stop in this village. It is near the post office.

The fact that it does not seem to make sense to relate the underlined pronoun in (54a) to the underlined indefinite, is usually described in terms of logico-syntactic constellation: anaphoric links must not cross negations. It is therefore

---

[18] See Section 4.2 (based on van der Does 1996) for an approach along these lines.

to be expected that the corresponding anaphor in (54b) is illicit, which it isn't[19]. But it does come with a uniqueness condition which becomes more visible in:

(55)   It is not true that no honest man lives in this village. *He* is just away an business.

(55) strongly suggests that there is precisely one honest man among the inhabitants of the village – as predicted by an E-type account of the underlined pronoun.

The conclusion seems to be that, while the E-type strategy works fine for *inaccessible* pronouns and (certain cases of) plural anaphora, ordinary donkey and discourse anaphora lie outside the realm of classical quantifier semantics and should be handled by other – e.g. dynamic – means. But then the dynamic treatment of donkey sentences should not be seen as an alternative to but rather an *extension* of **GQ** theory. Let us briefly take this perspective.

According to present-day semantic folklore (Heim 1982)[20], the logical analysis of the donkey sentence (56a) involves a partition into three components:

(56)   a. Every farmer who owns a donkey beats it.

       b. *Quantifier*: every

       c. *Restrictor*: farmer who owns a donkey

       d. *Scope*: beats it

In order to obtain the correct truth conditions both restrictor and scope are then interpreted as binary relations – rather than (unary) properties as the traditional approach would have it. Roughly, the restrictor expresses the relation R that holds between given x and y iff x is a farmer and y is a donkey owned by x: and, under the relevant anaphoric resolution, the scope expresses the relation S of beating. The quantifier then combines R and S into a proposition. In particular, the quantifier *every* in (56a) must be construed as a relation between binary relations – rather than (unary) properties as the GQ approach would have it. Which relation could that be? Since (56a) is true iff $R \subseteq S$, the answer seems to be obvious: *every* expresses the subset relation. In other words, in the donkey sentence (56a) the quantifier *every* receives its ordinary interpretation but switches its domain: instead of quantifying over individuals, it now quantifies over pairs of individuals. Formally, the quantifier's type changes from $((et)((et)t))$ to $((e^2t)((e^2t)t))$[21]. And it is obvious what triggers this type switch: the very fact that it is used as a functor on binary relations. We thus seem to have a clear case of *type shifting* (or *coercion*) as a result of type mismatch.

---

[19] We regard *no* as reducible to (abstract) negation plus indefinite: *no bus stop* $\sim$ *not a bus stop*.

[20] It should be noted that the type-shifting analysis of donkey sentences presupposes a non-quantificational interpretation of indefinites and anaphoric pronouns. The analysis ultimately goes back to Lewis 1975 and can be seen to form the common core of virtually all later treatments of donkey anaphora, about which more is said in Marcus Kracht's contribution to this volume.

[21] Of course $a^n t$ is the type of n-tuples of objects of type a.

One problem with this analysis is that it does not smoothly generalize to other kinds of quantifiers. In particular, given the **GQ** analysis of *most,* one would expect a sentence like (57a) to be interpreted as (57b), i.e. as saying that there are more pairs consisting of farmers and donkeys they own and beat, than pairs of farmers they own but don't beat:

(57) a. Most farmers who own a donkey beat it.
      b. $(MOST < x, y > ([Fx \wedge Dy \wedge xOy], xBy)$

However, a look at extremely unbalanced scenarios – involving, say, one farmer beating each of his two hundred donkeys vs. two animal-respecting farmers with one donkey each – reveals that (57a) does not have a *symmetric* reading according to which *most* expresses the generalized quantifier MOST over pairs. Rather, the sentence means that most donkey-owning farmers beat all, or maybe some, of their donkeys. Instead of (57b), we would thus need one of the following formalizations:

(58) a. $(MOSTx)([Fx \wedge (\exists y)[Dy \wedge xOy]], [Fx \wedge (\forall y)[[Dz \wedge xOy] \rightarrow xBy])$
      b. $(MOSTx)([Fx \wedge (\exists y)[Dy \wedge xOy]], [Fx \wedge (\exists y)[[Dz \wedge xOy \wedge xBy])$

It is important to realize that both of these formalisations are compatible with the type shifting analysis of donkey sentences. What distinguishes them from (57b) is just the shift itself, not the type of the shifted quantifier. For instance, (57b) can be obtained by applying the following operation to the restrictor R and scope S defined by (56c) and (56d):

(59) $\lambda A \lambda B(MOSTx)((\exists y)xAy, (\forall y)[xAy \rightarrow xBy])$

This operation may be regarded as one way of type-shifting the quantifier *most* in (57a). And it is clear that (59) easily generalizes to other donkey sentences involving more indefinites and/or other quantifiers. It can also be applied to the original donkey sentence (57a), where it yields (60a), which is equivalent to the intended analysis (60b):

(60) a. $(ALLx)([Fx \wedge (\exists y)[Dy \wedge xOy]], [Fx \wedge (\forall y)[[Dz \wedge xOy] \rightarrow xBy])$
      b. $(\forall x)[Fx \wedge (\forall y)[[Dx \wedge xOy] \rightarrow xBy])$

It thus turns out that the universal quantifiers in the logical paraphrase (60b) of (the most likely reading of) the donkey sentence have different sources: the outermost one is due to the lexical meaning of the determiner *every* and thus disappears when the latter is replaced by a different determiner; the other universal quantifier, however, is the result of a type-shift applying to that determiner that is equally applicable in other cases, where it also leads to universal quantification. In particular, there is no need for a domain shift from individuals to pairs. In fact, the latter is somewhat suspicious anyway, because it does not conform to general principles of type shifting observed elsewhere[22].

---

[22] The reason is that the domain shift implicit in Lewis's (1975) treatment of donkeys is not de-

The construal (58b) of (57a) can also be obtained by type shifting, viz.:

(61) $\lambda A \lambda B(MOSTx)((\exists y)xAy, (\exists y)[xAy \wedge xBy])$

When applying the same procedure to the original donkey-sentence, the result is no longer equivalent to (60b) but gives the (sometimes) so-called *weak reading* according to which every donkey-owning farmer beats some donkey he owns[23].

4 The scope of dynamic logic

4.1 Dynamic predicate logic

This section is not intended as an introduction to dynamic predicate logic (DPL). We just want to remind the reader of the most basic facts of this system[24].

The syntax of DPL is the same as the syntax of first-order predicate logic (without constants), but the semantics differs.

Let $\mathcal{M} =< M, I >$ be a model for first-order predicate logic with domain M and interpretation function I. Let VAR be the set of individual variables and let $\mathcal{V}(M)$ be the set of assignments $g : VAR \rightarrow M$.

$g \sim_x h$ means: $g(y) = h(y)$ for all $y \neq x$.

Definition 7. The semantics of dynamic predicate logic (DPL).

a. $[\![R(x_1, \ldots, -x_n)]\!] = \{<g, g >: < g(x_1, \ldots, g(x_n) >\in I(R)\}$
b. $[\![x_1 = x_2]\!] = \{<g, g >: g(x_1) = g(x_2)\}$
c. $[\![\neg\phi]\!] = \{<g, g>: \neg\exists h :< g,h >\in [\![\phi]\!]\}$
d. $[\![\phi \wedge \psi]\!] = \{<g, h >: \exists k :< g, k>\in [\![\phi]\!] \wedge < k, h >\in [\![\psi]\!]\}$
e. $[\![(\exists x)\phi]\!] = \{<g, h >: \exists k \sim_x g :< k, h >\in [\![\phi]\!]\}$

The semantics of DPL validates the scheme (62a) for arbitrary ψ [25].

(62) $(\exists x)\phi \wedge \psi \Leftrightarrow (\exists x)(\phi \wedge \phi)$

Given the definition of $\phi \rightarrow \psi$ and $(\forall x)\phi$ in (63) one easily derives the donkey equivalence (64).

---

finable in (functional) type logic, whereas the above operations clearly are. Unfortunately, these observations are a far cry from a *theory* of type shifting that predicts precisely the readings given here. For more an these topics, the reader should consult Rooth 1987, van der Does 1996 and the literature cited in Kracht's contribution to this volume.

[23] Readers who doubt that (56a) has such a reading should consult (Chierchia 1995: 64) for a context in which it is even more prominent than (60b).

[24] For a detailed introduction to DPL see Marcus Kracht's contribution to this volume or Groenendijk & Stokhof 1991.

[25] In classical first order predicate logic scheme (62a) is valid provided x does not occur freely in ψ.

(63)   a. $\phi \rightarrow \psi := \neg(\phi \wedge \neg\psi)$
       b. $(\forall x)\phi := \neg(\exists x)\neg\phi$

(64) $(\exists x)\phi \rightarrow \psi \Leftrightarrow (\forall x)(\phi \rightarrow \psi)$

The sentences (65a) and (66a) are represented by the DPL-formulas in (65b) and (66b), respectively, which by (62) and (64) give the correct interpretations.

(65)   a. A man walks in the park. He whistles.
       b. $(\exists x)\,(man(x) \wedge walk - in - the - park(x)) \wedge whistle(x)$

(66)   a. Every farmer who owns a donkey beats it.
       b. $(\forall x)(farmer(x) \wedge (\exists y)(donkey(y) \wedge own(x, y)) \rightarrow beat(x, y))$

4.2 The Results of van der Does

In this section we will apply the theory of generalized quantifiers to the core of dynamic semantics – the interpretation of anaphoric dependencies. Van der Does's results show that the quantificational perspective allows for an understanding of the distinction between static and dynamic noun phrases as a reflection of logical properties that form the basis of generalized quantifier theory.

All quantifiers in this section are assumed to be binary and logical. To motivate the questions and the proposed answers of this section let us consider example (65a) from the point of view of a generalized quantifier approach[26].

(67)   **Some(man, walks – in – the – park). A(whistles).**

Here **A** represents a contextually restricted quantifier, which serves as interpretation of the pronoun *He*. Following a generalized E-Type approach the contextual restriction is given by the antecedent sentence. In example (67) for instance it is the intersection of the two arguments of the quantifier **Some**. This means that **A(whistles)** is just short for **A(man ∩ walks – in – the – park, whistles)**. The right hand side of (62a) represented in generalized quantifier notation is:

(68)   **Some(man, walks – in – the – park ∩ whistles).**

If we choose for **A** the quantifier **Some** it is immediate that under the given assumptions (67) and (68) are equivalent.

(69)   **Some(man, walks – in – the – park)**   ∧
         Some(man ∩ walks – in – the – park, whistles)
         ───
         Some(man, walks – in – the – park ∩ whistles)

Considering equivalence (62a) from this point of view naturally leads to the following question: Which quantifier **Q** satisfy schema (70) for a given **A**?

---

[26] We introduce brackets in the following examples in order to increase readability.

(70) $\dfrac{\mathbf{Q}XY \qquad \wedge \quad \mathbf{A}Z}{\mathbf{Q}X\,Y \cap Z}$

where $\mathbf{A}Z$ is short for $\mathbf{A}X \cap Y\,Z$.

This is a semantically interesting problem, because it also raises the question for which $\mathbf{Q}$ the method of scope extension is empirically successful.

Before we prove some of the formal results in detail let us first see more examples where the above equivalence holds and some where (70) fails.

(71) $\dfrac{\text{All men played the guitar.} \qquad\qquad \text{They sang.}}{\text{All men played the guitar and sang.}}$

This is an instance of (70) where *they* is interpreted as the universal quantifier restricted to the set **man ∩ played – the – guitar.**

If $\mathbf{Q}$ is conservative we always have one direction of (71):

(72) $\mathbf{Q}XY \qquad X \cap Y \subseteq Z$
$\Rightarrow \mathbf{Q}X\,Y \cap Z$

But here is an example where the converse fails.

(73)   Some men played the guitar and sang.
         $\nRightarrow$ Some men played the guitar. They sang.

To see this consider the premise written in set notation. It is true iff

> **man ∩ played – the – guitar ∩ sang** $\neq 0$.

It follows that

> **man ∩ played – the – guitar** $\neq 0$.

But the clause corresponding to *They sang* does not follow from the premise.

> **man ∩ played – the – guitar** $\subseteq$ **sang.**

This shows that the premise is true in a situation where not all guitar playing men sang, but the conclusion is false in such a situation; it requires that all guitar playing men are also singers.

This example also illustrates the general observation that the first part of the conclusion is implied whenever $\mathbf{Q}$ in (70) is monotone increasing. Here are some more examples:

(74)   Five men bought whiskey. Five got drunk.
         $\Leftrightarrow$ Five men bought whiskey and got drunk.

An easy calculation shows that equivalence (74) is valid if *five* is interpreted as *at least five* but invalid if it is interpreted as *exactly five*.

The equivalence in example (75) however is invalid irrespective of the interpretation of *five*.

(75)   Five men bought whiskey. Some got drunk.
        ⇎ Five men bought whiskey and got drunk.

The last example is a little bit more complicated.

(76)   Most men went to the party. Most had fun.
        ⇎ Most men went to the party and had fun.

Although *Most men went to the party and had fun*, which is true if $| M \cap (P \cap F) | > | M \setminus (P \cap F) |$, implies *Most men went to the party. Most had fun.*, i.e. $| M \cap P | > | M \setminus P |$, $| (M \cap P) \cap F | > | (M \cap P) \setminus F |$, the converse is not true.

This example is important, because it shows that requiring **Q** and **A** to be one and the same monotone increasing quantifier is not enough to validate (70), since **Most** is monotone increasing. In order to characterize those quantifiers for which (70) is correct it is therefore necessary to investigate a subclass of the monotone increasing quantifiers. It turns out that this is the class of *restrictive* quantifiers.

Consider the following schemata:

(77) $\dfrac{QX\ Y\cap Z}{QXY}$ $\dfrac{QX\ Y\cap Z}{QX\cap Y\ Z}$

The first scheme in (77) is familiar. A quantifier satisfies this scheme iff it is monotone increasing. The second is restrictivness. An example is provided by (78):

(78) $\dfrac{\text{Most books are yellow and expensive.}}{\text{Most yellow books are expensive.}}$

Therefore **Most** is an example of a restrictive quantifier. Restrictivness is a rather week property. For example it is weaker than intersectivity. The following scheme (79) is equivalent to restrictiveness.

(79) $\dfrac{QXY\ Y\subseteq Z}{QX\cap Z\ Y}$

Proof: Assume the second scheme of (77) is satisfied by quantifier **Q** and QXY, $Y \subseteq Z$. Then $QX\ Z\cap Y$ and therefore by (77) $QX\cap Z\ Y$

Conversely assume quantifier **Q** satisfies (79) and $QX\ Y\cap Z$. Then by (79) $QX\cap Y\ Y\cap Z$, since $Y \cap Z \subseteq Y$. $QX\cap Y\ Y\cap Z$ iff (CONS) $QX\cap Y\ X\cap Y\cap Z$ iff (CONS) $QX\cap Y\ Z$.

We will prove now in detail the first major result of van der Does. Roughly put this result says that logical **A** have property (70) iff the only determiners which validate (70) are the same as **A** modulo a cardinality restriction of the first argument. For a more precise statement of this result we need:

Definition 8. *Let θ be a class of cardinals. The quantifier $\mathbf{Q}^\theta$ is defined by:*

$$\mathbf{Q}^\theta XY \Leftrightarrow |X| \in \theta \wedge \mathbf{Q}XY$$

Theorem 1. A is *logical and has property (70), iff for all logical* Q: Q *has property (70) iff* $Q = A^\theta$ *for some class of cardinals* θ.

The proof of theorem 1 proceeds via two lemmas. The first is:

Lemma 3. *Let A be restrictive. For each non-empty[27] quantifier* Q *which satisfies (70) we have:* $AX = QX$.

Proof: We first prove $Q \subseteq A$. Assume Q has property (70), then $QXY \Leftrightarrow_{CONS}$ $QX\ X \cap Y \Rightarrow_{(70)} AX \cap X\ Y \Leftrightarrow AXY$.

We now prove $A \subseteq Q$ for non-empty Q. Therefore assume $QX \ne \emptyset$ and AXY. There is a Z with QXZ. From (70) follows that Q is monotone increasing. Hence we have: $QX\ Z \cup Y$. Since A is restrictive and $Y \subseteq Z \cup Y$ we get with (79) $AX \cap (Z \cup Y)\ Y$. Since we have shown $QX\ Z \cup Y \wedge AX \cap (Z \cup Y)\ Y$ property (70) implies $QX\ (Z \cup Y) \cap Y$. But $(Z \cup Y) \cap Y = Y$ and we have: QXY.

Lemma 3 allows us to partially describe the quantifiers Q which satisfy (70); they are those quantifiers which are monotone increasing and are subsets of A. In general we can't have equality, because Q may be empty. But the concept in Definition 8 allows to prove the following lemma:

Lemma 4. *Let A be logical and restrictive. If a logical quantifier* Q *has (70), then* $Q = A^\theta$ *for some class of cardinals* θ.

Proof: Assume that Q has (70). Define:

$$\theta = \{\kappa \mid \exists X(QX \ne \emptyset \wedge |X| = \kappa)\}$$

We first prove $Q \subseteq A^\theta$. Assume QXY. Then $|X| \in \theta$ and since $Q \subseteq A$ we have $A^\theta XY$.

To show the converse we assume $A^\theta XY$. From this assumption follows that $|X| \in \theta$ and AXY. Next we derive from the definition of θ the existence of a set X' with $|X'| = |X|$ and $QX' \ne \emptyset$. Lemma 3 derives

$$\Diamond \qquad \text{For all } Y': QX'Y' \Leftrightarrow AX'Y'.$$

Since $|X| = |X'|$ there exists a bijection $\pi : X \to X'$ with the following properties[28]:

$$|X \cap \overline{(X \cap Y)}| = |X' \cap \pi(\overline{X \cap Y})| \text{ and}$$
$$|X \cap Y| = |X' \cap \pi(X \cap Y)|.$$

We now have the following equivalences[29]: $AXY \Leftrightarrow_{logicality} AX'\pi(X \cup Y) \Leftrightarrow_{\Diamond}$ $QX'\pi(X \cap Y) \Leftrightarrow_{logicality} QXY$.

Since most quantifiers Q are not of the form A^θ Lemma 4 makes clear that preservation of meaning under scope extension is rare. The question is, whether

---

[27] A quantifier Q is non-empty iff $QX \ne \emptyset$.

[28] Note that the sets $X \setminus Y$ and $X \cap Y$ determine the behaviour of logical Q.

[29] Note that logicality includes conservativity.

the quantifiers which have (70) are enough for natural language anaphora resolution.

It is now easy to prove theorem 1:

Proof of theorem 1: Assume first that **A** is logical and has property (70). Such
an **A** is restrictive and A^{θ} is logical if **A** is. Lemma 4 informs us that all we have
to prove is that A^{θ} has (70) with respect to logical **Q**.

$$A^{\theta} XY \wedge AX \cap Y Z$$
$$\Leftrightarrow |X| \in \theta \wedge AXY \wedge AX \cap Y Z$$
$$\Leftrightarrow_{A \ has \ (70)} |X| \in \theta \wedge AX \ Y \cap Z$$
$$\Leftrightarrow A^{\theta} X \ Y \cap Z$$

Conversely if the logical quantifiers which satisfy (70) are precisely A^{θ} for some
θ then A must have (70) as well, since

$$A = A^{\{\kappa: \ \kappa = \kappa\}}.$$

From now an we will not bother to prove van der Does's results in detail, but
concentrate on sketching the most important points of the argumentation, if
possible by way of examples.

Before we go on developing the theoretical machinery we show how to apply Theorem 1 to a simple example. Singular *some* or *a*, which are assumed to
be treated alike, come in two variants.

(80)   a. **some** $XY \Leftrightarrow X \cap Y \neq 0$
        b. **some**^{s} $XY \Leftrightarrow X \cap Y \neq 0 \wedge |X| = 1$

The definitions correspond to Russell's view of *a* and *the*. Consider now:

(81)   A man walks in the park. He whistles.
        _____
        A man walks in the park and whistles.

When does the equivalence in (81) hold? Theorem 1 allows us to derive the
following answers. The equivalence holds if both *a* and *he* are interpreted as
some, both as **some**^{s}, or *a* is interpreted as the description **some**^{s} and *he* as **some**. The equivalence does not hold if *a* is an existential and *he* a singular definite description.

We therefore arrive at the conclusion that the interpretation of singular pronouns via the mechanism of scope extension (70) has to be restricted to certain
parts of **some**[30]. The question arises whether this strategy accounts for all singular anaphoric links. We will first sketch van der Does's positive answer to this
question and then discuss the plural case.

The first task is to determine those NPs which are possible antecedents for
singular anaphora. This task is solved by providing a constraint for the denota-

---

[30] See the appendix for a note an choice functions.

tions of singular antecedents. This constraint will exclude all NPs as singular antecedents except those whose determiner is one in the following list:

some^s, a, just one, the, one of the, one ... out of –.

All these can be interpreted as **some**$^\theta$ where θ is a set of cardinals. This result shows that the mechanism of scope extension is adequate for singular anaphora.

Van der Does proposes the *singular dynamicity constraint* (short: *SDYN*) as a restriction on the denotation of singular antecedents. This constraint corresponds to the common intuition that singular antecedents introduce a possible referent for the anaphor.

SDYN $\mathbf{Q}_M XY \Rightarrow \exists y \in Y : \mathbf{Q}_M X \{y\}$

Note that under conservativity, which is assumed here, since we presuppose that all quantifiers are logical, *SDYN* is equivalent with: $\mathbf{Q}_M XY \Rightarrow \exists y \in X \cap Y :$ $\mathbf{Q}_M X \{y\}$

It is assumed that singular antecedents satisfy *SDYN*, but not that all quantifiers satisfying *SDYN* are singular antecedents.

Restriction 7. *All singular antecedents satisfy SDYN.*

There is still something vague about Restriction 7. Do we want singular antecedents to satisfy *SDYN* locally, i.e. for given M, X, Y, or globally, which means for all M, X, Y? The answer to this question has empirical consequences, since, for example, on a particular universe *every* may mean the same as say *just one*. Therefore the local variant does not exclude the anaphoric link in (82):

(82)   Every man walks in the park. He whistles.

The global version however excludes this link. We therefore assume that Constraint 7 is satisfied globally. This allows us to conclude that no non-empty SDYN-determiner is monotone decreasing. Since each non-empty *SDYN* – $\mathbf{Q}_M$ with $\mathbf{Q}_M XY$ implies $X \neq 0 \neq Y$, but for a non-empty monotone decreasing quantifier we get $\mathbf{Q}_M X0$ for some X, this shows that under a global interpretation of Restriction 7 there can be no anaphoric link in (83).

(83)   No man walks in the park. He whistles.

We will therefore be concerned from now on with the behaviour of quantifiers with different monotonicity properties. In order to be able to work with van Benthem trees let us assume Restriction 6 (FIN) here. $\mathbf{Q}^\theta$ will now be written as $\mathbf{Q}^A$ where A is a set of natural numbers.

With respect to monotone increasing singular antecedents there is no problem, since we have

Theorem 2. *The only monotone increasing singular antecedents are. those of the form* **some**^{A} *where A is a set of natural numbers.*

Proof: We will give some of the details of the proof of Theorem 2, since it is an excellent illustration of the use of van Benthem trees.

some^A certainly satisfies *SDYN* and is monotone increasing. So we assume that a monotone increasing **Q** is given. We have to show that such a **Q** = **some**^{A}. Since we assume FIN and furthermore that **Q** is logical, **Q** can be considered as a relation **q** between numbers. The rest of the proof just inspects the effects of *SDYN* and monotonicity on van Benthem trees.

Let us first describe *SDYN* in the tree of numbers. It corresponds to the following clause:

$$\mathbf{q}nm \Rightarrow m \geq 1 \wedge \mathbf{q}(n + m - 1)\,1$$

Note that $n+m$ *is* the size of the first argument of **Q** in the tree of numbers; and the first argument of **q** is $|\,X \setminus Y\,|$, the second $|\,X \cap Y\,|$. So if we know **q**13 we also know by *SDYN* **q**.

Monotone increasing quantifiers have the following property in the tree of numbers. If we have a point in **q**, then all points to the right of this point are in **q** as well. Formally:

$$\mathbf{q}nm \Rightarrow \forall k(m \leq k \leq n + m \Rightarrow \mathbf{q}(n + m - k)k$$

This follows easily from the fact that $\mathbf{Q}XY \wedge Y \subseteq Y' \Rightarrow \mathbf{Q}XY'$ implies $|\,X \setminus Y\,| \geq |\,X \setminus Y'\,|$ and $|\,X \cap Y\,| \leq |\,X \cap Y'\,|$.

Since by *SDYN* we have **q**m0 for no m, we get partial information about monotone increasing quantifiers satisfying *SDYN* [31]. The first step gives us the following picture:

$\|X\|=0$								
$\|X\|=1$			..		?			
$\|X\|=2$		−		?		?		
$\|X\|=3$		.-	?		?		?	
$\|X\|=4$	−		?		?		?	?
$\|X\|=5$	−	?		?		?		?	?

Again with *SDYN:* for very line $n+1$ at which **q** has a + we have **q**n1.

---

[31] We continue to use + for a node in the tree of numbers that is an element of **q**, − for a node that isn't and ? for a node which is undetermined with respect to elementhood.

only if:

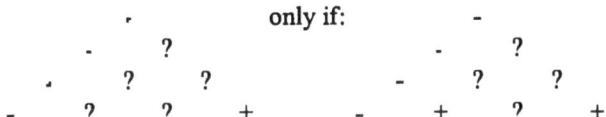

If we combine this pattern with the fact that **Q** is monotone increasing we derive for all m and $n \geq 1$: qmn.

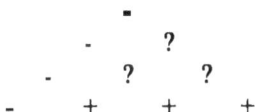

Now let $A = \{n : \mathbf{q} \text{ has a } + \text{ at some row } n\}$. The resulting pattern is then that of **some**^{A}.

By the discussion so far we know that if there are any problematic singular antecedents satisfying $SDYN$, then these are bound to be non-monotonic.

By inspecting the proof of Theorem 2 we get the additional information that SDYN-Quantifier are supersets of **exactly one**^{A}.

Corollary 1. *For each SDYN* **Q** *it is true that:* **exactly one**$^A \subseteq$ **Q**, *where A is a set of natural numbers.*

The most important class of non-monotonic determiners which constitute singular antecedents are the indefinites, defined as follows:

Definition 9. *A quantifier* **Q** *is an indefinite iff it satisfies:*

$$\mathbf{Q}XY \leftrightarrow |X \cap Y| \in \mathbf{N},$$

where **N** *is a set of natural numbers.*

For example a singleton set $\{n\}$ gives **just n** and **at least n** is $\{k \mid n \leq k\}$. We will write $< \mathbf{N} > XY$ for indefinites.

The following theorem, which we will not prove here, characterises the non-empty, non-monotonic, weakly intersective $SDYN$ quantifiers. This result makes clear that singular indefinite antecedents are not problematic for the scope extension strategy.

Theorem 3. *The only non-empty, non-monotonic, weakly intersective, SDYN* **Q** *are those of the form* $< \{1\} \cup \mathbf{N} >^A$ *with $A \neq \emptyset$,* **N** *a set of natural numbers such that:*

    (i) $0 \notin \mathbf{N}$.
    (ii) $\exists k > 1 : k \notin \mathbf{N}$.

However this result does not give a complete characterization of singular ante-cedents, since there are determiners denoting quantifiers $< \{1\} \cup N >^A$ which are not possible singular antecedents. One example of such a determiner is given in (84).

(84)   One or five students sang. *He was clever.

Therefore we have to conclude that the converse of Constraint 7 is false.

Empirical investigations suggest that the only non-monotonic singular ante-cedents are of the form $< \{1\} > (= \textbf{just one})$[32], apart from the monotone increa-sing $\textbf{some}^A$, which can be equivalently defined as $< N >$, with $N = \{n \mid n \geq 1\}$.

So, given the inclusion ordering $< \{1\} >^A \subseteq < \{1\} \cup N >^A \subseteq \textbf{some}^A$ it seems that only the weakest and the strongest elements of this ordering can figure as singular antecedents. From this discussion we conclude that the method of scope extension is adequate for the singular case.

Let us now turn to plural antecedents and anaphora. We will first give some cases were scope extension works and then concentrate on more problematic examples.

Standard examples of NPs which are interpreted as anaphora, include defi-nites like *they, the student, those four professors.*

We now consider the following numberless, singular and plural forms of the quantifier **all**.

(85)   a. $\textbf{all}XY \subseteq Y.$
         b. $\textbf{all}^S XY \subseteq Y \wedge |A| = 1.$
         c. $\textbf{all}^P XY \subseteq Y \wedge |A| > 1.$

The determiner *the is* interpreted as $\textbf{all}^S$ or as $\textbf{all}^P$ and the denotation of *they is* $\textbf{all}$ or $\textbf{all}^P$. Each of these quantifiers satisfy (70) with $A = \textbf{all}$.

(86)   The books are expensive.   They are old.
          ――
          The books are expensive and old.

The sentences in (86) are equivalent if *the* and *they* are both interpreted as in (85) or if *the* denotes $\textbf{all}^P$ and *they* **all**.

If we could interpret *the* as **all** and *they* as the plural in (85c), then the above equivalence would not be true, as an easy calculation shows; hence the inference from bottom to top is no longer valid.

Definition 10. A *quantifier* Q *is maximal iff for all* M: $Q_M \subseteq \textbf{all}_M$

For the case where $A = \textbf{all}$ theorem 1 implies that the only quantifiers that satis-fy (70) are the maximal monotone increasing ones. These are the quantifiers of form A^θ. Examples of such determiners are *the four, the four ... or more.* Note that the equivalence in the following example holds in accordance with the corollary implied by Theorem 1.

―――――――――――――――――――――――――――
[32] This corresponds to Definition 9 with $N = \emptyset$.

(87)　　The four books are expensive.　　　　They are old.
　　　　———————————————————————————
　　　　The four books are expensive and old.

If we assume that *they* is interpreted as (85c), i.e. as pluralic, the above equivalence is still valid. This case is covered by Theorem 1 too, since this theorem implies that the only quantifiers for which the scheme (70) where $\mathbf{A} = \mathbf{all}^\theta$ is valid are the quantifiers $\mathbf{all}^\theta$ with $\theta' \subseteq \theta$.

We will now turn to the analysis of numerals. Here we will encounter examples which are somewhat problematic for the scope extension strategy.

Consider examples (88) and (89).

(88)　　Five women went to a bar.　　　　Five had a beer.
　　　　———————————————————————————
　　　　Five women went to a bar and had a beer.

(89)　　Four women went to a bar.　　　　They had a beer.
　　　　———————————————————————————
　　　　Four women went to a bar and had a beer.

If *five is* interpreted as **at least five,** then the equivalence in (88) certainly holds. For $\mathbf{A} = \mathbf{five}$ scheme (70) holds for **five** and similarly for other numerals as predicted by Theorem 1.

However if we interpret *four* as the quantifier **four** and *they* according to (85c), the equivalence (89) is not valid, since **four** is not of the form $\mathbf{all}^\theta$ required by Theorem 1. Therefore this case is not covered by scope extension. But of course there are ways out. Numerals may be viewed in a quantificational, referential or adjectival way[33]. (89) is valid if *four* is interpreted referentially. In this case *four* is interpreted as $\mathbf{all}^4$ defined in (90).

(90)　　$\mathbf{all}^4\, X{\cap}C\, Y \Leftrightarrow X \cap C \subseteq Y \wedge \mid X \cap C \mid = 4.$

It is easy to see that under this interpretation of *four* (89) is valid. The difference between the referential and adjectival use is subtle. Consider the following recipe to transform an arbitrary determiner $\mathbf{Q}$ into an adjective (Kamp & Reyle 1993):

(91)　　$ADJ(\mathbf{Q})XY \Leftrightarrow \exists X' \subseteq X\,[\mathbf{Q}XX' \wedge X' \subseteq Y].$

The following observations show that this is different from the referential use, since recipe (91) invalidates (89). Observe first (van Benthem 1986) $ADJ(\mathbf{Q})$ is always right monotone increasing: $ADJ(\mathbf{Q})XY \wedge Y \subseteq Y'$ iff $\exists X' \subseteq X\,[\mathbf{Q}XX' \wedge X' \subseteq Y] \wedge Y \subseteq Y'$. It is clear that this implies $ADJ(Q)XY'$. Moreover $ADJ(Q) = Q$ iff Q is conservative and right monotone increasing. Before we prove this simple fact let us first show how it explains the difference between the referential and the adjectival use.

---

[33] For more information about the different uses of numerals the reader is advised to consult van der Does 1994.

Note that $ADJ(\textbf{just } n) = ADJ(\textbf{at least } n)$, since $\exists X' \subseteq X [| X \cap X' | = 4 \wedge X' \subseteq Y]$ implies $\exists X' \subseteq X [| X \cap X' | \geq 4 \wedge X' \subseteq Y]$ and conversely. Since **at least** n is conservative and right monotone increasing we have $ADJ(\textbf{at least } n) = $ **at least** n. Putting things together we conclude that $ADJ(\textbf{just } n) = $ **at least** n, which means that we are back at the quantificational interpretation of *four*, which invalidates (89). Let us now prove Lemma 5.

Lemma 5. $ADJ(\textbf{Q}) = \textbf{Q}$ *iff* $\textbf{Q}$ *is conservative and right monotone increasing.*

Proof: Assume $< X, Y > \in ADJ(\textbf{Q})$. We want to show that $< X, Y > \in \textbf{Q}$. $< X, Y > \in ADJ(\textbf{Q})$ *iff* $\exists X' \subseteq X [\textbf{Q}XX' \wedge X' \subseteq Y]$. Since $\textbf{Q}$ *is* right monotone increasing we have $\textbf{Q}XY$.

Conversely assume that $< X, Y > \in \textbf{Q}$. Since $\textbf{Q}$ *is* conservative this holds *iff* $\textbf{Q}X\ X \cap Y$. This then implies $\exists X' \subseteq X [\textbf{Q}XX' \wedge X' \subseteq Y]$. Therefore $< X, Y > \in ADJ(\textbf{Q})$.

We now briefly turn to the discussion of numerals in second-order DRT (Kamp & Reyle 1993) and a problem with *just four*.

A sentence like *Four women went to a bar* would be translated in the DRS (92).

(92) $\quad X [| X | = 4 \wedge X \subseteq \textit{women} \wedge X \subseteq \textit{went to a bar}]$.

The variable X would then be bound by the discourse operator $\exists$. During the discourse (86) the structure (92) is transformed into:

(93) $\quad X [| X | = 4 \wedge X \subseteq \textit{women} \wedge X \subseteq \textit{went to a bar} \wedge X \subseteq \textit{had a beer}]$.

Under this analysis (89) is valid, since (94) and (95) – the respective representations of the top and bottom lines of (89) – are of course equivalent.

(94) $\quad \exists X [| X | = 4 \wedge X \subseteq \textit{women} \wedge X \subseteq \textit{went to a bar} \wedge X \subseteq \textit{had a beer}]$

(95) $\quad \exists X [| X | = 4 \wedge X \subseteq \textit{women} \wedge X \subseteq \textit{went to a bar} \cap \textit{had a beer}]$

A problem occurs however if we change *four* to *just four* in (89). The resulting equivalence is invalid.

(96) $\quad$ <u>Just four women went to a bar. $\qquad\qquad$ They had a beer.</u>

$\qquad\quad$ Just four women went to a bar and had a beer.

In DRT *just four* is analysed either as a quantifier or as an adjective. If *just four* is considered as a quantifier, Theorem 1 implies that it does not allow anaphoric links outside its scope. But *They* in *They had a beer* can certainly be anaphoric to *Just four women*. However if we interpret *Just four* as the adjectival $ADJ(\textbf{just four})$ we change the meaning of *just four* to that of *at least four*, since $ADJ(\textbf{just four}) = $ **at least four**.

This problem can be solved if one changes the adjectival interpretation of determiners according to the recipe (97).

(97) $\quad adj\ (\textbf{Q})XY \Leftrightarrow \exists X' [\textbf{Q}XX' \wedge \textbf{X'} = X \cap Y]$.

It is easy to show that the equality $adj\ (Q) = Q$ holds iff Q is conservative. Note that adj does not allow to reduce *just n* to ***at least n*** and that (89) is valid under this interpretation.

The DRS for the top of (96) is now (98).

(98) $\exists X\ [|\ X\ | = 4 \wedge X = women \cap went\ to\ a\ bar \wedge X \subseteq had\ a\ beer.$

But this formula is equivalent to (99).

(99) $|\ women \cap went\ to\ a\ bar\ | = 4 \wedge women \cap went\ to\ a\ bar \subseteq had\ a\ beer.$

Under this interpretation (96) is no longer valid, since $|\ X \cap Y \cap Z\ | = 4$ and $|\ X \cap Y\ | = 4 \cap X \cap Y \subseteq Z$ are not equivalent. But structure (99) results from interpreting the pronoun *they* as contextually restricted universal quantification. It is quite clear that the scope of *just four* is not extended in this case. We therefore achieve the correct result if we interpret the pronoun *they* as **all**[p] with the first argument restricted to the context set provided by the discourse *Just four women went to a bar*, i.e. the set *women $\cap$ went to a bar*. So van der Does's generalisation of Evans's E-type approach – his Q-type theory of anaphora resolution – seems to be required for an adequate account of plural anaphora. Using van der Does's slogan we may conclude:

[…] plural anaphora are bound to be Q-types.
van der Does 1996, p. 48.

5 Conclusion

Generalized Quantifier Theory is generally considered one of the big success stories of logical semantics. It not only gave rise to a surprisingly coherent and homogeneous picture of semantics by focussing on quantification, rather than predication, as the elementary form of judgement; it could also account for various seemingly syntactic phenomena in largely semantic terms, thus paving the way to an explanatory approach to the syntax/semantics interface. Some of the appeal of that approach is hopefully reflected in our account in Section 2 above. However, with the advent of dynamic semantics, the unified approach to noun phrase meaning appeared to have had its day: not all noun phrases quantify; rather, some of them denote or express properties, or (dynamically speaking) introduce discourse referents. And though there were attempts to reconcile donkey sentences and discourse anaphora with a quantificational analysis of indefinites (and descriptive pronominalisation), they did not seem to be entirely successful. All that was left for Generalized Quantifier Theory, then, was the relatively small area of truly (static) quantificational noun phrases; in particular, the theory could no longer form the core of a unified theory of judgement. This, we take it, is the received view, at least among those of the dynamic persuasion.

We hope to have shown that this view is not correct. There is plenty of room for GQT within the dynamic framwork(s), and not just in the classification of determiners. On the one hand, by depriving indefinites of their quantificational force, dynamic semanitcs makes quantification an almost ubiquous operation, as witnessed by constructions like adverbial quantification or existential closure; and it turns out that the study of these operations can benefit from the insights of GQT. Some of this has been indicated at the end of Section 3 above. On the other hand, and more dramatically, the very core of dynamic semantics – the interpretation of anaphoric dependencies can itself be approached from a quantificational perspective; and here it turns out that, what originally looked like an arbitrary, if deep-rooted distinction between static and dynamic noun phrases, may be seen as the reflection of the kind of logical properties that form the basis of GQT. This, we take it, is the upshot of van der Does's important results discussed in Section 4. Contrary to superficial impressions, then, generalized quantifier theory still has a central place even in dynamic or discourse-oriented natural language semantics.

Appendix: Choice functions

Definition 11. *A function $f : \wp(A) \rightarrow A$ is a choice function for set A iff for all non-empty $X \subseteq A : f(X) \in X$.*

The quantifier Q_f determined by choice function f is defined as follows:

$$Q_f XY \Leftrightarrow X :\neq \emptyset \wedge f_M(X) \in Y$$

for all $X, Y \subseteq M$.

With the help of this definition we can now interpret anaphoric relations established by choice functions within quantifier theory. More precisely the anaphoric relation in $Q^i XY \wedge A_i Z$ is now formulated as (100).

(100) $\exists f : Q XY \wedge Q_f X \cap Y Z$.

We are therefore interested in those Q that satisfy the variant (101) of (70).

(101) $\exists f : Q XY \wedge Q_f X \cap Y Z$ iff $Q X Y \cap Z$ for all X, Y.

The following observation allows an immediate application of Theorem 1:

$$\exists f : Q_f XY \Leftrightarrow X \cap Y \neq \emptyset$$

This means that scheme (101) is valid for exactly those quantifiers Q which satisfy (70) for $A = $ **some.**
    We therefore have immediately from theorem 1:

Corollary 2. *The logical quantifiers Q which satisfy (101) are precisely those with $Q = $ some$^\theta$ for some class of cardinals θ.*

The results shows that if indefinites like *a man* in *a man walks in the park* are analysed as existentials, DRT, DPL and choice functions allow the same class of quantifiers to extend their scope. These are exactly the variants of **some** with cardinality restrictions on the first argument[34].

References

Barwise, J. & R. Cooper (1981): 'Generalized Quantifiers in Natural Language', *Linguistics and Philosophy* 4, *159–219*.

Barwise, J. & S. Feferman, eds, (1985): *Model-Theoretic Logics*. Springer, New York.

Beghelli, F. (1994): Structured Quantifiers. In: M. Kanazawa & C. Piñón eds, *Dynamics, Polarity and Quantification*. CSLI, Stanford.

Chierchia, G. (1995): *Dynamics of Meaning – Anaphora, Presupposition and the Theory of Grammar*. Chicago University Press, Chicago/London.

Dekker, P. (2001): Cases, Adverbs, Situations and Events. In: *Proceedings of the 1995 Prague/Bad Teinach Workshops an Context Dependence in Natural Language*. Elsevier, Amsterdam. to appear.

Evans, G. (1977): 'Pronouns, Quantifiers, and Relative Clauses I', *The Canadian Journal of Philosophy* 7, 467–536.

Fauconnier, G. (1979): Implication Reversal in Natural Language. In: F. Guenthner & S. Schmidt, eds, *Formal Semantics for Natural Language*. Reidel, Dordrecht.

Groenendijk, J. & M. Stokhof (1991): 'Dynamic Predicate Logic', *Linguistics and Philosophy* 14, 39–100.

Heim, I. (1982): The Semantics of Definite and Indefinite Noun Phrases. PhD thesis, University of Massachusetts at Amherst.

Heim, I. (1990): 'E-Type Pronouns and Donkey Anaphora', *Linguistics and Philosophy* 13, 137–178.

Hella, L., J. Väänänen & D. Westerståhl (1997): 'Definability of Polyadic Lifts of Generalized Quantifiers', *Journal of Logic, Language and Information* 6, 305–335.

Kadmon, N. (1990): 'Uniqueness', *Linguistics and Philosophy* 13, 273–324.

Kamp, H. & U. Reyle (1993): *From Discourse to Logic*. Kluwer, Dordrecht.

Keenan, E. (1987a): A Semantic Definition of Indefinite NP. In: J. Reuland & A. ter Meulen, eds, *The Representation of (In)Definiteness*. MIT-Press, Cambridge, MA, pp. 286–317.

Keenan, E. (1987b): Unreducible *n*-ary Quantifiers in Natural Language. In: P. Gärdenfors, ed., *Generalized Quantifiers*. Reidel, Dordrecht.

Keenan, E. (1992): 'Beyond the Fege Boundary', *Linguistics and Philosophy* 15, 199–221.

Keenan, E. (1996): The Semantics of Determiners. In: S. Lappin, ed., The *Handbook of Contemporary Semantic Theory*. Blackwell, Oxford.

Keenan, E. & D. Westerståhl (1997): Generalized Quantifiers in Linguistics and Logic. In: J. van Benthem & A. ter Meulen, eds, *Handbook of Logic and Language*. Elsevier, Amsterdam.

Keenan, E. & J. Stavi (1986): 'Semantic Characterization of Natural Language Determiners', Linguistics and *Philosophy* 9, 253–326.

Klima, E. (1964): Negation in English. In: J. Fodor & J. Katz, eds, *The Structure of Language*. Prentice-Hall, New York.

Ladusaw, W. (1979): Polarity Sensitivity as Inherent Scope Relations. PhD thesis, University of Texas, Austin.

Ladusaw, W. (1983): 'Logical Form and Conditions an Grammaticality', *Linguistics and Philosophy* 6, 373–392.

---

[34] For linguistic applications of choice functions see for instance von Heusinger 2000, von Stechow 2000 and Winter 1997.

Lasersohn, P. (1992): 'Bare Plurals and Donkey Anaphora', *Natural Language Semantics* 5, 79–86.

Lewis, D. (1975): Adverbs of Quantification. In: E. Keenan, ed., *Formal Semantics of Natural Language*. Cambridge University Press, Cambridge.

Lindström, P, (1966): 'First-order predicate logic with generalized quantifiers', *Theoria* 35, 186–195.

Mostowski, A. (1957): 'On a generalization of quantifiers', *Fund. Math.* 44, 12–36.

Mundici, D. (1985): Other Quantifiers: An Overview. In: J. Barwise & S. Feferman, eds, *Model-Theoretic Logics*. Springer, New York.

Nam, S. (1994): Another Type of Negative Polarity Item. In: M. Kanazawa & C. Piñón, eds, *Dynamics, Polarity and Quantification*. CSLI, Stanford.

Rooth, M. (1987): NP Interpretation in Montague Grammar, File Change Semantics and Situation Semantics. In: P. Gärdenfors, ed., *Generalized Quantifiers*. Reidel, Dordrecht.

Thijsse, E. (1984): Counting Quantifiers. In: J. van Benthem & A. ter Meulen, eds, *Generalized Quantifiers in Natural Language*. Foris, Dordrecht.

Väänänen, J. (1997): 'Unary Quantifiers on Finite Models', *Journal of Logic, Language and Information* 6, 275–304.

van Benthem, J. (1986): *Essays in Logical Semantics*. Reidel, Dordrecht.

van Benthem, J. (1989): 'Polyadic Quantifiers', *Linguistics and Philosophy* 12, 437–465.

van Deemter, K. (1984): Generalized Quantifiers: Finite versus Infinite. In: J. van Benthem & A. ter Meulen, eds, *Generalized Quantifiers in Natural Language*. Foris, Dordrecht.

van der Does, J. (1994): On Complex Plural Noun Phrases. In: M. Kanazawa & C. Piñón, eds, *Dynamics, Polarity and Quantification*. CSLI, Stanford.

van der Does, J. (1996): Quantification and Nominal Anaphora. In: K. von Heusinger & U. Egli, eds, *Proceedings of the Konstanz Workshop "Reference and Anaphorical Relations"*.

van der Does, J. & J. van Eijck (1996): Basic Quantifier Theory. In: J. van der Does & J. van Eijck, eds, *Quantifiers, Logic, and Language*. CSLI Publications, Stanford.

van der Wouden, T. (1994): Polarity and 'Illogical Negation'. In: M. Kanazawa & C. Piñón, eds, *Dynamics, Polarity and Quantification*. CSLI, Stanford.

van Rooy, R. (1997): Attitudes in Changing Contexts. PhD thesis, Universität Stuttgart.

von Heusinger, K. (2000): Tbe Reference of Indefinites. In: K. von Heusinger & U. Egli, eds, *Reference and Anaphoric Relations*. Kluwer, Dordrecht.

von Stechow, A. (2000): Some Remarks an Choice Functions and LF-Movement. In: K. von Heusinger & U. Egli, eds, *Reference and Anaphoric Relations*. Kluwer, Dordrecht.

Westerståhl, D. (1989): Quantifiers in Formal and Natural Languages. In: D. Gabbay & F. Guenthner, eds, *Handbook of Philosophical Logic*, Vol IV. Reidel, Dordrecht.

Westerståhl, D. (1995): Quantifiers in Natural Language. A Survey of Some Recent Work. In: M. Krynicki, M. Mostowski & L. Szczerba, eds, *Quantifiers: Logics, Models and Computation, Vol. I*. Reidel, Dordrecht.

Winter, Y. (1997): 'Choice Functions and the Scopal Semantics of Indefinites', *Linguistics and Philosophy* 20, 399–467.

Zucchi, A. (1992): Existential Sentences and Predication. In: P. Dekker & M. Stokhof, eds, *Proceedings of the Eightth Amsterdam Colloquium*. ILLC Publication, Amsterdam.

Zwarts, F. (1998): Three Types of Polarity. In: F. Hamm & E. Hinrichs, eds, *Plurality and Quantification*. Kluwer, Dordrecht.

Tübingen / Frankfurt   Fritz Hamm / Thomas Ede Zimmermann

Seminar für Sprachwissenschaft der Universität Tübingen, Kleine Wilhelmstr. 113, D-72074 Tübingen

Institut für dt. Sprache und Literatur II der Universität Frankfurt, Grüneburgplatz 1, D-60323 Frankfurt/M.

Links without Locations
Information Packaging: From Cards to Boxes

Herman Hendriks[1]

This paper is organized as follows. First, in Section 1, an outline is given of the theory of information packaging – i.e., the structuring of propositional content in function of the speaker's assumptions about the hearer's information state – as it is presented by Vallduví (1992, 1993, 1994), who identifies the informational primitives *focus* and *ground*, *link* and *tail*, adapted from the traditional pragmatic focus/ground and topic/comment approaches, and who concludes – as is explained in Section 2 – that the exploitation of information states of hearers by the information-packaging strategies of speakers reveals that these states have at least the internal structure of a system of file cards along the lines of Heim (1982, 1983): links, which correspond to what are traditionally known as topics and which are typically marked by L+H* pitch accents in English, say *where* – on which file card – the focal information goes, and tails indicate *how* it fits there. This conclusion is challenged in Section 3, where it is argued that it begs the question. *If* file card systems are assumed, *then* the information-packaging strategies do seem to contribute to efficient information exchange – however, the question is whether this assumption itself is justified. Moreover, it is shown that the idea that links specify a locus of update in information states that are systems of file cards is problematic for various reasons. Therefore, Section 4 offers an alternative account in terms of the discourse representation structures of Discourse Representation Theory (see Kamp 1981, Kamp and Reyle 1993), which are ontologically less committed than the 'dimensionally richer' file card systems, since discourse representation structures do not come with locations. The latter aspect raises the question what purpose links *do* serve if they. do not serve to specify a locus of update: a different perspective on the function of links is required. According to the perspective offered in Section 4, linkhood – and hence L+H* pitch accent in English – serves to signal non-monotonic anaphora: the discourse referent Y of a link is anaphoric to an antecedent discourse marker X such that $X \not\subseteq Y$. This hypothesis affects a wide

[1] The present paper is a merged, updated and extended version of 'Links without Locations' and 'Information Packaging: From Cards to Boxes', which appeared in P. Dekker and M. Stokhof (eds.), *Proceedings of the Tenth Amsterdam Colloquium*, Institute of Language, Logic and Computation, University of Amsterdam, pp. 339–358, and in T. Galloway and J. Spence (eds.), *Proceedings of Semantics And Linguistic Theory VI*. CLC Publications, Ithaca, New York, pp. 75–92, respectively. Section 3 of the present paper is largely based on joint work of Paul Dekker (ILLC/Department of Philosophy, University of Amsterdam) and the author, who would like to thank Paul Dekker, Elisabet Engdahl, Fritz Hamm, Sieb Nooteboom, Tanya Reinhart and Enric Vallduví for cooperation, discussion and stimulation. – A more recent version of this paper will appear in "Information Sharing", edited by Kees van Deemter and Roger Kibble and published by CSLI Publications of Stanford University.

range of phenomena. In addition to its contribution to an analysis of (non-)as-
sociation with focus, it is shown to subsume 'non-identity' anaphora, contrastive
stress, correction, pronoun referent resolution, and restrictiveness of relatives
and adjectives. In Section 5, finally, it is pointed out that the account of links
given here is consistent with and can actually be considered a partial execution
of the intonational-informational research program that is outlined in Pierrehumbert and Hirschberg (1990).

1 Information packaging

The notion of information packaging is introduced in Chafe (1976):

[The phenomena at issue] have to do primarily with how the message is sent and only secon-
darily with the message itself, just as the packaging of toothpaste can affect sales in partial independence of the quality of the tooth paste inside. (Chafe 1976: 28)

The basic idea is that speakers do not present information in an unstructured
way, but that they provide a hearer with detailed instructions on how to manipulate and integrate this information according to their beliefs about the
hearer's knowledge and attentional state:

To ensure reasonably efficient communication, [t]he speaker tries, to the best of his ability, to
make the structure of his utterances congruent with his knowledge of the listener's mental
world. (Clark and Haviland 1977: 5)

On all levels the crucial factor appears to be the tailoring of an utterance by a sender to meet
the particular assumed needs of the intended receiver. That is, information packaging in natural languge reflects the sender's hypotheses about the receiver's assumptions and beliefs and
strategies. (Prince 1981: 224)

For instance, sentences such as (1) and (2) are truth-conditionally equivalent in
that they express the same proposition, but each of them 'packages' this proposition in a prosodically different way:[2]

(1)   *The* **teacher** *loves* ICE CREAM

(2)   *The* **teacher** LOVES *ice cream*

Typically, speakers will use (1) if the hearer at the time of utterance knows
nothing about or is not attending to the teacher's relation to ice cream, while
they will use (2) if the hearer at the time of utterance knows that there exists a
relation between the teacher and ice cream, is attending to this relation, but does
not know what it is. Apparently, speakers are sensitive to such differences in the
hearer's knowledge and attentional state, and hearers rely on this:

---

[2] *Italics* are used for unaccented expressions; SMALL CAPS for expressions that bear a (focal)
H* pitch accent; and **boldface** is used for expressions that bear a L+H* pitch accent. This is the terminology of Pierrehumbert (1980). H* accent and L+H* accent are called A accent and B accent,
respectively, in Jackendoff (1972).

speakers not using this device systematically give their listeners a harder time. (Nooteboom and Terken 1982: 317)

Truth-conditionally equivalent sentences which encode different information packaging instructions are not mutually interchangeable *salva felicitate* in a given context of utterance: for example, of the above sentences, only the first one is a felicitous answer to the question *What does the teacher love?* It is this context-sensitivity that has traditionally placed information packaging within the realm of pragmatics, where two influential approaches can be distinguished, the 'topic/comment' approach and the 'focus/ground' approach.

According to the focus/ground approach, sentences consist of a 'focus' and a 'ground'[3]. The focus is the informative part of the sentence, the part that (the speaker believes) makes some contribution to the hearer's mental state. The ground is the non-informative part of the sentence, the part that anchors the sentence to what is already established or under discussion in (the speaker's picture of) the hearer's mental state. Although sentences may lack a ground altogether, sentences without focus do not exist.

The topic/comment (theme/rheme) approach splits the set of subexpressions of a sentence into a 'topic', the – typically sentence-initial – part that expresses what the sentence is about, and a 'comment', the part that expresses what is said about the topic. Topics are points of departure for what the sentence conveys, they link it to previous discourse. Sentences may be topicless: so-called 'presentational' or 'news' sentences consist entirely of a comment.

In Reinhart (1982), it is argued that the dimension of 'old'/'new' information is irrelevant for the analysis of sentence topics. Instead, the notion of 'pragmatic aboutness' is defined in terms of the organization of information. The set $PPA_{(S)}$ of Possible Pragmatic Assertions that can be made with a sentence S expressing proposition φ is defined as follows:

(3) $PPA_{(S)} = \{\varphi\} \cup \{\langle a, \varphi \rangle \mid a \text{ is the interpretation of an NP in S}\}$

A pragmatic assertion $\langle a, \varphi \rangle$ is assumed to be *about a*. The possibility for an NP interpretation a to serve as the topic of a pragmatic assertion $\langle a, \varphi \rangle$ is subject to further syntactic and semantic restrictions, cf. footnote 8 below.

Notice, by way of example .(adopted from Dahl 1974), that the sentence *The* **teacher** *loves* ICE CREAM gives rise to the parallel topic/comment and ground/focus partitions indicated in (4) if it answers the questions *What about the teacher? What does he feel?*, whereas it induces the partitions specified by (5) in the interrogative context *What about the teacher? What does he love?*

---

[3] The ground is also known as 'background', as 'presupposition' and as 'open proposition'. In phonology, the term 'focus' is often used for intonational prominence. That is, any constituent which bears pitch accent is said to be a focus. Although in general, (part of) the informational focus is marked by prosodic prominence, not every accented constituent is a focus in the informational sense. In particular, accented constituents may also be topics/links.

(4)

topic	comment
The **teacher**	*loves* ICE CREAM
ground	focus

(5)

topic	comment	
The **teacher**	*loves*	ICE CREAM
ground	focus	

The fact that the two informational articulations correspond to different partitions in (5) shows that neither of them is by itself capable of capturing all the informational distinctions present in the sentence. Therefore, the two traditional
binomial articulations of focus/ground and topic/comment are conflated into a
single trinomial and hierarchical one in Vallduví's account of information packaging (1992, 1993, 1994). The core distinction is the one between new information and anchoring, between focus and ground. In addition, the ground is further
divided into the 'link', which corresponds approximately to the topic in the traditional topic/comment approach[4], and the 'tail'[5]. In a picture:

(6)

topic		comment	'aboutness'
link	tail	focus	
ground		focus	'old'/'new'

Given this articulation, the answer *The* **teacher** *loves* ICE CREAM to the questions *What about the teacher? What does he love?* will receive the following
analysis:

(7)

The **teacher**	loves	ICE CREAM
link	tail	focus
ground		focus

Roughly speaking, the different parts – focus and ground, link and tail – of a
sentence S have the following informational functions in Vallduví's theory. The
focus encodes I_S, the *information* of S, which can be metaphorically described
as ϕ_S, the proposition expressed by S, minus K_h, the information (the speaker
presumes) already present in the hearer's information state.

The ground performs an *ushering* role – it specifies the way in which I_s fits
in the hearer's information state: links indicate *where* I_S should go by denoting a

---

[4] To the extent that links correspond to the topic in the traditional topic/comment distinction,
Vallduví's theory is quite similar to the analysis of sentence topics presented in Reinhart (1982),
where a pragmatic assertion of φ about a is formalized as $\langle a, \varphi \rangle$, in that a functions as a kind of 'locus of update' for φ (see below). The two approaches differ in that Reinhart allows assertions without α 'locus of update' (since also $\varphi \in PPA_{(s)}$) and topics that express new information.

[5] The hierarchy does not imply constituency or (even) continuity. In particular, the two parts
(link and tail) of the ground may not constitute a linear unit at the surface. Moreover, sentences may
have more than one link, and more than one element may constitute the tail.

location in the hearer's information state, and tails indicate how I_S fits there by signaling a certain mode of information update.

Of course, talking about ushering information to some location in the hearer's information state presupposes that this information state has some sort of internal structure. In this respect, Vallduví purports to

agree with Heim that there has to be some additional internal structure in the hearer's model of the common ground that plays an important role in natural language interpretation, even if this internal structure is of tangential relevance in truth value computation. It is this internal structure of information states which is, in fact, crucially exploited by the different information-packaging strategies used by speakers in pursuing communicative efficiency. (Vallduví 1994: 7)

2 Files in focus

In fact, Vallduví takes the metaphor of Heim's file change semantics (1982, 1983) literally, in that he assumes that the information in the hearer's model is organized in files, i.e., collections of file cards. Each file card represents a discourse entity: its attributes and its links with other discourse entities are recorded on the card in the form of conditions. Such a discourse entity may be known to the hearer but not salient at the time of utterance, it may be salient at the time of utterance, it may be completely new to the hearer, it may be inferable from what the hearer knows, etc. Discourse entities mediate between referring expressions (noun phrases) and entities in the real world: indefinite noun phrases prompt hearers to create a new file card, and definite noun phrases incite them to retrieve an already existing file card. Both definites and pronouns denote already existing file cards, but pronouns denote salient file cards, whereas (other) definites refer to non-salient ones.

File change comprises the above aspects of file card management, but it also involves content update, i.e., the incorporation of information conveyed by a given sentence into records on novel and familiar file cards, and this is where Vallduví lets information packaging come in.

Links are associated with so-called GOTO instructions. In file change semantics, the target location of such a declaration is a file card fc. A tail points at an information record – normally a (possibly underspecified) condition – on such a file card, RECORD(fc), and indicates that it has to be *modified* (or further specified) by the focus information I_S of the sentence. The associated instruction type is called UPDATE-REPLACE. In the absence of a tail, the focus information I_S of a sentence is simply *added* at the current location. The associated instruction type is called UPDATE-ADD.

Sentences may lack links and tails (recall that the focus is the only non-optional part of a sentence), so the following four sentence types can be distinguished:

(8)   a. link-focus
       b. focus
       c. focus-tail
       d. link-focus-tail

The respective sentence types in (8) are associated with the (compound) instruction types in (9):

(9)   a. GOTO(fc) (UPDATE-ADD(I_S))
       b. UPDATE-ADD(I_S)
       c. UPDATE-REPLACE(I_S,RECORD(fc))
       d. GOTO(fc) (UPDATE-REPLACE(I_S,RECORD(fc)))

The sentence and instruction types in (8) and (9) can be illustrated with the following examples, where links, tails and foci are specified by means of [$_L$...], [$_T$...] and [$_F$...] brackets, respectively, and accented expressions in foci and links are – as above – written in small caps (representing H* pitch accent) and boldface (for L+H* pitch accent), respectively:

(10)   a. link-focus: [$_L$ *The* **boss**] [$_F$*hates* BROCCOLI]
          GOTO(fc)(UPDATE-ADD(I_S))
       b. focus: [$_F$*He always eats* BEANS]
          UPDATE-ADD(I_S)
       c. focus-tail: [$_F$*He is* NOT][$_T$*dead*]
          UPDATE-REPLACE(I_S,RECORD(fc))
       d. Link-focus-tail: [$_L$ *The* **boss**] [$_F$HATES] [$_T$*broccoli*]
          GOTO(fc) (UPDATE-REPLACE(I_S,RECORD(fc)))

As regards the first example, suppose that a newly appointed temp is ordering dinner for the boss and asks the executive secretary whether there is anything that he should know about the boss' taste. The executive secretary gives the following answer:

(11)   [$_L$*The* **boss**][$_F$*hates* BROCCOLI]

Example (11) is a link-focus construction, and as such it is associated with a GOTO(fc) (UPDATE-ADD(I_S)) instruction. The link subject *the* **boss** specifies a locus of update fc, viz., the card representing the boss – card #25, say. The focus verb phrase *hates broccoli* specifies the information I_S that has to be added to this card. Suppose that broccoli is represented by card #136. Then, passing over some formal details, the UPDATE-ADD(I_S) instruction associated with the focus *hates broccoli* amounts to adding the condition 'hates(25,136)' to the locus of update, i.e., the boss' card #25. Moreover, the record ' $\overline{-\!*25}$ ', a pointer to the locus of update, is added to card #136, rendering the condition 'hates(25,136)' on card #25 'accessible' from card #136. Vallduví says that this linking mechanism, which designates a unique location for content update, is 'much more efficient' than straightforward multiple recording of information on cards.

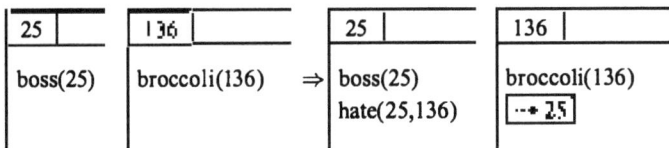

25	1 36		25	136
boss(25)	broccoli(136)	⇒	boss(25) hate(25,136)	broccoli(136) $\boxed{\cdots\!\rightarrow 25}$

(12)   [ₚHe always eats BEANS]

Example (12), an all-focus construction, is associated with a simple UPDATE-ADD(I_S) instruction. Here, this instruction involves the addition of the focus information I_S that the value of the current card always eats beans. That is: if it is interpreted immediately after example (11) and if its adverbially modified transitive verb phrase is left unanalyzed for simplicity, it amounts to adding the condition 'always eats beans(25)' to card #25.

The presence of a tail in a sentence signals a mode of update different from the straightforward UPDATE-ADD(I_S) instruction. A tail indicates that a (possibly underspecified) record on a file card has to be replaced (or specified further). The material in the tail serves the purpose of determining which record. Suppose, for example, that (13) is a reaction to the statement *Since John is dead, we can now split his inheritance*:

(13)   *I hate to spoil the fun, but* [ₚhe is NOT][ₜdead]

With this focus-tail example, the speaker instructs the hearer to replace the record on the current locus of update – card #17, say, for John – expressing that the value of card #17 is dead by one saying that he is not dead. In short, the tail serves to highlight a condition on file card #17, the one saying its value is dead. This condition is then modified in the way specified by the material in the focus.

In addition to the option of replacing a record on a file card, there is the possibility of further specifying an underspecified record, something which is assumed to be going on in the link-focus-tail example (14) given below. Suppose now that the newly appointed temp asks the executive secretary whether it was a good idea to order broccoli for the boss, and that the executive secretary gives the following answer:

(14)   [ₗThe **boss**][ₚHATES][ₜbroccoli]

The idea is that the temp has an underspecified record on his card for the boss, which says that the boss has some attitude towards broccoli. The lack of information about the nature of this attitude is reflected by the record 'ATT', and it is this record which is replaced by 'hate' after hearing the executive secretary's answer (14):

25	136		25	136
boss(25) ATT(25,136)	broccoli(136)	⇒	boss(25) hate(25,136)	broccoli(136) $\boxed{\cdots\!\rightarrow 25}$

Different languages choose different structural means to spell out the same informational interpretations. Vallduví studies the manifestation of information packaging in several languages, with an emphasis on Catalan and English. Cross-language comparison shows that in expressing information packaging, languages exploit word order and prosody in various ways. Roughly speaking, English structurally realizes information packaging by means of alternative intonational contours of identical strings, whereas Catalan has a constant prosodic structure and effectuates information packaging by means of string order permutations. In fact, Vallduví argues that languages such as Catalan supply empirical support for the representation of information packaging sketched above, since these languages package their information in a much more salient way than, for example, English. Thus, while informational interpretations may be expressed exclusively by prosodic means in English, information packaging instructions in Catalan are straightforwardly reflected in syntax.

In English, the focus is associated with a H* pitch accent (written in small caps), links are marked by a L+H* pitch accent (written in boldface), and tails are structurally characterized by being deaccented. One and the same string may be assigned different intonational phrasings in order to realize different informational interpretations. In particular, the focal pitch accent may be realized on different positions in the sentence. This is illustrated by the sentences (16), (18) and (20), construed as answers to the questions (15), (17) and (19), respectively:

(15)   *What did you find out about the company?*

(16)   [$_F$*The boss hates* BROCCOLI]

(17)   *What did you find out about the boss?*

(18)   [$_L$*The* **boss**][$_F$*hates* BROCCOLI]

(19)   *What does the boss feel about broccoli?*

(20)   [$_L$*The* **boss**][$_F$HATES][$_T$*broccoli*]

In Catalan, the situation is as follows. Metaphorically speaking, one can say that Catalan focal elements remain within a so-called 'core clause', but that ground elements are 'detached' to a clause-peripheral position. In particular, links are detached to the left, and non-link ground elements undergo rightdetachment. As a result of detaching both links and tails, the core clause (CC) is left containing only the focus of the sentence:

(21)   LINKS [$_{CC}$ FOCUS] TAILS

Consider the Catalan counterparts (22), (23) and (24) of (16), (18) and (20), respectively. The all-focus sentence (22) displays the basic verb-object-subject word order. In (23) and (24), the link subject *l'amo* has been detached to the left. In (24), moreover, the tail direct object *el bròquil* has been detached to the right, leaving a clitic (*l'*) in the focal core clause. Note that intonational structure plays

a part in Catalan too, albeit 'a rather lame one' (Vallduví 1993: 33): a focal H*
pitch accent is invariably associated with the last item of the core clause.

(22)   [$_F$*Odia el bròquil* L'AMO]

(23)   [$_L$*L'amo*][$_F$*odia el* BRÒQUIL]

(24)   [$_L$*L'amo*] [$_F$L'ODIA][$_T$*el bròquil*]

The above observations provide confirmation that information packaging involves syntax as well as prosody; hence any attempt to reduce information
packaging to either syntax (for Turkish, cf. Hoffman 1995) or prosody (for English, cf. Steedman 1991, 1992, 1993) is inadequate from a crosslinguistic point
of view[6]. Accordingly, Hendriks (1996) treats the range of variation in the
structural realization of information packaging as displayed by Catalan and
English by means of the sign-based categorial grammar formalism of Hendriks
(1994), which takes its inspiration from Oehrle's (1988, 1993) work on generalized compositionality for multidimensional linguistic objects and shares characteristics with HPSG (Head-Driven Phrase Structure Grammar – see Pollard
and Sag 1987, 1994). Basically, this formalism is a both intonationally/syntac-
tically and semantically/informationally interpreted version of a double 'dependency' variant (see Moortgat and Morrill 1991) of the non-associative Lambek (1961) calculus, enriched with the unary operators of Moortgat (1994). The
signs, the grammatical resources of this formalism, are Saussurian form-
meaning units which reflect the fact that the dimensions of linguistic form and
meaning contribute to well-formedness in an essentially parallel way:

(25)   intonational term ◁ type ▷ informational term

The treatment of information packaging in this formalism differs from many of
its predecessors (including other extensions of standard Lambek calculus such
as Oehrle 1991, Van der Linden 1991, and Moortgat 1993), in that it does not
employ focusing operators, but, instead, makes use of 'defocusing' operators
that license the presence of links and tails. Acccording to most approaches, focused constituents are semantic functors which take the nonfocused part of the
sentence as their argument. This analysis is based on such assumptions as made
in Szabolcsi (1981, 1983) and Svoboda and Materna (1987), where focus is not
only considered an information-packaging primitive but also an implicit truth-
conditional exhaustiveness operator, and on semantic studies of the phenomenon
of 'association with focus' as provided by Jacobs (1983), Rooth (1985), Krifka
(1991), and others who have argued that the quantificational structure of so-
called focus-sensitive operators is crucially determined by the traditional prag-

---

[6] Note, moreover, that the structural realization of information packaging in Catalan involves
both syntax *and* prosody. E.g., the informationally non-equivalent sentences [$_F$*Odia el bròquil*
L'AMO] and [$_F$*Odia* EL BRÒQUIL] [$_T$*l'amo*] differ only prosodically. The same holds for English,
where the structural realization of information packaging also may involve syntax: Reinhart (1982:
63) notes that a fronted NP such as *Felix* in the sentence *Felix, it's been ages since I've seen him*
must be a topic (i.e., link).

matic focus-ground partition. However, Vallduví argues convincingly that 'the claim that focused constituents truth-conditionally entail exhaustiveness leads to extreme positions' (1992: 170), and Vallduví and Zacharski (1993) show that 'association with pragmatic focus' is not an inherent semantic property of 'focus-sensitive' operators, which may express their semantics on partitions other than the focus-ground one – witness obvious cases of association with subsegments of the informational focus, with links, and with other parts of the ground. This dissociation of the pragmatic focus-background distinction from issues of exhaustiveness and focus-sensitivity dispels the need of analyzing focused constituents as operators which semantically take scope over the non-focused parts of the sentence, which can be considered an advantage. As sentences may lack links and tails, such analyses do not immediately reflect the core status of the focus, which is the only non-optional part of a sentence. In some sense, then, all-focus sentences constitute the basic case, and the cases where there is a ground are derived from such basic all-focus structures.

3 Cards and boxes

Vallduví has it that

[...] a proper understanding of information packaging, i.e., of the actual strategies used by human agents in effecting information update by linguistic means, will help us gain further insight into the structural properties of the cognitive states these dynamic strategies manipulate. (Vallduví 1994: 24)

As we have seen, the basic idea of information packaging is that in discourse, speakers not only present information to their interlocutors, but also provide them with detailed 'instructions' on how to manipulate and integrate this information. With respect to the role of these instructions in the determination of those aspects of the structure of information states which are relevent to natural language interpretation, Vallduví claims the following:

The use of these instructions reveals that speakers treat information states as highly structured objects and exploit their structure to make information update more efficient for their hearers. (Vallduví 1994: 3)

More specifically, concerning 'the internal structure of information states which is, in fact, crucially exploited by the different information-packaging strategies used by speakers in pursuing communicative efficiency' (1994: 7), it is argued that information packaging instructions contribute in two ways to the optimization of information update, since they provide means to

- designate a file card as the locus of information update and hence circumvent the redundancy of multiple update; and
- identify the information of the sentence and its relation to information already present in the hearer's model.

(Recall that the information of the sentence, I_S, is expressed by the focus, and that the ground has an ushering role with respect to I_S: links indicate where I_S goes, and tails indicate how it fits there.) So, summing up, Vallduví concludes that information states constitute systems that have at least the internal structure of a collection of file cards connected by pointers.

Though the presented arguments may appear to be intuitively quite appealing, it can be argued that, strictly speaking, they are not as compelling as they seem. Somehow, Vallduví is begging the question: 'talking about ushering I_S to a location in the hearer's model K_h [...] does not make much sense unless one assumes some sort of rich internal structure for K_h' (Vallduví 1994: 7). The relevant question, however, is whether this assumption of 'some sort of rich internal structure' itself makes sense of anything besides the ushering function of links.

If file card systems are assumed, *then* the information-packaging instruction types apparently do contribute to efficient information exchange. And if this assumption is warranted, it may even serve as an explanation of the fact that we do appear to find these ways of packaging information in a variety of languages. Nonetheless, the more theoretical question is whether this assumption itself is warranted, and whether the organization of linguistic information exchange really presupposes such information states. After all, ushers can be very useful, but there are also halls that have unnumbered seats! Maybe links really make no sense without files, but, for that matter, maybe we simply fail to understand what links do. The notion of 'ushering I_S to a location' may be just as metaphorical as the notion of 'file card collection'. For instance, files are, as Vallduví puts it, 'dimensionally richer' than the card-less discourse representation structures of Discourse Representation Theory (see Kamp 1981, Kamp and Reyle 1993), since each file card introduces its own 'representational space' where all its records are to be found while there is no sensible notion of location in discourse representation structures. Still, a hearer who employs discourse representation structures has an easier job from a bookkeeping perspective than a hearer whose information states are collections of file cards connected by pointers.

This can be illustrated as follows. Imagine an utterance made by Irene, a speaker who organizes her utterances on the basis of the assumption that her audience stores information using collections of file cards connected by pointers, to Hans, a hearer who employs discourse representation structures. Clearly, it would be inappropiate to say that Irene uses links to usher I_S to a location in the hearer's model K_h, since there is no sensible notion of location in Hans' discourse representation structures. Still, this does not at all preclude Hans from updating his discourse representation with the proposition that Irene attempts to get through. And worse, he has even got considerably less to do than a hearer who uses collections of file cards connected by pointers. Compare the following link-focus example:

(26)   [$_L$**Frank**$_5$][$_F$flew from Amsterdam$_9$ to Oslo$_8$ via STUTTGART$_2$]

Neglecting various details, if a file clerk is to update her file in order to represent the information expressed by example (26) in the way sketched above, she has to carry out the following sequence of instructions[7]:

(27)   GOTO(5)(UPDATE-ADD(flew(5,9,8,2)))
         GOTO(9)(UPDATE-ADD($\overline{\rightarrow 5}$))
         GOTO(8)(UPDATE-ADD($\overline{\rightarrow 5}$))
         GOTO(2)(UPDATE-ADD($\overline{\rightarrow 5}$))
         GOTO(5)

Hans, on the other hand, only has to carry out the following instruction:

(28)   PDATE-ADD(flew(5,9,8,2))

This example may serve as an indication that none of the data discussed above precludes the use of, say, Kampian discourse representation structures instead of Heimian files. Clearly, there may be evidence for assuming there to be files at work, and one of the last things this paper would like to claim is that people organize their information in simpler systems than collections of file cards (or discourse representation structures, for that matter). On the contrary. The only point is that the use of files does not appear to be imperative so far.

Notice that Vallduví's conclusion is, in some sense, unfalsifiable. Discourse representation structures can model precisely the same information as file card systems, except for one small difference. The only thing that discourse representation structures lack is a marked discourse referent corresponding to the file notion of 'current locus of update', i.e., the location where the file clerk happens to find herself. If we assume that discourse representation structures have a way of marking such a discourse referent j – by a condition 'CLERK_AT(j)', say –, then the two systems differ only in the way in which they display their information: in one big box, or on several cards connected by pointers. But, moreover, one can show that given Vallduví's specific use of pointers to file cards, there is actually a bijective correspondence between his files and the class of discourse representation structures with atomic conditions and one marked discourse referent for the current locus of update. For note that conditions 'REL(i_1, ... , i_n)' are invariably added on card i_1, inducing pointers ' $\overline{\rightarrow i_1}$ ' on the cards i_2, ... , i_n. Hence the following correspondence can be established:

---

[7] Assuming that establishing links to the locus of update is done via packaging instructions – of course, these links have to be established *somehow*. Note, by the way, that the file clerk's task would not be made easier by structure sharing (something suggested by Enric Vallduví (personal communication)), because also the structure sharing will itself have to be established somehow – in the following way, for example:

GOTO(5)(UPDATE-ADD($\boxed{1}$ flew(5,9,8,2)))
GOTO(9)(UPDATE-ADD($\boxed{1}$))
GOTO(8)(UPDATE-ADD($\boxed{1}$))
GOTO(2)(UPDATE-ADD($\boxed{1}$))
GOTO(5)

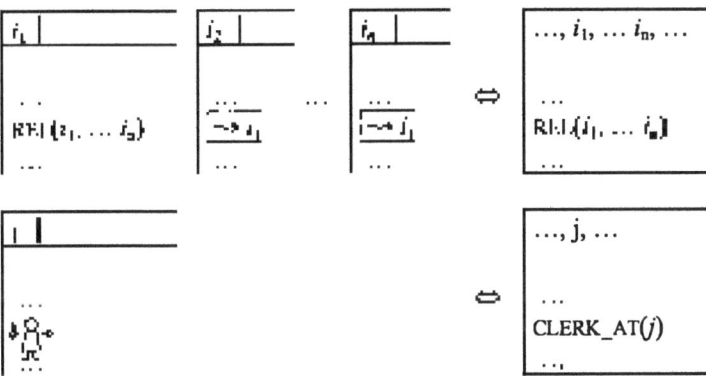

The idea that links specify a locus of update in information states that are collections of file cards connected by pointers is problematic for various reasons. First, it is unclear what locus of update must be associated with quantified, negative and disjunctive links, or – more in general – where and how quantified, negative and disjunctive information has to be put. Second, the existence of sentences with more than one link is enigmatic. Third, the replacement operation triggered by the presence of tails is complicated by the use of file cards. And fourth, the approach leads to the counterintuitive conclusion that pronouns form part of the focus. These issues will be addressed in the remainder of this section.

(a) Vallduví observes that files are 'dimensionally richer' than the discourse representation structures (DRSs) of Discourse Representation Theory. Now, this is true to the extent that each file card introduces its own 'representational space' where all records concerning that file card are to be found. In order to be actually richer, nonetheless, files must be adapted to model more than merely atomic conditions – i.e., individuals having properties and standing in relations at various spatio-temporal locations. Among other things, they should be able to model quantified, negative and disjunctive information. Discourse Representation Theory allows the construction of complex conditions from sub-DRSs, and these conditions – by an appropriate semantic interpretation procedure – model precisely such information. Heim, who explicitly speaks of files and file cards as metaphors (1982: 276 and 302ff.), spells out quantified, negative and disjunctive information in purely semantic terms, i.e., in terms of the domains and satisfaction sets of files. However, it is not clear how such information must be expressed in the non-metaphorical file card set-up of Vallduví (1994).

For one thing, what loci of update are specified by the links of sentences such as (29), (30) and (31)[8]? On what file card(s) – if any – should the information expressed by these sentences be put?

---

[8] Though 'links tend to be definite NPs' (1992: 77), Vallduví notes the 'restricted existence of indefinite links' (1992: 46). 'Sentences with *quantifier links* are' claimed to be 'less natural than others, causing raised eyebrows among some Catalan speakers. Sentences like *A tots els estudiants*₁

(29)   [$_L$**Every man**][$_F$WALKS]

(30)   [$_L$**No man**][$_F$WALKS]

(31)   [$_L$**John or Mary**][$_F$WALKS]

For another, how should this information be put? One might think of using sub-files, but then, where must these be put? Are they attached to a main file, or must they be attached to a main file's file card? Which one? Interestingly, Heim raises similar questions in her 1983 paper:

> Take a simple sentence [...]: *It is raining*. In the context of the file metaphor, one doesn't quite know how to deal with this sentence. As an informative sentence, it ought to call for an up-dating of the file somehow: but what exactly is the file clerk supposed to do? The information that it is raining does not belong on any particular file card, it seems, since each file card is a description of an individual, but *It is raining* is not about any individual. Should the file clerk perhaps write on some arbitrary card: 'is such that it is raining' ? Or should he write that on all cards? And what if the file so far doesn't contain any cards yet? [...] Quantified and negated propositions are similarly puzzling if we are so ambitious as to want to say what exactly the file clerk does in response to them. Under the modest aspect of domain and satisfaction set change, however, they pose no problem. (Heim 1983: 183–184)

It should be noted here that such a 'modest' position cannot be retained in the set-up of Vallduví (1994), because there the entities to be updated must be *files*, and *not* their domains and their satisfaction sets.

(*b*) Vallduví (1992: 104) notes that there is no structural restriction on the number of links in Catalan. "Sentences may have more than one link, as in the Catalan example (32).

(32)   [$_L$*El bròquil*] [$_L$a *l'amo*] [$_F$*l'hi* van REGALAR]
         the broccoli to the boss *obj-iobj 3p-past* give
         Approx.: 'The broccoli the boss (they) gave it to him (for free)'.

In these cases the speaker directs the hearer to go to two addresses and enter the information under both." (Vallduví 1992: 60, example number adapted). So, as-suming that 'they' have card #3 and that the boss and broccoli still possess their respective cards #25 and #136, this means that the sentence is not associated with the instruction (33)[9], but with an instruction along the lines of (34).

(33)   *GOTO(136)(GOTO(25)(UPDATE-ADD(give(3,136,25))))

(34)   GOTO(136)(UPDATE-ADD(give(3,136,25))
         GOTO(25)(UPDATE-ADD(give(3,136,25))

---

els$_i$ donen un CARNET t$_i$ "To all students they give an ID" *or A tothom$_i$ no el$_i$ tracten t$_i$* IGUAL "Everybody they don't treat the same" are extremely natural, some other sentences sound odder. Most sentences, however, are felicitous once the right context is construed, although in some cases it may require some sophistication' (Vallduví 1992: 153). Analogously, Reinhart notes that if they 'can be interpreted (pragmatically) as denoting sets, universally quantified NPs, as well as specific and generic indefinite NPs, can serve as topics' (1982: 65–66).

[9]   Note, by the way, that the 'GOTO(136)' constitutes a superfluous detour in instruction (33).

But this raises questions. What is the current locus of update after (34) has been carried out? Is the file clerk suddenly simultaneously working on two different file cards? If she isn't (suppose she is only working on card #25), does this then mean that (34) is equivalant to (35), the instruction associated with the one-link sentence (36)?

(35)   GOTO(25) (UPDATE-ADD(give(3,136,25)))
         GOTO(136)(UPDATE-ADD($\leadsto$ 25))
         GOTO(25)

(36)   [$_L A$ *l'amo*] [$_F hi$ *van regalar el* BRÒQUIL]]

But if (34) and (35) are equivalent, then why does Catalan allow multiple links at all? And how could (34) and (35) be non-equivalent – what sense could multiple loci of update make that pointers cannot?

(*c*) Above an informal sketch was given of Vallduví's analysis of tailcontaining sentences in terms of UPDATE-REPLACE instructions. It can be expected that various complications will arise when it comes to giving an explicit formalization of the replacement instructions associated with tails. Any attempt at giving an appropriate and fully general definition of these instructions will have to confront a number of questions. Thus, how exactly do you know which record has to be replaced or specified further? Is there guaranteed to be such a record? Is there a unique one, and what happens if there are more? Is it always one record that has to be replaced, or do we sometimes need to replace a group of records? What kind of match must there be between the material in a tail, and the material in the target record? Of course, these are tough nuts that have to be cracked when it comes to theories of belief revision.

Here we will just present a simple example which illustrates that the replacement operation triggered by the presence of tails is specifically complicated by the idea that information is organized in file card systems. Suppose that Louis van Gaal utters (37), whereupon Johan Cruijff reacts with saying (38):

(37)   [$_L$**Ajax**][$_F$WONI

(38)   [$_F No$, BARCELONA][$_T$won]

Assume the file cards #1 and #2 for Ajax and Barcelona, respectively. Now, clearly, Johan Cruijff here instructs Louis van Gaal to replace his record according to which Ajax won by one according to which Barcelona did. Presumably, this should not (only) be done on the card for Ajax. Instead of the straightforwardly simple (39), the complex instruction given in (40) seems to be needed.

(39)   *UPDATE-REPLACE(won(2),won(1))

(40)   UPDATE-REPLACE(won(2),won(1))
         GOTO(2) (UPDATE-ADD(won(2)))

(*d*) An example typical of the way in which Vallduví analyzes pronouns can be obtained by combining the above example sentences (11) and (12) into one text:

(41)   [$_L$*The* **boss**][$_F$*hates* BROCCOLI]
         [$_F$*He always eats* BEANS]

The first sentence is a link-focus construction, and therefore associated with an instruction to go to the file card of the boss, thereby turning it into the current locus of update, and to enrich that file card with the information that the boss hates broccoli (and the broccoli file card with a pointer to the file card of the boss). The second sentence is an all-focus construction, associated with the simple instruction to add the focus information that the value of the current locus of update always eats beans to the current locus of update. Hence if it is interpreted immediately after the first sentence, it amounts to adding the information that the boss always eats beans to the card of the boss.

Note that the pronoun *he* obviously does not induce replacement or shift the locus of update. Hence it cannot be a link or a tail, and this inevitably leads to the conclusion that it forms part of the focus. This is a counterintuitive result, however, since it is also clear that the interpretation of the pronoun is provided by the value of the current locus of update – which does not constitute new information, but can be assumed to be already present in the hearer's information state.

4 Non-monotonic anaphora

Let us wind up the discussion so far. It has been argued that the data discussed above do not enforce the conclusion that information states have at least the structure of a collection of file cards connected by pointers. For that matter, the phenomena can also be accounted for in terms of discourse representation structures, and it is very well possible that circumventing file cards might lead to the avoidance of the complications that were outlined in the previous section.

In view of these considerations, a card-less alternative will be defended in the present section, according to which information states are modeled by means of discourse representation structures, which are ontologically less committed than the 'dimensionally richer' file card system, in that discourse representation structures do not come with locations.

But if, as was argued above, the use of files does not appear to be imperative, then a question must be faced: what purpose *do* links serve if they do not serve to specify a locus of update by ushering to locations? What does 'ushering to a location' mean if representations do not come with locations? Thus a different perspective on the function of links is required. Below a tentative answer will be suggested that carries less presuppositions than the file metaphor.

This alternative perspective has its heuristic starting point in Kamp and Reyle (1993), who note that processing a plural pronoun does not always involve equating the discourse referent it introduces with one introduced earlier through the processing of some other plural NP. Kamp and Reyle consider the following example:

(42)   *John took Mary to Acapulco. They had a lousy time.*

Here, the plural pronoun *they* does not have a single NP for its antecedent. Rather, the 'antecedent' has to be 'constructed' out of various parts of the preceding text. Such examples, which are very common, seem to suggest that plural pronouns can pick up any antecedent that can be obtained from antecedent information by logical deduction. However, the deductive principles that are permitted in this context turn out to be subject to restrictions.

(43)   *Eight of the ten balls are in the bag. They are under the sofa.*

The pronoun *they* in (43) cannot be understood as referring to the two balls that are missing from the bag. Apparently, subtracting one set from another is not a permissible operation for the formation of pronominal antecedents.

The permissible process of antecedent formation displayed by (42) is called Summation: a new discourse referent is introduced which represents the 'union' of individuals (John and Mary) and/or sets represented by discourse referents that are already part of the discourse representation structure. Other permissible processes are Abstraction, exemplified by (44), which allows the introduction of discourse referents for quantified NPs (compare also footnote 8 above), and Kind Introduction, which introduces discourse referents for a certain 'genus' explicitly mentioned in the text by a (simple or complex) noun. If *they* in (45) refers to the (few) men who joined the (conservative) party, we are dealing with abstraction. The more natural reading, where *they* refers to men in general (and the party is presumably non-conservative), is a case of Kind Introduction.

(44)   *I found every book Bill needs. They are on his desk.*

(45)   *Few men joined the party. They are very conservative.*

In their discussion of the inferential processes available for the construction of antecedents for (plural) pronouns, Kamp and Reyle suggest the following generalization:

What sets the admissible inference processes of Summation, Abstraction and Kind Introduction apart from an inadmissible inference pattern such as set subtraction is that the former are [...] strictly *positive* (Kamp and Reyle 1993: 344),

or

'cumulative' in the following sense: the newly created discourse referent represents an entity of which the discourse referents used in the application of the rule represent (atomic or non-atomic) parts (Kamp and Reyle 1993: 394).

Notice that, when this generalization is taken in conjunction with a principle that anaphora invariably involves the addition of an equational condition 'X = Y' for an anaphoric expression with discourse referent Y and a – possibly inferentially created – antecedent discourse referent X (and such an equational approach is standard practice in Dicourse Representation Theory), the necessary result will be that anaphora is always (upward) monotonic: if an expression with discourse referent Y is anaphorically dependent on an expression with discourse referent X, then $X \subseteq Y$[10].

The latter result, however, does not seem to be borne out by the facts. For example, Van Deemter (1992, 1994a) presents cases of 'non-identity anaphora' along the lines of (46), as well as minimal pairs such as (47) and (48):

(46)   *Our neigbours are extremely nice* PEOPLE.
          He *is a* TEACHER, **she** *is a* HOUSEWIFE.

(47)   *John fed the* ANIMALS. *The cats were* HUNGRY.

(48)   *John fed the* ANIMALS. *The* **cats** *were* HUNGRY.

It can be observed that the pronouns **he** and **she** are anaphorically dependent on *our neighbours* in (46), but that the discourse referents of the pronouns represent entities which are proper subsets of the entity represented by the discourse referent of the antecedent: obvious cases of non-monotonic anaphora.

Moreover, whereas the reading of (47) where *the cats* is anaphoric to *the* ANIMALS strongly and monotonically suggests that all animals fed by John were cats, the reading of (48) where *the* **cats** is anaphoric to *the* ANIMALS does not. It even seems to imply that John fed at least one non-cat[11]. Again, we are dealing with non-monotonic anaphora.

Note that the texts (47) and (48) differ only in the assignment of L+H* accent to the noun phrase *the cats*, which is the distinguishing mark of links in English. Hence our alternative hypothesis concerning links:

(49)   *Non-Monotonic Anaphora Hypothesis (NAH):*
          Linkhood (marked by L+H* accent in English) serves to signal non-monotonic anaphora. If an expression is a link, then its discourse referent Y is anaphoric to an antecedent discourse referent X such that $X \not\subseteq Y$.

This hypothesis affects a range of phenomena. In Hendriks (*draft*) it is argued that a discourse-representational approach of information packaging such as the one sketched here provides a sound background for an adequate theory of the phenomena commonly referred to as 'association with focus' (Jacobs 1983, Rooth 1985, 1992, Krifka 1991), thereby contributing to the integration of pragmatic theories of information packaging with contemporary research in formal semantics. More in particular, the approach is capable of handling the non-marginal cases of association of 'focus-sensitive' operators such as *only*

---

[10] Let sets A and B be partially ordered by $\leq_A$ and $\leq_B$, repectively. In mathematics, a function $f: A \to B$ is called *monotonic* iff $a \leq_A b$ entails that $f(a) \leq_B f(b)$ for all a and b in A. Note that the same notion is involved here for (*i*) the function f: NP $\to$ DR which associates every occurrence of a noun phrase a with its discourse marker $f(a)$; (*ii*) $\leq_{NP}$ such that $a \leq_{NP} b$ iff a is the antecedent of anaphor b; and (*iii*) $\leq_{DR}$ such that X $\leq_{DR}$ Y iff $X \subseteq Y$.

[11] 'Strongly suggests' and 'seems to imply' instead of 'entails', since though the effects are quite strong, they are of a pragmatic, rather than a logico-semantic, nature. See also (*c*), an pronoun referent resolution, below.

with non-focal parts of the sentence that have been attested in the literature (Vallduví 1992, Partee 1994, Vallduví & Zacharski 1993). That is, not only the phenomenon of 'second occurrence focus' is accounted for, but also the link-sensitive behaviour of 'focus-sensitive' operators is given an analysis of which the approach to links given here is an essential ingredient. Below it will be shown that, in addition to this, the *NAH* subsumes not only the so-called 'non-identity' anaphora just exemplified and analyzed in Van Deemter (1992, 1994a), but also the cases of contrastive stress discussed in Rooth (1992) and Vallduví (1992, 1994), and the corrections mentioned by Pierrehumbert and Hirschberg (1990). It contributes to an explanation of the effect of pitch accenting on pronoun referent resolution noted in Cahn (1995), Kameyama (1994), Vallduví (1994), among many others, and it sheds light on the distinction between restrictive and non-restrictive relative clauses and adjectives (see Kamp & Reyle 1993).

(*a*) The relationship between non-identity anaphora and linkhood can be demonstrated even more saliently with relational nouns:

(50)   *Ten guys were playing basketball in the* RAIN.
         The fathers were having FUN.

(51)   *Ten guys were playing basketball in the* RAIN.
         The **fathers** *were having* FUN.

Thus, whereas (50) has an 'identity' reading where *the fathers* is anaphoric to *ten guys* which – monotonically – suggests that all ten guys playing basketball in the rain were fathers who were having fun, the reading of (51) where the **fathers** is anaphoric to *ten guys* does not. This reading seems to – non-monotonically – imply that the fathers who were having fun constitute a proper subset of the ten basketball-playing guys. Since *father* is a relational noun, there is, next to this 'subsectional' reading, also a – non-monotonic – 'relational' reading of (51) on which the fathers of the ten guys playing basketball in the rain were having fun.

Observe, by the way, that Kamp and Reyle's example (42) of Summation, a case of monotonic non-identity anaphora in which the pronoun *they* typically appears unaccented, shows that is not so much the 'non-identity' as the 'non-monotonicity' of the anaphora which is responsible for the L+H* accent (that is: the linkhood) of the anaphor.

(*b*) According to Rooth, contrast is the cornerstone of the interpretation of focus phenomena: 'Intonational focus has a semantic import related to the intuitive notion of contrast within a set of alternative elements' (1992: 113), and Vallduví gives the following example of 'contrastive' links (1993: 14):

(52)   *Where can I find the cutlery?*
         The **forks** are in the CUPBOARD, but
         The **knives** *I left in the* DRAWER.

Note, however, that contrast is not really necessary for L+H* accent[12]:

(53)   Where can I find the cutlery?
         *The **forks** are in the* CUPBOARD.

Mere non-monotonicity suffices.

(c) As Pierrehumbert and Hirschberg (1990) observe, L+H* accent often arises in corrections. Thus, sentence (55) is a natural way of correcting (54).

(54)   *John was stung by* MOSQUITOS.

(55)   *He was stung by* **bees**.

Interestingly, it can be observed that non-monoticity plays a role here too. Notice that a sentence such as (56) is less naturally uttered in the context of (54), even though, semantically (i.e., truth-conditionally) speaking, this sentence is an impeccable expression of the proposition entertained by a speaker who believes that John was actually stung by bees as well as mosquitos.

(56)   *He was stung by* **insects.**

In fact, a speaker of (54) who is 'corrected' by someone's utterance of (56) might very well react by uttering (57):

(57)   *Mosquitos* ARE *insects.*

Apparently, it is the fact that mosquitos are insects that thwarts the assignment of L+H* accent to *insects* in sentence (56).

(d) Many authors have paid attention to the effect of pitch accenting on pronoun referent resolution. The examples below stem from Lakoff (1971).

(58)   *Paul called Jim a Republican. Then he* INSULTED *him.*

(59)   *Paul called Jim a Republican. Then* **he** *insulted* **him.**

For grammatical reasons (syntactic parallellism), the preferred antecedents for the unstressed pronouns *he* and *him* in (58) are *Paul* and *Jim*, respectively. The preferences are reverse for the stressed pronouns **he** and **him** in (59)[13].

In the theory of Kameyama (1994), this phenomenon is accounted for in the following way:

- A grammar subsystem represents the space of possibilities and a pragmatics subsystem represents the space of preferences;
- Stressed and unstressed pronouns have the same denotational range – the same range of *possible* values;

---

[12] Nor is contrariety (as proposed in Van Deemter 1994b), witness:
Where can I find the cutlery?
The **forks** *are in the* CUPBOARD, *and the* **knives** TOO.

[13] The fact that (59) insinuates that calling someone a Republican is an insult is essentially due to the de-accenting of *insulted* in the second sentence of (59).

- *Complementary Preference Hypothesis (CPH)*: A stressed pronoun takes the complementary preference of the unstressed counterpart.

However, the *NAH* formulated in (49) is capable of *predicting* the *CPH* effects: adding L+H* accent to pronouns means the addition of a pragmatic signal that the anaphora involved is non-monotonic. In the case of singular antecedents with entity-representing discourse referents[14], this means that the anaphor does not *corefer* with its antecedent. Correspondingly, we have that pronominal stress turns the pragmatically determined preference for a certain grammatically possible antecedent into a pragmatically determined preference for non-coreference with that antecedent[15].

(*e*) The sentences (60) and (61) (taken from Kamp and Reyle 1993: 255) illustrate the familiar rule of English orthography that non-restrictive clauses are set apart from the surrounding text by commas, but that restrictive clauses are not.

(60)   *The son who attended a boarding school was insufferable.*

(61)   *The son, who attended a boarding school, was insufferable.*

Note that (60), in which the relative clause is used restrictively, suggests that there is more than one son, but only one who is boarding. In (61), where the relative clause is used non-restrictively, the suggestion is rather that there is only one son, of whom it is said not only that he was insufferable but also, parenthetically as it were, that he attended a boarding school. If the prosody of these sentences is taken into account, it will be clear that this pragmatic difference is in keeping with the *NAH* as formulated in (49). Similar observations can be made with respect to the (non-)restrictiveness of the adjectives and nouns in (64) (Kamp and Reyle 1993: 372).

(62)   *The **son who attended a boarding school** was* INSUFFERABLE.

(63)   *The **son**, who attended a* BOARDING SCHOOL, *was* INSUFFERABLE.

(64)   *John fed the* ANIMALS. *The young cats were* HUNGRY.
        John fed the ANIMALS. *The young **cats** were* HUNGRY.
        John fed the ANIMALS. *The **young** cats were* HUNGRY.
        John fed the ANIMALS. *The **young cats** were* HUNGRY.

---

[14] Or, equivalently, singleton-set-representing discourse referents.

[15] Thus let $\{p\}$, $\{j\}$, $\{x\}$, $\{y\}$ constitute the respective discourse referents of the noun phrases *Paul, Jim,* **he** and **him**. Then the grammar subsystem specifies $\{\{p\}, \{j\}\}$ as the range of possible values for $\{x\}$ and $\{y\}$, and the pragmatics subsystem (building an syntactic parallellism) specifies $\{p\}$ and $\{j\}$ as the respective preferred antecedents for the pronominal discourse referents $\{x\}$ and $\{y\}$. Since the pronouns are stressed, however, the respective preferences of $\{x\}$ and $\{y\}$ for $\{p\}$ and $\{j\}$ mean that $\{p\} \not\subseteq \{x\}$ and $\{j\} \not\subseteq \{y\}$, that is: $p \neq x$ and $j \neq y$.

5 Conclusion

In Pierrehumbert and Hirschberg (1990), 'The Meaning of Intonational Contours in the Interpretation of Discourse', it is proposed that speakers use tune to
specify a particular relationship between the 'propositional content' realized in
the intonational phrase over which the tune is employed and the mutual beliefs
of participants – speaker S and hearer H – in the current discourse, where tune,
or *intonational contour*, is taken to be a sequence of *low* (L) and *high* (H) tones,
made up from pitch accents, phrase accents and boundary tones, and tune
meaning is assumed to be built up compositionally. *Pitch accents* mark the lexical items with which they are associated as prominent: accented items are salient, not only phonologically but also from an informational standpoint. Pierrehumbert and Hirschberg follow Beckman and Pierrehumbert (1986) in
distinguishing six pitch accents: two simple tones, H* and L*, and four complex
ones, L*+H, L+H*, H*+L and H+L*, where the '*' indicates that the tone is
aligned with a stressed syllable. Pitch accents are believed to convey information about the status of the individual discourse referents, modifiers, predicates
and relationships specified by the lexical items with which the accents are associated.

(*a*) 'In general, we believe that all accent types can be used to convey information to H about
how the propositional content of the (perhaps partially) instantiated expression corresponding.
to the utterance is to be used to modify what H believes to be mutually believed' (1990: 289).

With respect to the two L+H pitch accents (L*+H and L+H*), it is observed
that:

(*b*) '[The L+H pitch accents] 'are employed by S to convey the salience of some *scale* (defined here [...] as a partial ordering) linking the accented item to other items salient in H's
mutual beliefs' (1990: 294), and 'S employs the L+H* accent to convey that the accented item
– and not some alternative related item – should be mutually believed' (1990: 296).

Finally, the most common use of L+H* in the data collected by Pierrehumbert
and Hirschberg

(*c*) 'is to mark a correction or contrast. In such cases S substitutes a new scalar value for one
previously proposed by S or by H – or for some alternative value available in the context'
(1990: 296).

By way of conclusion we may observe that the account of links detailed in the
present paper can actually be considered a partial execution – viz., for L+H*
pitch accent – of the intonational-informational program outlined in Pierrehumbert and Hirschberg (1990), for note that on the present account the following
analogous claims are assumed to hold:

(*a*) Pitch accent is an aspect of information packaging – i.e, the structuring of propositional
content in function of the speaker's assumptions about the hearer's knowledge and attentional
state;

(b)   L+H* pitch accent does invoke a scale, viz., the partial ordering '⊆' on discourse referents, and conveys that the antecedent the accented item finds itself 'linked to' is associated with a discourse referent that is not a subset of the discourse referent of the accented item; and

(c)   Correction and contrast are among the manifestations of the non-monotonic anaphora signaled by L+H* pitch accent, which were argued to involve (non-)association with focus, 'nonidentity' anaphora, contrastive stress, correction, pronoun referent resolution, and restrictiveness of relatives and adjectives.

References

[1] Beckman, M., & J. Pierrehumbert (1986): 'Intonational Structure in Japanese and English'. *Phonological Yearbook* 3, 15–70.

[2] Bosch, P. & R. van der Sandt (eds.) (1994): *Focus and Natural Language Processing. Proceedings of a Conference in Celebration of the 10th Anniversary of the Journal of Semantics.* Working Papers 6 (Vol. 1: Intonation and Syntax), 7 (Vol. 2: Semantics), and 8 (Vol. 3: Discourse) of the IBM Institute for Logic and Linguistics, Heidelberg.

[3] Cahn, J. (1995): 'The Effect of Pitch Accenting on Pronoun Referent Resolution'. Manuscript. MIT, Cambridge (Mass.).

[4] Chafe, W.L. (1976): 'Givenness, Contrastiveness, Definiteness, Subjects, Topics and Point of View'. In: C.N. Li (ed.) (1976), Subject and Topic, 25–55. Associated Press, New York.

[5] Clark, H.H. & S.E: Haviland (1977): 'Comprehension and the Given-New Contract'. In: R.O. Freedle (ed.) (1977), *Discourse Production and Comprehension,* 1–40. Lawrence Erlbaum Associates, Hillsdale (New Jersey).

[6] Dahl, Ö. (1974): 'Topic-Comment Structure Revisited'. In: Ö. Dahl (ed.) (1974), *Topic and Comment, Contextual Boundedness and Focus. Papers in Text Linguistics* 6. Helmut Buske, Hamburg.

[7] Deemter, K. van (1992): 'Towards a Generalization of Anaphora'. *Journal of Semantics* 9, 27–51.

[8] Deemter, K. van (1994a): 'What's New? A Semantic Perspective on Sentence Accent'. *Journal of Semantics* 11, 1–31.

[9] Deemter, K. van (1994b): 'Contrastive Stress, Contrariety and Focus'. In: P. Bosch & R. van der Sandt (eds.), 39–49.

[10] Engdahl, E. (ed.) (1994): *Integrating information Structure into Constraint-based and Categorial Approaches.* ESPRIT Basic Research Project 6852, Dynamic Interpretation of Natural Language. DYANA-2 Deliverable R1.3.B. ILLC, University of Amsterdam.

[11] Heim, I. (1982): *The Semantics of Definite and Indefinite Noun Phrases.* Ph.D. Dissertation University of Massachusetts, Amherst. Published in 1989 by Garland. New York.

[12] Heim, I. (1983): 'File Change Semantics and the Familiarity Theory of Definiteness'. In: R. Bäuerle, C. Schwarze & A. von Stechow (eds.) (1983), *Meaning, Use and Interpretation of Language.* De Gruyter, Berlin, 164–189.

[13] Hendriks, H. (1994): 'Information Packaging in a Categorial Perspective'. In: Engdahl (ed.), 89–116.

[14] Hendriks, H. (1996): 'Intonation, Derivation, Information'. In: C. Casadio (ed.), *Proceedings of the Third Roma Workshop on Proofs and Linguistic Categories.* University of Bologna.

[15] Hendriks, H. (*draft*): 'Information Packaging and "Association with Focus"'. Manuscript, Utrecht University.

[16] Hoffman, B. (1995): 'Integrating "Free" Word Order Syntax and information Structure'. Manuscript, University of Pennsylvania.

[17] Jackendoff, R. (1972): *Semantic Interpretation in Generative Grammar*. MIT Press, Cambridge (Mass.).

[18] Jacobs, J. (1983): *Fokus und Skalen: Zur Syntax und Semantik von Gradpartikeln im Deutschen*. Niemeyer, Tübingen.

[19] Kameyama, M. (1994): 'Stressed and Unstressed Pronouns: Complementary Preferences'. In: P. Bosch & R. van der Sandt (eds.), 475–484.

[20] Kamp, H. (1981): 'A Theory of Truth and Semantic Representation'. In: J. Groenendijk, T. Janssen & M. Stokhof (eds.) (1981), *Formal Methods in the Study of Language*. Mathematical Centre, Amsterdam. Reprinted in J. Groenendijk, T. Janssen & M. Stokhof (eds.) (1984*), Truth, Interpretation and Information. Selected Papers from the Third Amsterdam Colloquium*. Foris, Dordrecht.

[21] Kamp, H. & U. Reyle (1993): *From Discourse to Logic. Introduction to Modeltheoretic Semantics of Natural Language, Formal Logic and Discourse Representation Theory*. Kluwer, Dordrecht.

[22] Krifka, M. (1991): 'A Compositional Semantics for Multiple Focus Constructions'. *Linguistische Berichte, Suppl.* 4, 17–53.

[23] Lakoff, G., (1971): 'On Generative Semantics'. In: D. Steinberg & L. Jacobovitz (eds.) (1971), *Semantics*. Cambridge University Press, Cambridge, 232–296.

[24] Lambek, J. (1961): 'On the Calculus of Syntactic Types'. In: R. Jakobson (ed.) (1961*), Structure of Language and its Mathematical Aspects*. Providence.

[25] Linden, E.-J. van der (1991): 'Accent Placement and Focus in Categorial Logic'. In: S. Bird (ed.) (1991) *Declarative Perspectives on Phonology*. Edinburgh Working Papers in Cognitive Science. Eccs, Edinburgh.

[26] Moortgat, M. (1993): 'Generalized Quantification and Discontinuous Type Constructors'. In: W. Sijtsma and A. van Horck (eds.) (1993), *Proceedings of the Tilburg Symposium on Discontinuous Dependencies*. De Gruyter, Berlin.

[27] Moortgat, M. (1994): 'Residuation in Mixed Lambek Systems'. In: M. Moortgat (ed.) (1994), ESPRIT Basic Research Project 6852, Dynamic Interpretation of Natural Language, DYANA-2 Deliverable R1.1.B. ILLC, University of Amsterdam, and to appear in IGPL Bulletin.

[28] Moortgat, M. & G. Morrill (1991): 'Heads and Phrases. Type Calculus for Dependency and Constituent Structure'. OTS Research Paper, University of Utrecht.

[29] Nooteboom, S.G., and J.M.B. Terken (1982): 'What Makes Speakers Omit Pitch Accents?'. *Phonetica* 39, 317–336.

[30] Oehrle, R. (1988): 'Multidimensional Compositional Functions as a Basis for Grammatical Analysis'. In: R. Oehrle, E. Bach and D. Wheeler (eds.) *Categorial Grammars and Natural Language Structures*. Reidel, Dordrecht.

[31] Oehrle, R. (1991): 'Prosodic Constraints on Dynamic Grammatical Analysis'. In: S. Bird (ed.) *Declarative Perspectives on Phonology*. Edinburgh Working Papers in Cognitive Science. Eccs, Edinburgh.

[32] Oehrle, R. (1993): 'String-based Categorial Type Systems'. Manuscript. Department of Linguistics, University of Arizona, Tucson.

[33] Partee, B. (1994): 'Focus, Quantification, and Semantics-Pragmatics Issues. Preliminary Version'. In: P. Bosch & R. van der Sandt (eds.), 363–378.

[34] Pierrehumbert, J. (1980): *The Phonology and Phonetics of English Intonation*. Ph.D. Disertation. MIT, Cambridge (Mass.). Distributed by the IULC.

[35] Pierrehumbert, J. & J. Hirschberg (1990): 'The Meaning of Intonational Contours in the Interpretation of Discourse'. In: P. Cohen, J. Morgan & M. Pollack (eds.) *Intentions in Communication*, MIT Press, Cambridge.

[36] Pollard, C. & I. Sag (1987): *Information-Based Syntax and Semantics. Vol. I*: Fundamentals. CSLI, Stanford.

[37] Pollard, C. & I. Sag (1994): *Head-Driven Phrase Structure Grammar*. University of Chicago Press, Chicago, and CSLI, Stanford.

[38] Prince, E. (1981): 'Toward a Taxonomy of Given-New Information'. In: P. Cole, *Radical Pragmatics*. Academic Press, New York, 233–255.

[39] Reinhart, T. (1982): 'Pragmatics and Linguistics: An Analysis of Sentence Topics'. *Philosophica* 27, 53–94.

[40] Rooth, M. (1985): *Association with Focus*. Ph.D. Dissertation University of Massachusetts, Amherst.

[41] Rooth, M. (1992): 'A Theory of Focus Interpretation'. *Natural Language Semantics* 1, 75–116.

[42] Steedman, M. (1991): 'Structure and Intonation'. *Language* 67, 260–296.

[43] Steedman, M. (1992): 'Surface Structure, Intonation and "Focus" '. In: E. Klein and F. Veltman (eds.) *Natural Language and Speech. Symposium Proceedings, Brussels, November 1991*. Springer, Berlin.

[44] Steedman, M. (1993): 'The Grammar of Intonation and Focus'. In: P. Dekker & M. Stokhof (eds.) (1993), *Proceedings of the Ninth Amsterdam Colloquium, December 14–17, 1993*, Part III. ILLC, University of Amsterdam.

[45] Svoboda, A. & P. Materna (1987): 'Functional Sentence Perspective and Intensional Logic'. In: R. Dirven & V. Fried (eds.) *Functionalism in Linguistics*. John Benjamins, Amsterdam.

[46] Szabolcsi, A. (1981): 'The Semantics of Topic-Focus Articulation'. In: J. Groenendijk, T. Janssen & M. Stokhof (eds.) (1981), *Formal Methods in the Study of Language*. Mathematical Centre, Amsterdam.

[47] Szabolcsi, A. (1983): 'Focussing Properties, or the Trap of First Order'. In: *Theoretical Linguistics* 10, 125–145.

[48] Vallduví, E. (1992): *The Informational Component*. Garland, New York.

[49] Vallduví, E. (1993): 'Information Packaging: A Survey'. Report prepared for *Word Order, Prosody, and Information Structure*. Centre for Cognitive Science and Human Communication Research Centre, University of Edinburgh.

[50] Vallduví, E. (1994): 'The Dynamics of Information Packaging'. In: Engdahl (ed.), 1–27.

[51] Vallduví, E. & R. Zacharski (1993): 'Accenting Phenomena, Association with Focus, and the Recursiveness of Focus-Ground'. In: P. Dekker & M. Stokhof (eds.) (1993) *Proceedings of the Ninth Amsterdam Colloquium, December 14–17, 1993*, Part III. ILLC, University of Amsterdam.

Duivendrecht   Herman Hendriks

Utrecht Institute of Linguistics OTS, Utrecht University, Trans 10, 3512 JK Utrecht, The Netherlands, phone: +31-30-2539152, fax: +31-30-2536000, hendriks@hum.uva.nl

ILLC/Department of Philosophy, University of Amsterdam, Nieuwe Doelenstraat 15, 1012 CP Amsterdam, The Netherlands, phone: +31-20-5254509, fax: +31-20-5254503, Herman.Hendriks@let.ruu.nl

Faculty of Philosophy, Utrecht University, Heidelberglaan 8, 3584 CS Utrecht, The Netherlands, phone: +31-30-253 77 80, fax: +31-30-253 28 16, Herman.Hendriks@phil.uu.nl

Dynamic Semantics

Marcus Kracht[1]

1 Introduction

Dynamic semantics is called 'dynamic' because it assumes that the meaning of a sentence is not its truth condition but rather its impact on the hearer. In contrast to standard semantics in terms of predicate logic (from now on also called *static semantics*), where formulae are interpreted as conditions on models, dynamic semantics interprets formulae as update functions on databases. The change from the static to the dynamic view was necessitated by problems concerning extrasentential anaphors, but nowadays many more applications of this new semantics have been found. We will begin however with the classical problem. Consider the following examples.

(1)   There is a fat man at the metro entrance. He is selling souvenirs.

(2)   If Alfred has a car, he washes it every weekend.

In Montague semantics, following the philosophical tradition, a sentence expresses a proposition. A proposition corresponds to a closed formula in predicate logic. Using some self-explanatory abbreviations, the above sentences may be rendered as follows.

(1a) $(\exists x)(\textbf{fat-man}(x) \wedge \textbf{at-metro-entrance}(x) \wedge \textbf{sell-souvenirs}(x))$

(2a) $(\forall x)(\textbf{car}(x) \wedge \textbf{own}(a, x) \rightarrow \textbf{wash-every-week}(a, x))$

In the translation we have ignored certain details such as tense. The problem is to arrive at the given translations in a systematic way, that is, using λ-expressions as in Montague semantics. Let us illustrate this with (1). (1) is composed from two sentences; each of them is translated by a closed formula. If we assume that the meaning of two sentences in sequence is simply the conjunction of the meanings of the individual sentences we get the following translation.

(1b.1) $(\exists x)(\textbf{fat-man}(x) \wedge \textbf{at-metro-entrance}(x))$

(1b.2) $(\exists x)\textbf{sell-souvenirs}(x)$

(1b) $(\exists x)(\textbf{fat-man}(x) \wedge \textbf{at-metro-entrance}(x)) \wedge (\exists x)\textbf{sell-souvenirs}(x)$

[1] I have benefitted from enlightening discussions with Fritz Hamm, Peter Staudacher, Kees Vermeulen and Albert Visser.

The transliteration of (1b) is *there is a fat man at the metro entrance and there is someone selling souvenirs* – which is not the meaning of (1). The problem is that (1b) can be satisfied when there is a fat man at the metro entrance and someone different, who is not fat but sells souvenirs. Notice that the choice of the variable in (1b.1) and (1b.2) is completely immaterial. We can replace x by any other variable.

Obviously, the problem lies in the translation of the pronoun. In our previous attempt we have tacitly assumed that a pronoun is to be translated by a variable. This strategy fails. Similar problems arise with sentence (2) above. Now what can be done? One solution is to interpret a pronoun as a covert definite description. Let us consider again example (1). After hearing the second sentence we may ask ourselves who is meant by *he*. The obvious answer is: *the fat man at the metro entrance*. So, rather than picking up a referent by means of a syntactic variable we may pick it up by a suitable definite description. Without going into details we may note that under this strategy (1) turns out to be synonymous with (3).

(3)   There is a fat man at the metro entrance. The fat man at the metro entrance is selling souvenirs.

This, however, is not without problems. For suppose there are two fat men at the metro entrance and only one is selling souvenirs. Then (1) is still true, while (3) is false since the definite description *the fat man at the metro entrance* fails to refer.

Another possibility is to use open formulae as translations. Rather than translating (1) as (1a) we may simply translate it as

(1c)   **fat-man**(x) $\wedge$ **at-metro-entrance**(x) $\wedge$ **sell-souvenirs**(x)

This allows to derive (1c) in a systematic way from the meaning of the two sentences, which we give as (1c.1) and (1c.2)

(1c.1)   **fat-man**(x) $\wedge$ **at-metro-entrance**(x)

(1c.2) $y = x$ $\wedge$ **sell-souvenirs**(y)

Here, *selling souvenirs* is rendered as **sell-souvenirs**(y), where y is a fresh variable, and the pronoun *he* is rendered $y = x$. Again we will not go into details here. The truth conditions for (1c) are different from the standard conditions in predicate logic, where a free variable is treated as if universally quantified. Rather, a free variable is treated as if *existentially quantified*. Let us say that (1c) is true in a model $\mathfrak{M}$ under a valuation g if there exists a valuation h differing from g in at most x such that (1c) is true in $\mathfrak{M}$ under the valuation h. This is, modulo some minor variation, the solution presented in Discourse Representation Theory (DRT) (see [4]). Note especially how it assigns truth conditions to an implication such as (2). Namely, an implication $\phi \Rightarrow \psi$[2] is true in a model

---

[2] We write $\Rightarrow$ for the implication and ; for the conjunction of DRT in order not to get confused with the standard symbols of predicate logic.

$\mathfrak{M}$ under a valuation g if for every valuation h differing from g in at most the free variables of ϕ that makes ϕ true there is a valuation k differing in at most the free variables of ψ that are not free in ϕ such that that k makes ψ true. Let us apply this to the translation of (2), (2c).

(2c) $\mathbf{car}(x); \mathbf{own}(a, x) \Rightarrow y = x; \mathbf{wash\text{-}every\text{-}week}(a, y)$

(2c) is true in $(\mathfrak{M}, g)$ if for every h differing from g in at most x, such that h assigns for example j to x and j is a car and Alfred owns it in $\mathfrak{M}$, then there is a valuation k differing from h in at most y such that $k(y) = k(x) (= j)$ and Alfred washes $k(y)$ every day. So, (2c) is true if Alfred washes every car that he owns every week. This is exactly as it should be.

This definition of truth anticipates certain features of dynamic semantics. Although it still employs the static notion of satisfaction (or truth) in a model it already works with dynamically changing assignments. In predicate logic, only the truth conditions for quantifiers allow for a change in assignments, while in DRT the standard logical connectives may also change them. Compare, for example, the truth condition for an implication in predicate logic with that of DRT. In the former, $\phi \rightarrow \psi$ is true in $(\mathfrak{M}, g)$ if either ϕ is false or ψ is true in it. The dynamic character of the simple connectives also allows DRT to dispense with the usual quantifiers. For notice that $(\exists x)\phi(x)$ is equivalent to $\phi(x)$ and $(\forall x)\phi(x)$ is equivalent to $x = x \Rightarrow \phi(x)$. Consequently, DRT dispenses with quantifiers and only introduces a separate head section in a DRS to annotate for which variables the valuation may be changed. So, rather than $\phi(x)$ we write $[x : \phi(x)]$. In this way we can distinguish between a contextually unbound variable (corresponding to an indefinite description) and a contextually bound variable (for example in translating a pronoun by an expression $y = x$, where x has appeared already).

2 Dynamic predicate logic

In DRT, we have no quantifiers, only conditions on assignments. This may solve the problem for the indefinite expressions and the existential quantifiers. However, DRT has no analogue for the universal quantifier. The reduction of the universal quantifier to an implication is merely a formal trick and can in fact not be used for other quantifiers. Several people have noticed independently that the problems of anaphoric reference can only be solved if we allow to memorize the value given to a certain variable. In DRT this is achieved by simply removing the quantifier and readjusting the satisfaction clauses for free formulae. Yet another path was followed by Peter Staudacher and, somewhat later but independently, Jeroen Groenendijk and Martin Stokhof. (See [9] and [1]. A comparison of the two approaches can be found in [10].) Hence our basic vocabulary consists of

1. a set *Var* of variables over individuals,
2. a set *Con* of constants for individuals,
3. some atomic relation symbols,
4. the boolean connectives $\top$, $\bot$, $\neg$, $\wedge$, $\vee$, $\rightarrow$,
5. the quantifiers $\exists$ and $\forall$.

(That we have no function symbols is just a question of simplicity. In the formal definitions we will also often ignore the constants to keep the notation simple.) As usual, a well-formed formula (simply called a *formula*) is defined by induction.

1. If R is an n-ary relation symbol and $u_i \in Var \cup Con$ for all $1 \leq i \leq n$, then $R(u_1, \ldots, u_n)$ is a formula.
2. $\top$ and $\bot$ are formulae.
3. If ϕ is a formula, so is $\neg\phi$.
4. If ϕ and ψ are formulae then so are $\phi \wedge \psi$, $\phi \vee \psi$ and $\phi \rightarrow \psi$.
5. If x is a variable and ϕ a formula then $(\exists x)\phi$ and $(\forall x)\phi$ are formulae.

Definition 1. *A* **model** *is a pair (D, I), where D is a set, called the* **domain**, *and I a function, the* **interpretation function**, *assigning to each constant an element of D and to each n-ary relation R of the language a subset of D^n. An* **assignment** *or* **valuation** *is a function g : Var $\rightarrow$ D. The set of all assignments into D is denoted by $\mathbb{V}(D)$.*

We write $(\mathfrak{M}, g) \vDash \phi$ if ϕ is true in $\mathfrak{M}$. This is defined by induction. On the basis of that we define the **static meaning** of ϕ, $[\phi]_{\mathfrak{M}}$ or simply $[\phi]$, to be

$$[\phi] := \{g : \langle \mathfrak{M}, g \rangle \vDash \phi\}$$

Let us write $g \sim_x h$ if $g(y) = h(y)$ for all $y \neq x$.

Definition 2 (Static Meaning). *Given a model $\mathfrak{M}$, the static meaning of a formula ϕ is computed as follows.*

$$
\begin{aligned}
[R(x_1,\ldots,x_n)] &:= \{g : \langle g(x_1),\ldots,g(x_n)\rangle \in I(R)\} \\
[\top] &:= \mathbb{V}(D) \\
[\bot] &:= \varnothing \\
[\neg\phi] &:= \mathbb{V}(D) - [\phi] \\
[\phi \vee \psi] &:= [\phi] \cup [\psi] \\
[\phi \wedge \psi] &:= [\phi] \cap [\psi] \\
[\phi \rightarrow \psi] &:= (\mathbb{V}(D) - [\phi]) \cup [\psi] \\
[(\exists x)\,\phi] &:= \{g : \text{exists } h \sim_x g : h \in [\phi]\} \\
[(\forall x)\,\phi] &:= \{g : \text{for all } h \sim_x g : h \in [\phi]\}
\end{aligned}
$$

The idea of the dynamic interpretation is to keep the full syntax of predicate logic and instead change the underlying notion of truth. Rather than talking of an assignment g in a model $\mathfrak{M}$ making a formula true we will now talk of ϕ being processable or unprocessable under the assignment g. If ϕ is processable we may further speak of ϕ taking us from the assignment g to an assignment h. We will assume that the meaning of a formula ϕ of predicate logic is a *binary relation* on the set of assignments of variables. We discuss this with our examples (1) and (2). We translate (1) and (2) now as follows.

(1d) $(\exists x)(\textbf{fat-man}(x) \wedge \textbf{at-metro-entrance}(x)) \wedge \textbf{sell-souvenirs}(x)$

(2d) $(\exists x)(\textbf{car}(x) \wedge \textbf{own}(a, x)) \rightarrow \textbf{wash-every-week}(a, x)$

Notice that the last occurrence of x in (1d) is outside the scope of the quantifier. Likewise the last occurrence of x in (2d). Notice furthermore that in (2d) the indefinite expression is translated by an existential quantifier; we will see that this nevertheless gives the right analysis. All three facts are vital for the possibility to arrive at the translation in a compositional manner, but we will defer the details for later. We shall assume now the following: the denotation of a formula ϕ in a model $\mathfrak{M}$ is a relation between assignments. We denote it by $[\phi]_{\mathfrak{M}}$ or usually by $[\phi]$. We usually write $g \xrightarrow{\phi} h$ rather than $(g, h) \in [\phi]$. (Actually, to make the dependency on the model $\mathfrak{M}$ explicit we would have to write $g \xrightarrow{\phi}_{\mathfrak{M}} h$, but we refrain from using an overly pedantic notation.) $g \xrightarrow{\phi} \sqrt{}$ means that there exists a k such that $g \xrightarrow{\phi} k$. If $g \xrightarrow{\phi} \sqrt{}$ we say that ϕ is *processable* in g.

Definition 3 (Dynamic Meaning). *Given a model $\mathfrak{M}$, the dynamic meaning of ϕ in $\mathfrak{M}$ is computed as follows.*

$$
\begin{aligned}
[R(x_1, \ldots, x_n)] &:= \{\langle g, g \rangle : \langle \mathfrak{M}, g \rangle \vDash R(x_1, \ldots, x_n)\} \\
[\top] &:= \{\langle g, g \rangle : g \in \mathbb{V}(D)\} \\
[\bot] &:= \varnothing \\
[\phi \wedge \psi] &:= \{\langle g, h \rangle : \text{for some } k : g \xrightarrow{\phi} k \xrightarrow{\psi} h\} \\
[\phi \vee \psi] &:= \{\langle g, g \rangle : g \xrightarrow{\phi} \sqrt{} \text{ or } g \xrightarrow{\psi} \sqrt{}\} \\
[\phi \rightarrow \psi] &:= \{\langle g, g \rangle : \text{ for all } h : \text{ if } g \xrightarrow{\phi} h \text{ then } h \xrightarrow{\psi} \sqrt{}\} \\
[\neg \phi] &:= \{\langle g, g \rangle : \text{ not } : g \xrightarrow{\phi} \sqrt{}\} \\
[(\exists x)\phi] &:= \{\langle g, h \rangle : \text{ exists } k \sim_x g : k \xrightarrow{\phi} h\} \\
[(\forall x)\phi] &:= \{\langle g, g \rangle : \text{ for all } h \sim_x g : h \xrightarrow{\phi} \sqrt{}\}
\end{aligned}
$$

In Figure 1 further below we show the dynamic meaning of two formulae, namely $Q(x, y) \wedge (\exists x)(\exists y)(x = y)$ and $Q(x, y)$. We assume $Var = \{x, y\}$, $D = \{a,b\}$ and $I(Q) = \{\langle a, a \rangle, \langle a, b \rangle, \langle b, b \rangle\}$. The assignments are listed as pairs $\langle g(x), g(y) \rangle$.

Definition 4. *Let ϕ and ψ be two formulae. ϕ is called a **tautology** if $[\phi] = [\top]$, and a **contradiction** if $[\phi] = \bot$. We say that ϕ and ψ are **equivalent** and write $\phi \approx \psi$ if $[\phi] = [\psi]$.*

Notice that $[\phi] = [\psi]$ means that for all models $\mathfrak{M}$, $[\phi]_{\mathfrak{M}} = [\psi]_{\mathfrak{M}}$, which in turn means that for all $\mathfrak{M}$ and all assignments g and h, $g \xrightarrow{\phi} h$ iff $g \xrightarrow{\psi} h$.

Definition 5. *Given a model $\mathfrak{M}$ and a formula ϕ, ϕ is **true** under the assignment g iff ϕ is processable in g iff there is a k such that $\langle g, k \rangle \in [\phi]_{\mathfrak{M}}$. The set of all g such that ϕ is true under g is denoted by $\backslash \phi \backslash_{\mathfrak{M}}$. Dually,*

$$/\phi/_{\mathfrak{M}} := \{g : exists\ k : k \xrightarrow{\ \phi\ } g\}$$

$\backslash \phi \backslash_{\mathfrak{M}}$ is also called the *satisfaction set* in [1]. We skip the motivation for these definitions and turn directly to our examples. (1d) is true in a model under an assignment g iff there are assignments h and k such that $g \xrightarrow{\ (1.d\,.1)\ } h \xrightarrow{\ (1.d\,.2)\ } k$.

(1d.1) $(\exists x)(\textbf{fat-man}(x) \wedge \textbf{at-metro-entrance}(x))$
(1d.2)   **sell-souvenirs**(x)

Now $g \xrightarrow{\ (1.d\,.1)\ } h$ iff for some m differing in at most x, the pair (m, m) is in the interpretation of **fat-man**$(x) \wedge$ **at-metro-entrance**(x) and $m = h$. This is the case simply when $h = m$ and $m(x)$ is a fat man in the metro entrance in $\mathfrak{M}$. So, $g \xrightarrow{\ (1.d\,.1)\ } h$ iff h differs from g in at most x and $h(x)$ is a fat man in the metro entrance. $h \xrightarrow{\ (1.d\,.2)\ } k$ iff $k = h$ and $h(x)$ is selling souvenirs. This is as desired.

Now take (2d). The relation $[(2d)]$ is exactly the set of all $\langle g, g \rangle$ such that (2d) is true under g. (2d) is true under the assignment g if for every h such that $g \xrightarrow{\ (2.d\,.1)\ } h$ there is a k such that $h \xrightarrow{\ (2.d\,.2)\ } k$.

(2d.1) $(\exists x)(\textbf{car}(x) \wedge \textbf{own}(a, x))$

(2d.2)   **wash-every-week**(a, x)

Now, $g \xrightarrow{\ (2.d\,.1)\ } h$ iff h differs from g at most in x and $h(x)$ is a car that Alfred owns. $h \xrightarrow{\ (2.d\,.2)\ } k$ iff $k = h$ and Alfred washes $h(x)$ every week. Thus, $g \xrightarrow{\ (2.d)\ } g$ iff for every x which is a car that Alfred owns, Alfred washes x every week. This is as it should be.

So, the translations which we have given for the sentences turn out to be correct. Let us see now that we can assign these translations to sentences in a compositional way. We will highlight only the relevant details here. The assumption is that a phrase of the form *some NP* or *a(n) NP* is translated by $(\exists x)\phi$ where (a) x is a fresh variable and (b) ϕ is the translation of *NP*. The condition on freshness of the variable is problematic (see Section 5), so we assume that the input for the translation algorithm is a sentence enriched with indices which tell us which variable to use. So the input for the translation are the sentences

(1')   *There is [a fat man]^1 at the metro entrance. He$_2^1$ is selling souvenirs.*

(2')   *If Alfred^1 owns [a car]^2 then he$_1$ washes it$_2$ every day.*

Here the superscripts are used for newly introduced referents and the subscripts for already existing referents. Pronouns have both a superscript and a subscript, so they pick up a previously introduced referent and introduce a new one. The translation now works exactly as in Montague semantics. Let $(-)^{\dagger}$ be the translation from natural language into λ-expressions. Then the pronoun he^i_j is assigned the meaning $x_i = x_j$; likewise for the other pronouns *she, it.* Case endings are ignored. We give some sample translations for verbs, adjectives and nouns. (Here, $\mathcal{P}$ is a variable of type $\langle e, t \rangle$.)

$$
\begin{array}{lll}
(he_j)^\dagger & :- & \lambda\,\mathcal{P}.\exists x_i.x_i = x_i \wedge \mathcal{P}(x_i) \\
(a\,(n)\,NP^i)^\dagger & := & \lambda\,\mathcal{P}.\exists x_i.NP^\dagger(x_i) \wedge \mathcal{P}(x_i) \\
(every\,NP^i)^\dagger & := & \lambda\,\mathcal{P}.\forall x_i.NP^\dagger(x_i) \rightarrow \mathcal{P}(x_i) \\
own^\dagger & ;- & \lambda x.\lambda y.\mathbf{own}(y, x) \\
sell\,souvenirs^\dagger & := & \lambda x.\mathbf{sell\text{-}souvenirs}(x) \\
fat^\dagger & := & \lambda\mathcal{P}.\lambda x.\mathbf{fat}(x) \wedge \mathcal{P}(x) \\
man^\dagger & :- & \lambda x.\mathbf{man}(x) \\
(if\,S\,then\,T)^\dagger & :- & S^\dagger \rightarrow T^\dagger \\
(S.\,T)^\dagger & :\cdot & S^\dagger \wedge T^\dagger
\end{array}
$$

From these translations we derive the following formulae for (1') and (2'):

(1e) $(\exists x_1)(\mathbf{fat}(x_1) \wedge \mathbf{man}(x_1) \wedge \mathbf{at\text{-}metro\text{-}entrance}(x_1)) \wedge$
        $(\exists x_2)(x_1 = x_2 \wedge \mathbf{sell\text{-}souvenirs}(x_2))$

(2e) $(\exists x_2)(\mathbf{car}(x_2) \wedge \mathbf{own}(a, x_2)) \rightarrow$
        $(\exists x_3)(x_3 = a \wedge (\exists x_4)(x_4 = x_2 \wedge \mathbf{wash\text{-}every\text{-}week}(a, x_4)))$

This translation is somewhat more detailed than the one we gave earlier. It is easily checked that the satisfaction sets of the translations are the same as before. Therefore, with respect to the truth conditions we have succeeded in giving a compositional semantics. However, the situation is nevertheless not entirely ideal. We repeat (1d) with x_1 replacing x.

(1d) $(\exists x_1)(\mathbf{fat\text{-}man}(x_1) \wedge \mathbf{at\text{-}metro\text{-}entrance}(x_1)) \wedge \mathbf{sell\text{-}souvenirs}(x_1)$

Although (1d) and (1e) are truth requivalent, they do not have the same meaning in terms of the relation. That is to say, we have $\backslash(1d)\backslash = \backslash(1e)\backslash$ but we do not have $[\![(1d)]\!] = [\![(1e)]\!]$. Likewise for (2d) and (2e). Suppose for the sake of the argument that the variable x in (1d) is the same variable as x_1 in (1e).[3] Suppose we have the assignment $g : x_1 \mapsto$ John, $x_2 \mapsto$ Paul. Suppose further that John and Paul are different and that John is fat and standing at the metro entrance selling souvenirs. Let $h : x_1 \mapsto$ John, $x_2 \mapsto$ John. Then it turns out that $g \xrightarrow{(1.e)} h$ but not $g \xrightarrow{(1.d)} h$. The reason is easily identified: (1e) allows to change the value of x_1 and x_2 while (1d) allows to change only x_1. It may be thought that this is an effect of the translation of variables as existentially quantified expressions rather than simply variables. However, this is not so. Consider for simplicity the two formulae $(\exists x_1)\phi(x_1)$ and $(\exists x_2)\phi(x_2)$. (Think of ϕ as the translation of (1d).)

Proposition 6. *Let ϕ be an expression with only one variable. Then for all models $\mathfrak{M}$:*

$$\langle (\exists x_1)\phi(x_1) \rangle_{\mathfrak{M}} = \langle (\exists x_1)\phi(x_2) \rangle_{\mathfrak{M}}$$

---

[3] In fact, if they were not identical, matters would be quite the same.

However in general

$$[(\exists x_1)\phi(x_1)]_{\mathfrak{M}} \neq [(\exists x_2)\phi(x_2)]_{\mathfrak{M}}$$

Proof. Put $\chi_1 := (\exists x_1)\phi(x_1)$ and $\chi_2 := (\exists x_2)\phi(x_2)$. Assume $g \xrightarrow{\chi_1} \sqrt{}$. Then there exists a h such that $h \sim_{x_1} g$ and $h(x_1)$ satisfies ϕ in $\mathfrak{M}$. Put $k(x_2) := h(x_1)$. Then $k \sim_{x_2} g$ and $k(x_2)$ satisfies ϕ in $\mathfrak{M}$. So, $g \xrightarrow{\chi_2} k$. This shows one inclusion. The other is similar. For the other assertion, let $\mathfrak{M}$ have at least two elements, a and b. Let $g : x_1 \mapsto a, x_2 \mapsto b$. Assume that a satisfies ϕ but not b. Then $g \xrightarrow{\chi_2} g$ but not $g \xrightarrow{\chi_1} g$. Q.E.D.

This is a pervasive feature of the dynamic interpretation and is a direct consequence of what the dynamic semantics sought to achieve. The meaning of an expression not only encodes its truth conditions but also its context behaviour. The previous theorem is a direct consequence of this fact: while the two formulae are true in the same models, they are nevertheless not substitutable in all contexts without changing the truth. Here is a concrete example. Suppose that Peter is watching John but not Albert. John is on the balcony. The valuation g is such that $g(x_2) = Albert$. Now under g (4) turns out to be false, while (5) is true.

(4)   *Someone[1] is standing on the balcony. Peter watches him[2].*

(5)   *Someone[2] is standing on the balcony. Peter watches him[2].*

Here, the first sentence is translated by

$$(\exists x_{1/2})(\textbf{stand-on-balcony}(x_{1/2}))$$

while the second is translated by

$$\textbf{watch}(p, x_2)$$

Indeed, in (4) the existential quantifier sets x_1 to John. Everything else remains the same. Therefore, under this new valuation x_2 is still set to Albert. But Peter does not watch Albert. Therefore, (4) is false. In (5), however, the existential quantifier allows to change g to h, where $h(x_2) = John$. Peter watches $h(x_2)$, which is John. So, (5) is true.

We still owe the reader a definition of the *logic* corresponding to this new interpretation.[4] Matters are a little bit difficult here. First of all, we will not define a relation between sets of formulae and a formula but between sequences of formulae and a single formula.

Definition 7 (Dynamic Consequence). *Let ϕ_i, $1 \leq i \leq n$, and ψ be formulae. Then $\phi_1; \phi_2; \ldots ; \phi_n \vDash^d \psi$ if for all $(\mathfrak{M}, g)$:*

$$g \xrightarrow{\phi_1} g_1 \xrightarrow{\phi_2} g_2 \ldots \xrightarrow{\phi_n} g_n \text{ implies } g_n \xrightarrow{\psi} \sqrt{}$$

*This relation is called the **dynamic consequence relation**.*

---

[4] This section is not essential for the understanding of this paper and may be skipped.

The reader may verify that the dynamic consequence relation satisfies very few of the postulates for ordinary consequence relations. For example, if Φ is a sequence and ϕ occurs in Φ then we ordinarily have $\Phi \vDash \phi$; but this fails for the dynamic consequence relation. Also, the sequence ϕ_1; ϕ_2 and the sequence ϕ_2; ϕ_1 have different dynamic consequences. These facts easily fall out of the results of the next section once some elementary facts are noted.

Proposition 8 (Deduction Theorem)

$$\phi_1;\ \phi_2;\ \ldots;\ \phi_n \vDash^d \psi \qquad \textit{iff} \qquad \phi_1;\ \phi_2;\ \ldots;\ \phi_{n-1} \vDash^d \phi_n \cdot \psi$$

Proposition 9

$$\phi_1;\ \ldots;\ \phi_i;\ \phi_{i+1};\ \ldots;\ \phi_n \vDash^d \psi \qquad \textit{iff} \qquad \phi_1;\ \ldots;\ \phi_i \wedge \phi_{i+1};\ \ldots;\ \phi_n \vDash^d \psi$$

The last theorem allows to reduce the dynamic consequence relation to a relation between formulae. (In view of the deduction theorem we can even reduce this to a set of theorems.) Two other relations between formulae come to mind, namely the static entailment and the meaning inclusion.

Definition 10. *Let ϕ and ψ be two formulae. ϕ statically implies ψ if $\backslash\phi\backslash \subseteq \backslash\psi\backslash$. ψ is meaning included in ϕ if $[\phi] \subseteq [\psi]$.*

It follows that $\phi \approx \psi$ iff ϕ is meaning included in ψ and ψ is meaning included in ϕ. Notice that a dynamic tautology is a formula ϕ such that $\vDash^d \phi$. In other words, ϕ is a tautology iff it is processable in every assignment iff $\backslash\phi\backslash = V(D)$ iff ϕ is statically implied by $\top$. However, this is *not* equivalent with $[\phi] \supseteq [\top]$. Here we see once again that the dynamic notion of truth is quite counterintuitive and should not be seen as superseding the static notion of truth.

3 Taking a closer look

In order to have a better grip on the mechanism of PDL we will prove some theorems about it and illustrate its relationship with static predicate logic. First, however, we will introduce some simplification according to Albert Visser. Namely, we will change the syntax of the existential quantifier in the following way. If x is a variable then $\exists x$ is an expression. Furthermore, we let

$$[\exists x] := \{\langle g, h \rangle : g \sim_x h\}$$

Then note the following:

$$[\exists x \wedge \phi] = \{\langle g, h \rangle : \text{exists } k : g \xrightarrow{\exists x} k \xrightarrow{\phi} h\}$$
$$= \{\langle g, h \rangle: \text{exists } k : g \sim_x k \text{ and } k \xrightarrow{\phi} h\}$$

This is exactly the semantics of $(\exists x)\phi(x)$. This rather strange change in the syntax can actually be rather nicely motivated from the ideology of dynamic semantics. In the dynamic setting a formula can also be seen as a program to change the state of the hearer. The statement $g \xrightarrow{\phi} h$ means that the hearer may change from g into h upon being told that ϕ. We may also think of a formula as denoting a nondeterministic program, exactly as in Dynamic Logic.[5] So, in this view, the formula $\phi \wedge \psi$ is the consecutive execution of the programs ϕ and ψ; it allows to change first via ϕ and next via ψ. Consequently, we may interpret $\exists x$ as a *random reset* of x. Under this interpretation, $\exists x \wedge \phi$ is the instruction to first reset x randomly and then to execute ϕ.

Definition 11 (Visser Style Syntax). *Let ϕ be a formula of dynamic predicate logic. Then its translation, $\phi^\S$, is defined by*

$$
\begin{aligned}
R(x_1, \ldots, x_n)^\S &:= R(x_1, \ldots, x_n) \\
\top^\S &:= \top \\
\bot^\S &:= \bot \\
(\neg\phi)^\S &:- \neg\phi^\S \\
(\phi \wedge \chi)^\S &:= \phi^\S \wedge \chi^\S \\
(\phi \rightarrow \chi)^\S &:- \phi^\S \rightarrow \chi^\S \\
(\phi \vee \chi)^\S &:- \phi^\S \vee \chi^\S \\
((\exists x)\phi)^\S &:- \exists x \wedge \phi^\S \\
((\forall x)\phi)^\S &: \exists x \rightarrow \phi^\S
\end{aligned}
$$

We will in sequel prefer the Visser style syntax. Furthermore, we note that

$$\phi \wedge (\psi \wedge \chi) \approx (\phi \wedge \psi) \wedge \chi$$

Therefore – to save space – we will write '.' instead of $\wedge$ and drop brackets. So, $\exists x.\phi.\psi$ denotes either of $((\exists x)\phi) \wedge \psi$ or $(\exists x)(\phi \wedge \psi)$. Let us also note the following equivalences, which allow us to reduce the set of basic logical symbols rather drastically.

$$
\begin{aligned}
(\forall x)\phi &\approx \exists x \rightarrow \phi \\
\neg\phi &\approx \phi \rightarrow \bot \\
\phi \wedge \psi &\approx \neg\phi \rightarrow \psi
\end{aligned}
$$

The first equivalence has already been used implicitly to define the translation of the universal quantifier. So, all connectives can be defined from $\exists$, $\bot$, $\rightarrow$ and $\wedge$. The logic of DPL is rather unusual otherwise. Various theorems of static logic fail to hold. For example, $\wedge$ is not commutative and not idempotent. That is to say, we neither have $\phi \wedge \psi \approx \psi \wedge \phi$ nor $\phi \wedge \phi \approx \phi$ for all ϕ and ψ. Here are some counterexamples.

$$
\begin{aligned}
\exists x.P(x).\,\exists x.\neg P(x) &\not\approx \exists x.\neg P(x).\exists x.P(x) \\
P(x).\exists x.\neg P(x).\,P(x).\exists x.\neg P(x) &\not\approx P(x).\exists x.\neg P(x)
\end{aligned}
$$

In fact, consider the set $D = \{a, b\}$ and let P be true of a but not of b. Put $g(x) := a$ and $h(x) := b$, $g(y) = h(y)$ for all $y \neq x$. We have

$$
h \xrightarrow{\exists x} g \xrightarrow{P(x)} g \xrightarrow{\exists x} h \xrightarrow{\neg P(x)} h
$$

---

[5] This connection has already been noted in [1].

and

$$g \xrightarrow{\exists x} h \xrightarrow{\neg P(x)} h \xrightarrow{\exists x} g \xrightarrow{P(x)} g$$

On the other hand, $\langle g, g \rangle \notin [\exists x.P(x).\exists x.\neg P(x)]$ and $\langle h, h \rangle \notin [\exists x.\neg P(x).\exists x.P(x)]$. The reason is simply that otherwise in the first case we must have $\langle g, k \rangle \in [\exists x.P(x).\exists x]$ for some k and $\langle k, g \rangle \in [\neg P(x)]$. But since $g(x) = a$, which does

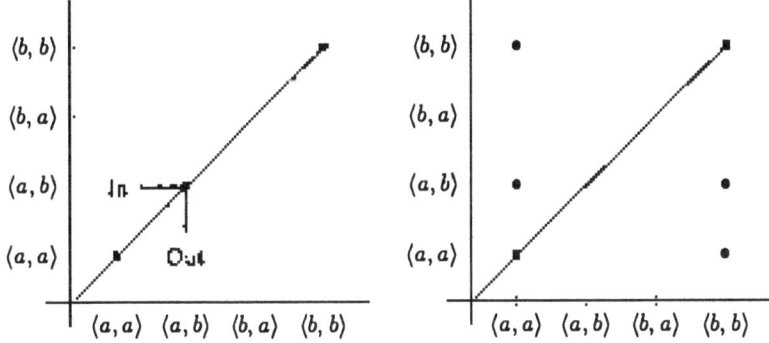

Figure 1: Dynamic Meaning:
$D = \{a, b\}$, $I(Q) = \{\langle a, a \rangle, \langle a, b \rangle, \langle b, b \rangle\}$ and $Var = \{x, y\}$.

not satisfy P, the latter cannot hold. Turning now to the second example notice that the lower left hand side is a contradiction. For $P(x).\neg P(x)$ is a contradiction and – as the reader may check – if ϕ is a contradiction, so is $\chi.\phi$ and $\phi.\chi$. But we have

$$g \xrightarrow{P(x)} g \xrightarrow{\exists x} h \xrightarrow{\neg P(x)} h$$

An important characteristic of some connectives is the ability to change the valuation. For example, we can have $g \xrightarrow{\phi} h$ for some $h \neq g$; take $\phi = \exists x_1.\mathbf{car}(x_1)$. Think of the formula ϕ in this context as picking up g and returning h. (Note that due to the relational character, a formula may return many valuations.) If ϕ is a complex formula, then this scheduling of picking up valuations and returning other valuations can in fact become rather complex. For notice that not all formulae return a different valuation; one example is $\neg \phi$. Therefore, the following definition is introduced.

Definition 12. *A formula ϕ is a* **test** *if for all models* $\mathfrak{M}$, $g \xrightarrow{\phi} h$ *implies* $g = h$.

The *diagonal* is the set $\{\langle g, g \rangle : g \in V(D)\} = [\top]$. A formula is a test iff its meaning is a subset of the diagonal. The diagonal is inserted in both pictures of Figure 1. Tests have a blob only along the diagonal. So, $Q(x, y)$ *is* a test but $Q(x, y).\exists x.\exists y.x = y$ is not. Tests behave in much the same way as their static companions. To see this, note first of all the following.

Proposition 13. *If $\phi \approx \psi$ then $\backslash\phi\backslash = \backslash\psi\backslash$ and $/\phi/ = /\psi/$. However, $\backslash\top\backslash = \backslash\exists x\backslash$ and $/\top/ = /\exists x/$ but $[\top] \neq [\exists x]$.*

(For those who like to see a proper PDL example, the formula $(\exists x)\top$ does the trick instead of $\exists x$.)

Proposition 14. *For tests ϕ and ψ the following holds*:

$$\backslash\phi\backslash = \backslash\psi\backslash \quad \text{iff} \quad /\phi/ = /\psi/ \quad \text{iff} \quad [\phi] = [\psi]$$

For a proof note that

$$[\phi] = \{\langle g, g\rangle : g \in \backslash\phi\backslash\} = \{\langle g, g\rangle : g \in /\phi/\}$$

All formulae of the following kind are tests:

1. Atomic formulae,
2. $\neg\phi$, $\phi \to \psi$ and $\phi \vee \psi$,
3. $\forall x.\phi$,
4. $\phi.\psi$, given that ϕ and ψ are tests.

We may now note the following.

$$
\begin{array}{lcl}
\backslash\neg\phi\backslash & \cdots & \mathbb{V}(D) - \backslash\phi\backslash \\
\backslash\phi \vee \psi\backslash & - & \backslash\phi\backslash \cup \backslash\psi\backslash \\
\backslash\phi \to \psi\backslash & \blacksquare & (\mathbb{V}(D) - \backslash\phi\backslash) \cup \backslash\psi\backslash \\
\backslash(\forall x)\phi\backslash & = & \{g : \text{for all } h \sim_x g : h \in \backslash\phi\backslash\}
\end{array}
$$

These are exactly the clauses of static predicate logic if we read $\backslash\phi\backslash$ simply as $[\phi]$. Furthermore, if ϕ and ψ are tests then

$$\backslash\phi.\psi\backslash = \backslash\phi\backslash \cap \backslash\psi\backslash$$

This notion of a test can be further refined. A change in valuation can be either internal or external to the formula. In the formula $\phi.\psi$, ϕ can reset the valuation, for example if $\phi = \exists x_1.\chi$. The new value is then passed on to ψ. Because of this behaviour we call $\wedge$ *internally dynamic*. Furthermore, ψ may also change the valuation, and this latter change persists. That is to say, a formula to the right of $\phi.\psi$ picks up the valuation from ψ, so to speak. Therefore we call $\phi \wedge \psi$ *externally dynamic*. By contrast, $\phi \vee \psi$ is not internally dynamic (and so we say it is *internally static*). For whatever change ϕ may produce, ψ cannot pick up that new valuation; rather, it is evaluated against the same valuation as is ϕ. $\phi \vee \psi$ is also not externally dynamic: a formula at the right end of $\phi \vee \psi$ also starts at the same valuation as did $\phi \vee \psi$. Hence, $\phi \vee \psi$ is externally static. Externally static

	EXTERNAL	INTERNAL
$\wedge$	+	+
$\vee$	−	−
$\rightarrow$	−	+
$\neg$	−	
$\exists$	+	
$\forall$	−	

Table 1: Dynamic properties of connectives

formulae are exactly the tests. We can summarize the behaviour in Table 1. Of course, the concept of internal dynamicity does not apply to unary connectives. If ϕ is a formula, then $\neg\neg\phi$ is a test. Moreover, we calculate that

$$[\neg\neg\phi] = \{\langle g, g \rangle : g \xrightarrow{\phi} \sqrt{}\} = \{\langle g, g \rangle : g \in \backslash\phi\backslash\}$$

Namely, $[\neg\phi] = \{\langle g, g \rangle : not\ g \xrightarrow{\phi} \sqrt{}\}$, that is, the set of pairs $\langle g, g \rangle$ such that ϕ is not processable in g. Hence, $[\neg\neg\phi]$ is the set of all pairs such that $\neg\phi$ is not processable in g, which is the set of all $\langle g, g \rangle$ such that ϕ is processable in g.

Proposition 15. *Let ϕ be a formula. Then $\neg\neg\phi$ is a test and* $\backslash\neg\neg\phi\backslash = \backslash\phi\backslash$.

We call $\neg\neg\phi$ the *static counterpart* of ϕ. In this way we can define new connectives which are externally static, for example an externally static conjunction ($\neg\neg(\phi.\psi)$) and an externally static existential quantifier ($\neg\neg(\exists x.\psi)$). Likewise, we can remove the internal dynamicity of a connective. For example, the following connectives are internally static.

$$\phi \dot\wedge \phi \quad .- \quad \neg\neg\phi.\psi$$
$$\phi \dot{\cdot} \dot\phi \quad :- \quad \neg\neg\phi . \psi$$

And thirdly, the internal and external dynamicity can be cancelled together. In this way, we get totally static connectives. The static conjunction and the static implication are as follows.

$$\phi \wedge' \psi \quad :- \quad \neg(\neg\phi \vee \neg\psi)$$
$$\phi \ '\psi \quad :- \quad \neg\phi \vee \psi$$

It is however impossible to introduce a dynamicity into a connective. For example, the connective $\neg\phi \rightarrow \psi$ is an internally and externally static disjunction (equivalent to $\phi \vee \psi$). So there is no way to dynamify essentially static connectives. In a sense, this has to be expected. It is not clear a priori what for example an externally dynamic implication should be like. In fact, implication, disjunction and universal quantifiers are not externally dynamic. We give examples.

(6)   *If someone[1] is watching you, then you must be careful. *He[1] is from the mafia.*

(7)   *Either I am stupid or someone[1] is watching me. *He[1] is from the mafia.*

(8)   *Be careful with [everyone who watches you].[1] *He$_1$ is from the mafia.*

Notice that if the second sentence is in subjunctive mood (e.g. *He might be from the mafia.*) then the continuation is generally acceptable (see [8]). This means that the second sentence is attached not on the main level of discourse but rather added into (generally) the second subformula. However, this addition is in that case not a mere conjunction, so it is futile to try to incorporate that into the present semantics. Here are the (somewhat liberal) renderings of the sentences into predicate logic, showing the unacceptability of the pronoun in the second sentence.

(6a) $(\exists x_1.\mathbf{watch}(x_1, \mathbf{you}) \rightarrow \Box\mathbf{beware\text{-}of}(\mathbf{you}, x_1)).\mathbf{mafioso}(x_1)$

(7a) $(\mathbf{stupid}(\mathbf{me}) \vee \exists x_1.\mathbf{watch}(x_1, \mathbf{me})).\mathbf{mafioso}(x_1)$

(8a) $(\forall x_1)(\mathbf{watch}(x_1, \mathbf{you}) \rightarrow \Box\mathbf{beware\text{-}of}(\mathbf{you}, x_1)).\mathbf{mafioso}(x_1)$

It has however been noted that disjunction can behave internally dynamic.

(9)   *Either Albert has not written any letter[1] or it$_1$ has been delayed.*

(9a) $\neg(\exists x_1.\mathbf{wrote}(a, x_1)) \vee \mathbf{delayed}(x_1)$

Formally, the translation, being of the form $\neg\phi \vee \psi$ does not allow to export the value of ϕ to ψ. Hence, in dynamic logic the anaphoric reference is blocked. Notice that by the laws of classical logic $\neg\phi \vee \psi$ is equivalent to $\phi \rightarrow \psi$, so in this special circumstance we may resort to the translation $\phi \rightarrow \psi$ in place of $\neg\phi \vee \psi$. In the latter the sharing of a referent between ϕ and ψ is legitimate and also possible in dynamic logic. There are however problems with compositionality. We may alternatively define a dynamic disjunction as follows.

$$[\phi \vee^d \psi] := \{\langle g, g\rangle : g \xrightarrow{\phi} \sqrt{}, \text{ or else not } g, \xrightarrow{\phi} h,$$
$$\text{but } h \xrightarrow{\psi} \sqrt{}\}$$

Notice that $\vee^d$ is a new connective, not definable from the previous ones.

4 Dynamic binding and scope

Recall from predicate logic the notion of the *scope* of a quantifier. Scope is a structural notion designed to capture the domain within which occurrences of the same variable invariably are interpreted as the same object in the model. We will define again the scope of a quantifier and then proceed to the extended binding domains of the dynamic quantifiers. We define the notion of a subformula in the usual way. ψ is a subformula of ϕ if either $\varphi = \psi$ or $\phi = \neg\chi$ and ψ is a subformula of χ, or $\phi = \chi_1 \vee \chi_2$ or $\phi = \chi_1 \rightarrow \chi_2$ or $\phi = \chi_1 \wedge \chi_2$ and ψ is a subformula of χ_1 or of χ_2, or $\phi = (\exists x)\chi$ or $\phi = (\forall x)\chi$ and ψ is a subformula of χ. In Visser style syntax, $\exists x$ is a formula and so the clauses for the quantifiers can be dropped.

Definition 16. *Let $Q \in \{\forall, \exists\}$. Let ϕ be a formula and $(Qx)\chi$, ζ be subformulae of ϕ. ζ is said to occur in the **scope** of Qx in ϕ iff it occurs as a subformula of χ. Qx **binds** a variable x iff it is the quantifier with smallest scope containing x. A **static binding pair** of ϕ is a pair of occurrences of Qx and x, where Qx binds x.*

The dynamic notions are somewhat more roundabout. The definition of scope remains the same, except for the Visser style syntax, in which it is obsolete.

Definition 17. *Let ϕ be a formula. The dynamic accessibility relation of ϕ is a relation between occurrences of subformulae of ϕ, and it is defined as follows. χ is **dynamically accessible for** ξ (in ϕ) if*

1. *$\chi \rightarrow \xi$ is a subformula of ϕ or*
2. *$\chi.\xi$ is a subformula of ϕ or*
3. *ξ occurs in μ and χ is dynamically accessible for μ or*
4. *$\chi.\chi'$ is a subformula of ϕ and $\chi.\chi'$ is dyamically accessible for ξ or*
5. *$\chi'.\chi$ is a subformula of ϕ and $\chi'.\chi$ is dynamically accessible for ξ.*

*If χ is dynamically accessible for ξ we also say that ξ is **dynamically accessible from** χ.*

The dynamic accessibility relation is used mainly with respect to atomic subformulae so that the bracketing of a conjunction is mostly irrelevant. In a sequence $\phi_1. \phi_2..... \phi_n$, the formula ϕ_i is accessible for all subsequent ones, that is, for all ϕ_j with $j > i$. Further, in $\phi \rightarrow (\chi \rightarrow \psi)$, ϕ and χ are accessible for ψ, and

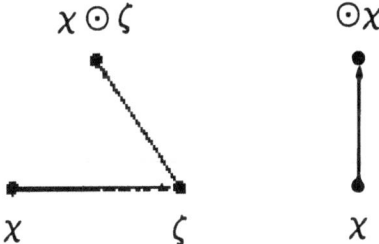

Figure 2: Immediate accessibility

ϕ is accessible for χ. The same applies to $(\phi.\chi) \rightarrow \psi$. By contrast, look at $(\phi \rightarrow \chi) \rightarrow \psi$. Here, ϕ is dynamically accessible for χ but not for ψ. Roughly speaking, the connective $\rightarrow$ in the antecedent $\phi \rightarrow \chi$ destroys the accessibility of ϕ and χ for other formulae.

Definition 18. *Let ϕ be a formula. A **dynamic binding pair** of ϕ is a pair of occurrences of Qx and x such that either (A) $Q = \forall$ and the pair is a static binding pair or (B) $Q = \exists$ and either (i) the least formula containing $\exists x$ also contains x or (ii) there is a ξ such that x occurs in ξ and ξ is dynamically acces-*

sible from $\exists x$. *If* $\exists x$ *and* x *form a dynamic binding pair of* ϕ *we say that that* $\exists x$ **dynamically binds** x.

The following is an immediate consequence.

Proposition 19. *Let* ϕ *be a formula. Then if* $\exists x$ *and* x *form a static binding pair they also form a dynamic binding pair.*

The reader may check the following fact. Suppose ϕ is a formula and $\phi^{\S}$ its translation into Visser style syntax. $\exists x$ and x form a dynamic binding pair of ϕ iff they form a dynamic binding pair of $\phi^{\S}$. This allows us to use both notations interchangeably when talking about binding. The dynamic accessibility relation can be defined purely in terms of the internal and external dynamicity of the connectives. This is what we will do now; it gives us a deeper understanding of these definitions and allows us to generalize them to formulae with other connectives. Let $\odot$ be a binary connective and $\chi \odot \zeta$ a formula. If $\odot$ is internally dynamic, we say that ζ is *immediately accessible* from χ. If $\odot$ is not internally dynamic, we say that ζ is *inaccessible* from χ.[6] If $\odot$ is externally dynamic we say that $\chi \odot \zeta$ is *immediately accessible* from ζ. If $\odot$ is not externally dynamic, $\chi \odot \zeta$ is *inaccessible* from ζ. Now let $\odot$ be a unary connective and χ a formula. Then $\odot \chi$ is a formula. If $\odot$ is externally dynamic, $\odot \chi$ is *immediately accessible* from χ; if $\odot$ is not externally dynamic, $\odot \chi$ is *inaccessible* from χ. The immediate accessibility relation might be pictured as in Figure 2 and Table 2. The internal dynamicity is 'horizontal', going in the direction of the time-arrow, the external dynamicity is 'vertical', going in the direction of the architecture of the formula. Now, say that ζ is accessible[1] from χ in ϕ if there exists a chain of (occurrences of) subformulae $\xi_1, \xi_2, ..., \xi_n$ such that $\xi_1 = \chi$ and $\xi_n = \zeta$, and ξ_{i+1} is immediately accessible from ξ_i for $1 \leq i < n$. It may happen that $n = 1$, in which case $\zeta = \chi$. Hence, accessibility[1] is the reflexive and transitive closure of immediate accessibility. Finally, we can give the following characterization.

Proposition 20. *Let* ϕ *be a formula, and* ζ, χ *subformulae of* ϕ. ζ *is dynamically accessible from* χ *if there exist a subformula* $\zeta_1 \odot \chi_1$ *of* ϕ *such that* ζ *is a subformula of* ζ_1, χ *a subformula of* χ_1, χ_1 *accessible[1] from* χ, *and* $\odot$ *is internally dynamic.*

This is again somewhat lengthy but quite a practical definition. Notice first that if ζ is accessible[1] from χ and does not contain χ (as a subformula) then it is accessible from χ. Hence another characterization is as follows. ζ is dynamically accessible from χ if (i) ζ does not contain χ, and (ii) is a subformula of ζ_1 which is accessible[1] from χ.

---

[6] To be accurate, we would have say that ζ is not immediately accessible from χ. However, it will turn out that under the definition of dynamic accessibility these two will turn out to be the same for the formula occurrences in question.

We give an example. Let α be the formula

$$((\zeta \vee \eta). \neg (\theta.\phi)) \rightarrow (\chi \vee \psi)$$

The accessibility relation for α is as follows.

$\{\langle\zeta \vee \eta, \neg(\theta.\phi)\rangle, \qquad \langle\zeta \vee \eta, \theta\rangle, \qquad \langle\zeta \vee \eta, \phi\rangle,$
$\langle\zeta \vee \eta, \chi \vee \psi\rangle, \qquad \langle\zeta \vee \eta, \chi\rangle, \qquad \langle\zeta \vee \eta, \psi\rangle,$
$\langle\neg(\theta.\phi), \chi \vee \psi\rangle, \qquad \langle\neg(\theta.\phi), \chi\rangle, \qquad \langle\neg(\theta.\phi), \psi\rangle,$
$\langle(\zeta \vee \eta). \neg(\theta.\phi), \chi \vee \psi\rangle, \quad \langle(\zeta \vee \eta). \neg(\theta.\phi), \chi\rangle, \quad \langle(\zeta \vee \eta). \neg(\theta.\phi), \psi\rangle\}$

5 Referent systems

The advantage of DPL over static predicate logic is that it can handle the trans-sentential anaphors of the type exemplified in (1) and (2). However, as we have noted, one has to annotate the words in the sentences with indices in order to get a systematic (= compositional) translation from surface structure into DPL. The

$\odot$	Immediate accessibility
$\wedge$	$\{\langle\chi, \zeta\rangle, \langle\zeta, \chi \wedge \zeta\rangle\}$
$\rightarrow$	$\{\langle\chi, \zeta\rangle\}$
$\vee$	$\varnothing$
$\neg$	$\varnothing$
$\exists$	$\{\langle\zeta, (\exists x)\zeta\rangle\}$
$\forall$	$\varnothing$

Table 2

problem arises exactly as in Montague semantics with the pronouns and the quantifiers. Rather than having only one quantifier and only one pronoun we have infinitely many of them and we must be told beforehand (by means of annotation) which one to choose. This state of affairs is rather unsatisfactory because Montague semantics is otherwise successful in exploiting λ-calculus to get the variable management right. To see the effect of the λ-calculus, suppose we said that the meaning of *man* is $\mathbf{man}(x)$ rather than $\lambda x.\mathbf{man}(x)$. Then every time we calculate the meaning of an expression containing the word *man* we have to check which variable we have to use in place of x. So we would have to decide whether to put in $\mathbf{man}(x)$ or $\mathbf{man}(y)$, for example. Likewise if we chose to translate *tall* by $\mathbf{tall}(x)$ rather than $\lambda P.\lambda x.(\mathbf{tall}(x) \wedge P(x))$. To take an easy example, the expression *tall man* could in principle be translated as $\mathbf{tall}(y) \wedge \mathbf{man}(x)$ rather than $\mathbf{tall}(x) \wedge \mathbf{man}(x)$ or $\mathbf{tall}(y) \wedge \mathbf{man}(y)$. To prevent this, we have to see to it that whatever variable we use to translate *tall* that same variable is used to translate *man*. In Montague semantics this problem does not arise by choice of the translation (and the λ-calculus, which renames variables automatically for us when needed). But while Montague semantics solves this problem elegantly, it nevertheless cannot solve the problem of quantifiers and pronouns as we have seen. DPL actually is a step back from Montague semantics insofar as it allows accidental capture of free variables and therefore cannot rely entirely on λ-calculus. (Notice, however, that this effect was intended, though not in all of its consequences, as Peter Staudacher has brought to my attention.) There is another problem of DPL, namely the accidental loss of variables. Suppose we have the following text (10a) and we translate accidentally by (10b) rather than by (10c).

(10)   a. There is a dog in the garden. There is a cat in the garden.
       b. $\exists x.\textbf{dog}(x).\textbf{in-garden}(x).\exists x.\textbf{cat}(x).\textbf{in-garden}(x)$
       c. $\exists x.\textbf{dog}(x).\textbf{in-garden}(x).\exists y.\textbf{cat}(y).\textbf{in-garden}(y)$

The truth conditions of (10b) and (10c) are in fact the same. However, in (10b) we have lost the possibility to refer back to the dog. Hence, the dynamic meanings of the two formulae are not identical. This is rather unfortunate. What can be done?

   A solution to this circle of problems was outlined by Kees Vermeulen and Albert Visser in [13] and [14]. Since the second paper is rather advanced and technical we will concentrate on the first one, which introduces the so-called *referent systems*. Referent systems will solve the problem only partly but that will be enough for our purposes. Our solution is clearly intended by [13] and [14] though the actual details might differ. First of all, referent systems take a step back from Montague semantics in using no λ-expressions. The variable management that was left implicit in Montague semantics is now made fully explicit. So we will actually translate *tall* by $\textbf{tall}(x)$ and *man* by $\textbf{man}(x)$. The expression *tall man* will be translated by the merge of the two translations. The secret lies in the definition of the merge of representations. Basically, merge should be seen as conjunction; each lexical entry provides some information and these pieces of information are piled up. However, lexical items do also provide information about the syntactic structure, and this information is ancillary in finding the meaning of the sentence. For example, Montague semantics uses the syntactic structure to steer the semantic translation. By virtue of the fact that both words form a constituent and the adjective precedes the noun, the expression *tall man* is translated as

$$(\lambda \mathcal{P}.\lambda x.\textbf{tall}(x) \wedge \mathcal{P}(x))(\lambda x.\textbf{man}(x)) \rightsquigarrow \lambda x.\textbf{tall}(x) \wedge \textbf{man}(x)$$

The linear order is directly visible whereas the syntactic structure is not. While this is not such an apparent problem for English since constituents are as a rule continuous segments of speech (text), in other languages the situation is not so favourable. Take Latin. The following are acceptable sentences.

(11)   *Illustrem habet Cicero servum.*
(11')   *Cicero has a famous slave.*

(12)   *Magno fuerunt in horto.*
(12')   *They were in a big garden.*

In both cases, the Latin constituents highlighted by boldface type are not continuous segments in contrast to their English counterparts. This shows that constituency is defined by other criteria than simply contiguity.[7] To simplify the matter rather greatly, we may say that in Latin the *agreement suffixes* define the constituency. To implement this, we introduce the notion of a *referent system*.

Definition 21. *Let N be a set. A referent system over N is a triple* $\mathfrak{R} = \langle I, R, E \rangle$, *where R is a set, called the set of* **referents**, *I is a partial injective function from N to R, called the* **import function**, *and E a partial injective function from R to N, called the* **export function**. *N is the set of* **names**.

When $E(r) = A$ we say that $\mathfrak{R}$ *exports r under the name A*, and when $I(B) = r$ we say that $\mathfrak{R}$ *imports r under the name B*. It is not required that $A = B$! Meaning units are pairs $\mathfrak{E} = \langle \mathfrak{R}, \Phi \rangle$ where $\mathfrak{R} = \langle I, R, E \rangle$ is a referent system over some appropriate set of names and Φ a set of formulae using only the referents from R. Let $\langle D, I \rangle$ be a model. An *assignment* is a map from a set of referents into D. $\langle \mathfrak{R}, \Phi \rangle$ is *satisfied* in a model under the assignment h if h assigns a value to each referent from $\mathfrak{R}$ and all formulae from Φ are true under h. Hence, the satisfaction clauses are pretty much those of DRT. The consequence is that the renaming of referents does not change satisfiability in a model.

Let $\mathfrak{E}_i = \langle \mathfrak{R}_i, \Phi_i \rangle$, $i \in \{1, 2\}$, be meaning units. The merge $\mathfrak{E}_1 \circ \mathfrak{E}_2$ is defined as follows. We define the merge $\mathfrak{R}_3 := \mathfrak{R}_1 \bullet \mathfrak{R}_2$ of referent systems plus injective functions $\iota_1 : R_1 \to R_3$, $\iota_2 : R_1 \to R_3$, and then put

$$\mathfrak{E}_1 \circ \mathfrak{E}_2 := \langle \mathfrak{R}_3, \iota_1[\Phi_1] \cup \iota_2[\Phi_2] \rangle$$

We are left with a definition of the merge. We say first of all given two referents $r \in R_1$ and $s \in R_2$ that r *supervenes* s if $I_2(E_1(r)) = s$. Supervenience is a relation $\subseteq R_1 \times R_2$. Let U be the set of supervened elements of R_2. Then we put

$$R_1 \quad :- \quad (R_1 \times \{1\} \cup R_2 \times \{2\}) - U \times \{2\}$$
$$\iota_1\{r\} \quad - \quad \langle r, 1 \rangle$$
$$\iota_2\{s\} \quad \begin{cases} \langle r, 1 \rangle & \text{if } s \text{ is supervened by } r \\ \langle s, 2 \rangle & \text{else} \end{cases}$$

Say that r *I-preempts* s if there is an $A \in N$ such that $I_1(A) = r$ and $I_2(A) = s$; and that s *E-preempts* r if $E_2(s) = E_1(r)$. Notice that r can both I-preempt and supervene s. Finally, for a partial function f we write $f(x) = \uparrow$ if f is undefined on x, and $f(x) = \downarrow$ if f is defined. The import and export functions are now as follows.

$$[A : r : B] \quad \bullet \quad [B : s : C] \quad = \quad [A : \langle r, 1 \rangle : C]$$
$$[- : r : B] \quad \bullet \quad [B : s : C] \quad - \quad [- : \langle r, 1 \rangle : C]$$
$$[A : r : B] \quad \bullet \quad [B : s : -] \quad - \quad [A : \langle r, 1 \rangle : -]$$
$$[- : r : B] \quad \bullet \quad [B : s : -] \quad \multimap \quad [- : \langle r, 1 \rangle : -]$$

Table 3: The merge of referent systems

---

[7] Even English has discontinous constituents. For example in *He rang me up.* or in *A man talked to me who had an extraordinarily long beard.*

$$I_s(A) \quad :- \quad \begin{cases} \langle r, 1 \rangle & \text{if } I_1(A) = r \\ \langle s, 2 \rangle & \text{if s is not I-preempted and } I_2(A) = s \\ \uparrow & \text{else} \end{cases}$$

$$E_u(u) \quad :- \quad \begin{cases} E_2(s) & \text{if } u = \langle t,1 \rangle \text{ and } t \text{ supervenes } s \\ E_2(s) & \text{if } u = \langle s, 2 \rangle \text{ and } s \text{ is not supervened} \\ E_1(r) & \text{if } u = \langle r,1 \rangle, E_1(r) = \downarrow \text{ and is not E-preempted} \\ \uparrow & \text{else} \end{cases}$$

Some options are summarized in Table 3. We write $[A : r : B]$ if r is a referent that is imported under A and exported under the name B. We write $[- : r : B]$ if r has no import name, and similarly $[A : r : -]$ and $[- : r : -]$. The table does not show the effect of the preemption. It can happen that two referents compete for the same import (export) name. In that case they must be from different referent systems by injectivity of the functions. Then the referent from the first system wins the import name; if they compete for the export name, the one from the second system wins the export name.

With the referent systems the Latin examples can be accounted for; as names we choose the cases, and the verbs and prepositions are simply referent systems importing referents under certain names, while inflected nouns export referents under a given name. For example, Latin *horto* and *magno* are translated by

$[- : r : abl]$
garden(r)

$[abl : r : abl]$
big(r)

Their merge is – according to the definition above –:

$[- : \langle r,1 \rangle : abl]$
garden($\langle r, 1 \rangle$)
big($\langle r,1 \rangle$)

This is the translation of *horto magno*. Notice that *magno horto* would in this system not get the right translation. We need to assume in fact that lexical entries are associated with sets of referent systems, thereby allowing for different word order (and the fact that both *magno* and *horto* can also be dative). Obviously, this model is very simplistic, but it shows how one can incorporate morphological information about the syntactic structure into the semantics.

How would referent systems handle our examples (1) and (2)? We will present a solution, which is based on the following insight. Pronouns pick up their referent not by an index (such an index is simply not part of the language) but rather by the information that is resident in the semantics of the antecedent, the gender of the pronoun and more. To make matters simple, we assume that we only use gender information. Then the set of names consists of combinations of gender and case. However, one or both of gender and case can be absent, and this is represented by $*$. Hence the set of names is as follows:

$$\{M, F, N, *\} \times \{N, A, *\}$$

(Here, N abbreviates *nominative*, A *accusative*, and F, M and N are the genders.) A particular pair is written like a vector, for example (M, A). Notice that (M, *) is a name in the technical sense, likewise (*, *) and (*, A). The cases will be used to steer the syntactic translation, and the gender is used to get at the binding. To make the whole thing work we have to play with the * to switch the assignment of gender and case on and off. For example, the pronouns *he* and *him* have the following semantics:

$[(M, *) : x : (M, N)]$	$[(M, A) : x : (M, *)]$
$\varnothing$	$\varnothing$

The difference is that *he* has no case to the left and nominative to the right, while *him* has accusative to the left and no case to the right. The semantics of **fat, man** (nominative) and *man* (accusative) are as follows:

$[(\alpha, \gamma) : x : (\alpha, \gamma)]$	$[(M, *) : x : (M, N)]$	$[(M, A) : x : (M, *)]$
fat(x)	man(x)	man(x)

Here the variable is instantiated to any appropriate value (in this case, genders or * for α and case or * for γ). This is an extension of the original proposal; what we argue is that the variables are part of the lexical representation and get instantiated after the representation has been inserted into the structure. The indefinite determiner *a(n)* wipes out the gender to the left. It has the semantics

$[(*, \gamma) : x : (\alpha, \gamma)]$
$\varnothing$

Finally, the transitive verb *see* looks as follows

$[(\alpha, N) : x : (\alpha, *)]$
$[(\beta, *) : y : (\beta, A)]$
see(x, y)

We now take the sentence (1) in a slightly modified form. The bracketing (plus case assignment) is given by the syntax.

(13)   Susan (sees (a fat man (at the metro entrance))). He (is selling souvenirs).

We continue our policy to leave the phrases 'at the metro entrance' and 'is selling souvenirs' unanalyzed. Putting together the object noun phrase and renaming the referents suitably gives

$[(*, A) : x : (M, *)]$
fat(x), man(x)
at-metro-entrance(x)

So the first sentence is translated thus:

$$\boxed{\begin{array}{c} [(F,*: x : (F, N)] \\ \hline x = s \end{array}} \cup \left(\boxed{\begin{array}{l} [(\alpha, N) : x : (\alpha, *)] \\ [(\beta, *) : y : (\beta, A)] \\ \text{see}(x, y) \end{array}} \quad \circ \quad \boxed{\begin{array}{l} [(*, A) : x : (M, *)] \\ \text{fat}(x), \text{man}(x) \\ \text{at-metro-entrance}(x) \end{array}} \right)$$

$$\simeq \boxed{\begin{array}{l} [(F, *) : x : (F, *)] \\ [(*, *) : y : (M, *)] \\ x = s, \text{fat}(y), \text{man}(y) \\ \text{at-metro-entrance}(y) \\ \text{see}(x, y) \end{array}}$$

Here, α is instantiated to F and β to M. $\simeq$ means that the structures are equal only after some renaming of referents. The point is now that the referents are open to anaphoric reference, but are syntactically inert since they carry the case description *. Subsequently they can only be picked up by a pronoun. For example, we can merge with

$$\boxed{\begin{array}{c} [(M, *) \quad x : (M, *)] \\ \hline \text{sell-souvenirs}(x) \end{array}}$$

This gives

$$\boxed{\begin{array}{l} [(F, *) : x : (F, *)] \\ [(*, *) : y : (M, *)] \\ x = s, \text{fat}(y), \text{man}(y) \\ \text{at-metro-entrance}(y) \text{ see}(x, y) \\ \text{sell-souvenirs}(y) \end{array}}$$

In order to be able to judge the success and failure of referent systems, compare the result with a slightly different sentence.

(14)   Paul sees a fat man at the metro entrance. He is selling souvenirs.

What will happen is that the phrase 'a fat man at the metro entrance' will get a referent that is different from that for Paul. This is due to the fact that the determiner blocks the gender to the left. But the referent also E-preempts the referent for Paul since they export the same name before merge, (M, *).[8] The pronoun 'he' can therefore not refer back to Paul. Hence referent systems do not handle the facts correctly. In this case it is because the space of names is too small to make enough distinctions. However, the fact that anaphoric reference is blocked by antecedents which are less distant is not so far off the mark. This is a topic that deserves attention. The analogue of example (2) is less straightforward, since we have no means to represent the implication.

---

[8] Here is also a point where one has to be careful with the variables for names. We will not explore that theme further, though.

6 Outlook

This article is only an introduction into dynamic semantics. A survey of the various developments can be found in [7]. We will end with a few remarks about the relationship between dynamic predicate logic and DRT as well as other uses of DPL. First, with respect to DRT note that both DPL and DRT encode the linearity of the text into the notion of accessibility. In DRT as well as in DPL, in a formula $\phi \rightarrow \chi$, referents introduced in ϕ may be used in χ and not vice versa. In $\phi \vee \chi$, neither can χ access referents from ϕ (because $\vee$ is internally static) nor can ϕ access referents from χ (since connectives work from left to right). We have already mentioned the fact that disjunction may occasionally be internally dynamic (but left-to-right). We will comment on the left-to-right character of connectives below. DRT differs from DPL in the way in which conjunction and existential quantification is treated. The existential quantifier is not so much a problem. DRT employs an implicit quantifier, namely the head section of the box. Recall that a DRS looks like this

$x\,y$
$\phi(x)$
$\chi(x,y)$
$\zeta(y,z)$

Here, we may treat the variables of the upper section (x and y) as quantified existentially (by a dynamic existential quantifier). So, the DRS is translated by

$$\exists x.\exists y.\phi(x).\chi(x,y).\zeta(y,z)$$

Conversely, $\exists x$ of DPL is like putting x into the head section of the just created DRS. The biggest difference is however conjunction. DRT has no conjunction in the sense of the word, but we may for our purposes say that the joint occurrence of formulae in a DRS means in practice that they are occurring in a conjunction. Hence, we may read the DRS above also as

$x\,y$
$\phi(x) \wedge \chi(x,y) \wedge \zeta(y,z)$

If read in this way, DRT conjunction is fully commutative, in contrast to DPL conjunction. However, notice that in the present circumstances no difference arises. The reader may namely check the following.

Proposition 22. *Let χ_1 and χ_2 be atomic formulae. Then*

$$[\![\chi_1.\chi_2]\!] = [\![\chi_2.\chi_1]\!]$$

Therefore, when no quantifier intervenes in a conjunction, full commutativity holds in DPL as well, and so we may disregard the order between the conjuncts, as is done in DRT.

The left-to-right character of DRT and DPL is in many instances a problematic feature and is not observed as rigorously as one may think. Several cases may be noted. First, from a syntactic point of view, anaphors inside sentences disregard the order of elements. They are only sensitive to the syntactic structure. This at least is the claim in Government and Binding theory. We will not comment on the validity of the last claim (it is doubtful as well) but simply note the following examples.

(15)   a. Albert[1] looks quite funny with his$_1$ hat.
       b. With his$_1$ hat, Albert[1] looks quite funny.

(16)   a. Albert gave Pete[1] a photograph with his$_1$ family on it.
       b. Albert gave a photograph with his$_1$ family on it to Pete[1].

(17)   a. Everybody[1] likes his$_1$ friends.
       b. His$_1$ friends, everybody[1] likes.

In all examples, the pronoun can precede its antecedent. Moreover, it is known that texts and dialogues are structured and that pronouns may only refer to objects that are available at the right structural level. This structuring is not reflected in DPL. (See [2].)

Finally, it has often been noted that there is a close connection between anaphora and presupposition. Technically, the domains of accessibility turn out to be those that are used in the projection algorithm for presuppositions. For example, the (a) sentences are said to be free of presupposition because the sentence of the left implies the presupposition of the sentence to the right. By contrast, the (b) sentences contain a presupposition since the first sentence contains a presupposition.

(18)   a. The series $1 + 2^n$ is convergent. The limit of $1 + 2^n$ is 1.
       b. The limit of the series $1 + 2^n$ is 1. The series $1 + 2^n$ is convergent.

(19)   a. If (a_n) is convergent then the limit of $(1 + a_n)$ is $1 + \lim(a_n)$.
       b. If the limit of $(1 + a_n)$ is not $1 + \lim(a_n)$ then (a_n) is not convergent.

The first to notice this connection is Rob van der Sandt in [11]. He in facts uses DRT to give an integrated account for presupposition and anaphora. Jan van Eijck (see e.g. [12]) actually tries to lift DPL to a three valued dynamic logic whereby replicating observations by Lauri Karttunen ([5]) and Irene Heim ([3]) in a dynamic setting. For a discussion about the use of three-valued logic and dynamics in this connection see [6].

References

[1] Jeroen Groenendijk & Martin Stokhof. Dynamic Predicate Logic. *Linguistics and Philosophy*, 14: 39–100, 1991.

[2] B. Grosz & C. Sidner. Attention, intention and the structure of discourse. *Computational Linguistics*, 12, 175–204, 1986.

[3] Irene Heim. On the projection problem for presuppositions. In: M. Barlow and D. Flickinger, D. Westcoat (eds.), *Proceedings of the 2nd West Coast Conference on Formal Linguistics*, 114–126, Stanford University, 1983.

[4] Hans Kamp & Uwe Reyle. *From Discourse to Logic, Introduction to Modeltheoretic Semantics of Natural Language, Formal Logic and Discourse Representation Theory*. Kluwer, Dordrecht, 1993.

[5] Lauri Karttunen. Presuppositions and linguistic context. *Theoretical Linguistics*, 1: 181–194, 1974.

[6] Marcus Kracht. Logic and control: How they determine the behaviour of presuppositions. In: Jan van Eijck and Albert Visser (eds.), *Logic and Information Flow*, pp. 88–111. MIT Press, Cambridge, Massachusetts, 1994.

[7] Reinhard Muskens, Johan van Benthem & Albert Visser. Dynamics. In: Johan van Benthem & Alice ter Meulen (eds.), *Handbook of Logic and Language*, 587–648. Elsevier, 1997.

[8] Craige Roberts. Modal Subordination and Pronominal Anaphora in Discourse. *Linguistics and Philosophy*, 12: 683–723, 1989.

[9] Peter Staudacher. Zur Semantik indefiniter Nominalphrasen. In: Brigitte Asbach-Schnitker & Johannes Roggenhofer (eds.), *Neuere Forschungen zur Wortbildung und Historiographie der Linguistik. Festgabe für Herbert E. Brekle zum 50. Geburtstag*, 239–258. Gunter Narr Verlag, Tübingen, 1987.

[10] Peter Staudacher. PLA and Dynamic Predicate Logic (PDL). Unpublished manuscript, 1996.

[11] Rob A. van der Sandt. Presupposition as anaphora resolution. *Journal of Semantics*, 9: 333–377, 1992.

[12] Jan van Eijck. The dynamics of descriptions. *Journal of Semantics*, 10: 239–267, 1993.

[13] Kees F. M. Vermeulen. Merging without Mystery or: Variables in Dynamic Semantics. *Journal of Philosophical Logic*, 24: 405–450, 1995.

[14] Kees F. M. Vermeulen & Albert Visser. Dynamic bracketing and discourse representation. *Notre Dame Journal of Formal Logic*, 37: 321–365, 1996.

Berlin   Marcus Kracht

II. Mathematisches Institut, Freie Universität Berlin, Arnimallee 3, D-14195 Berlin, kracht@math.fu-berlin.de

The Logic of Internal and External Observations

Uwe Mönnich

1 Introduction

In recent years, the contours have become visible of an approach to the semantics of natural languages that does not limit itself to a compositional device of denotation types*. This conception of a more fine-grained "meaning algebra" is in sharp contrast with the general aims of the Montagovian paradigm as epitomized by Richmond Thomason:

> But we should not expect a semantic theory to furnish an account of how any two expressions belonging to the same syntactic category differ in meaning. (Thomason 1974, 48)

Prominent among the attempts at developing a richer model of semantics is the field of generalized quantifiers where it has been possible to delineate more sharply the range of quantificational meanings that are attestable in natural languages. Semantics has thus attained the level of explanatory adequacy and its highly constrained hypotheses have achieved the status of falsifiable predictions.

The goals of such a more fine-grained conception of semantics can be classified by looking at different uses of the term *Logical Form*. Disregarding the difference between their representational systems – many-sorted first-order logic vs. higher-order intensional logic – both Davidson and Montague concentrate their efforts on determining the logical type of expressions at the expense of defining their meanings. On this view, the different propositional attitudes expressed by believing and knowing e.g. turn out to have the same logical type, and the foremost task, according to this construal of a semantic theory, consists in explicating the logical syntax of these expressions and the attendant consequences that are validated solely on the basis of these formal specifications. The fact that believing and knowing support different inferences is a major problem for this sort of overly homogeneous treatment. Montague avails himself of special meaning postulates to accommodate the divergent inferential patterns of expressions belonging to the same logical type. This strategy leads to a piecemeal collection of stipulations whose only purpose is to reintroduce enough "grain" into lexical semantics to be able to account for the classical cases of intensional phenomena.

* I would like to thank Susanne Schüle and Fritz Hamm for helpful discussions on this paper. Rosemary Drescher has spotted innumerable linguistic infelicities. I owe her a great debt of gratitude.

Logical Form (LF) has assumed a completely different rôle in recent incarnations of generative linguistics. This approach regards LF as an interface from the language faculty to the cognitive module of conceptual interpretation. LF has to comply with specific conditions on interpretation that have their origin in the cognitive module to which LF feeds its structural descriptions. In particular, the theory of LF requires that each of its components is in correspondence with a constituent or an operation of the conceptual module. Since LF is not similarly constrained by a relation between its constituents and entities in the real world questions about its structure have to be answered within a conceptualist framework.

This last statement does not imply that we think that a conceptualist theory without an objectivist component, a component that accounts for the relation between our cognitive states and states in the world, would ever be complete. Our claim, rather, is that our particular psycho-physiological endowment, our "faculty of concepts", is the determining factor in constraining the structure that we impose on our mental representations of things in the outer or the inner world.

This complementarity of an objectivist and a conceptualist component has another consequence that needs to be emphasised. In a recent article, Barbara Abbott (1997) tries to defend truth-conditional model-theoretic semantics against criticisms articulated within cognitivist and conceptualist approaches to semantics whose most prominent proponents are Lakoff and Jackendoff, respectively. The criticism Barbara Abbott tries to invalidate takes its inspiration from Putnam's famous paradox concerning the stability of referential relations. Whether one takes the paradox as a definite proof that model-theoretic semantics rests on insecure foundations depends crucially on the assumption that model-theory itself can be held accountable for the stability of the relation between elements of a syntactic signature and elements of a corresponding model-theoretic structure. Once this assumption is given up – and we believe that it would not only be difficult to defend it, but that it even runs counter to the spirit of model-theoretic semantics – cognitivist and conceptualist approaches are amenable to model-theoretic analysis. Under this perspective, the present paper can be read as an attempt at providing model-theoretic support for analyses that were arrived at through a concern with the influence of our sensory and motor systems on how we construe scenes that we perceive.

Even though model-theoretic semantics has been very successful in providing detailed descriptions for certain types of natural language constructions – an example being the already mentioned quantificational phrases – other areas, especially those where language reflects external inputs in a fairly direct way, have not fared well. A particularly clear case of this situation is provided by the wide range of perception reports. For this type of construction no one has even succeeded in isolating the right logical type, not to mention the individual content of lexical entries for different kinds of sense modalities. The technical device of possible worlds has turned out to imply identity criteria for propositions that do not accord with well entrenched inference patterns, an observation which counts against construing perception verbs as relations between individuals and propositions in their conceptual reading. In their more concrete perceptual reading – seeing understood as visual representation, not as cognitive comprehension – the usual logical calculi are deficient in their syntactic categories, since they do not seem to have at their disposal a category that would correspond to a seen situation or scene.

As a possible way out we shall try to follow a methodological principle that relates verbal strategies and conceptual structures to each other, its purpose being the isolation of those points of contact between form and content which mark fix-points in an open range of structural correspondences. The UNITYP group in Cologne strictly adheres to such a methodological principle and their work on what they call 'dimensions' will guide us in our analysis of perception reports. They understand by a dimension the total set of verbal strategies in natural languages that are attested as solutions for a particular type of task which consists in finding an articulated expression for a specific component of our conceptualization of our social and physical surroundings. The possession relation, the participation in an event and the apprehension of particulars are examples of such components which have been the object of investigations with respect to their verbal realizations across a wide range of genealogically and typologically unrelated languages.

We shall consider in the next section the perceptual contact with the outer and inner realm as a fundamental task in the above sense which is reflected in a range of verbal strategies in every language of the world. Along this dimension of verbal strategies a characteristic point is identifiable through a range of formal and semantic properties. We shall discover a unifiying principle for the semantic properties in the concept of a mental model as developed by the Cambridge school of psychology. The "manipulatory" attributes of these models correspond to the formal characteristics of verbal strategies that constitute the just mentioned specific point on the dimension of perceptual contact. Further independent evidence for the stability and coherence of this scheme encoding the perceptual relation on both the syntactic and the semantic level is provided by a family of fundamental principles that govern the so-called logic of observations. The last section will be devoted to a model-theoretic justification of this cluster of formal and semantic properties. The different types of evidence from universal grammar, cognitive psychology, non-classical logic and model theory converge towards a common conclusion to the effect that the relation of perception provides an ideal testbed for the kind of semantics mentioned above that tries to give equal weight to the input from the outside world and to the structure of our conceptual system.

2 The dimension of perception

2.1 The concept of dimension

Our overall goal consists in characterizing the semantic regularities of spontaneous perceptions in such a way that the empirically observable patterns come
out as obvious consequences of the general characterization. In pursuing this
goal we follow the methodological guidelines of the approach to universal
grammar that has been developed by the UNITYP group. According to that
conception linguistic realization and cognitive intention have to be regarded as a
structural whole in which the interaction between inductive ascent from verbal
form and abductive descent from conceptual content supports a dialectical bal-
ance. We saw already that the technical term 'dimension' denotes a unifying
principle which comprehends a variety of verbal strategies that subtend a common conceptual specification.

Within the dimension of possession which was mentioned above the range of
possible verbal renderings extends from simple juxtaposition (*Peter('s) house*)
to the explicit predication of appurtenance (*The house belongs to Peter*). This
continuum of verbal strategies, whose endpoints are indicated by simple juxtaposition and explicit attribution, respectively, in the case of the possession dimension, can be seen at work in other dimensions as well. Generally, a dimension seems to be determined in its linguistic aspect by two converse factors, that
of indicativity and that of predicativity. Predicativity is dominant as long as the
task of how to express a fundamental aspect of our orientation in the world is
solved by the use of a specific lexical item that signifies that aspect. We just saw
the example of the appurtenance relation and the verb *belong*. At the predicative
endpoint of a variety of verbal strategies it is *said* which salient aspect of our
life as a social or physical being is at issue whereas at the other endpoint the
solution to the task of how to put that very same aspect of our life into words is
only *shown*. To refer once more to the example of possession: at the indicative
pole the device of juxtaposition is indicating instead of expressing the relation
of appurtenance. Surveying the indicative poles of other dimensions, it turns out
that they are represented by grammatical constructions which tend to be more
absolute, less marked, highly grammaticalized, open for pragmatic factors and
displaying an overall coherent pattern. In contrast with this situation the constructions at the predicative pole exhibit a greater degree of freedom for substi-
tutions, they are more marked, less grammaticalized, more entrenched against
pragmatic factors and displaying a less coherent pattern. These two tendencies
towards indicativity and towards predicativity are not exclusive of one another,
but they exert their force in inverse proportion on the dimensional continuum
and at the endpoints of such a continuum one of the two tendencies clearly
dominates the other.

Given this interplay between indicativity and predicativity one would expect a *turning point* on the continuum where both factors are equally strong. In the dimension of possession this point is exemplified by constructions that lie on the borderline between nominal and verbal phrases and that show a clear affinity with indications of locality. Constructions which exhibit these proportions are e.g. *Das Buch ist meins* (This book is mine) and *Ce livre est à lui* (This book is his). The same transition from the nominal into the verbal field is also the defining feature of the turning point within another dimension, the dimension of junction (Raible 1992). In French, the junction with an aim or purpose is realized at this turning point by means of prepositional groups that govern either the infinitive (*de manière à*), a nounphrase (*à l'adresse de*) or both. We shall see below that relative to the dimension of perception the same kind of "Janus-face" (Raible 1992) is displayed at the turning point by the simultaneous availability of event-centred (*Peter saw Mary cross the street*) and actant-centred constructions (*Peter saw Mary crossing the street*).

The remark about the relationship with locality in the case of the possessive dimension directs the attention to a third principle which is less prominent than indicativity and predicativity, but which plays nevertheless an important rôle within the internal organization of a dimensional continuum. This principle is called iconicity. It unfolds its influence preferably around the turning point and, as betrayed by its name, is based on an abstract similarity relation which includes the just mentioned locality. What makes a relation a similarity relation is notoriously difficult to explain. A structured expression or a picture is called similar to a part of the world just in case it can be mapped onto that part of the world under appropriate conventions that transform the representational form homomorphically onto the section of the world it is supposed to stand for. Needless to say, the representational conventions and the associated similarity relations are beset with a high degree of indeterminacy, which, inevitably, entails a fair amount of fluctuation in the range of verbal strategies that enter into the sphere of influence exercised by the principle of iconicity.

2.2 The dimension of perception

As far as we know there has been no previous attempt at ordering along a dimensional continuum the expressional means which serve to report our perceptual contact with the world. One has not even approached the question whether the specific connection with the world that is mediated through the five sense modalities and the corresponding linguistic strategies can be considered to form that sort of dialectical unity which is amenable to an analysis under the auspices of dimension theory. Particular problems derive from the fact that under normal circumstances constructions in natural languages that serve to express a perceptual relation do contain a constituent naming this relation and, thus, belong to the predicative pole according to the organizational principles of a continuum we reviewed a moment ago. Another problem is connected to the question which components of a dimension belong to its core and which components are allowed to vary freely once the relevant subdimensions have been specified. The example of the dimension of possession again can be adduced to illustrate the point. The notion of appurtenance comprehends a rather heterogeneous family of binary relations. They extend from relations to one's body parts, via kinship relations to cases of ownership. In spite of this motley collection it is undeniable that they are held together by a unifying idea. Can that sort of unity be claimed for the difference between sensual and conceptual perception? Is there a unifying principle to be detected that stands behind both intuitional and non-intuitional representation and which proves them to be different species of a common genus?

We shall try to sketch a positive answer to the last question in the conclusion. Most of the other questions and methodological problems have to be left open and will be the topic of another paper. But even if the following argument for the dimensional status of perception constructions should be found wanting the negative consequences should not be too detrimental to our endeavour as long as the cluster of properties which characterize the hypothesized turning point is articulated enough to support a richer conception of semantics.

The fundamental task which requires on the content side the indication of a conceptual structure and on the expression side the delineation of a continuum of verbal strategies originates in the process of perception and its object, where it is immaterial at this stage of the discussion whether the object is a concrete particular or an abstract entity. The verbal strategies which offer different solutions to the task of representing by linguistic means the perceptual relation to our inner and outer world fall into an obvious pattern that spans a range of alternatives from the juxtaposition of independent sentences via a variety of intermediate forms to the governed occurrence of a nominal term that fills an obligatory argument rôle. At the indicative pole the fact that Peter actually sees the scene with a child crossing the street is not expressed but would be inferred on a normal reading of the second example below. In the previous example the inference is less clear-cut and needs further pragmatic evidence to lead to the same conclusion. It is generally agreed among the students of dimension theory that the central relation of a dimension has to be overtly expressed at the predicative pole. The following list contains illustrative examples from three European 'model' languages and does not claim to give a representative picture of the variety of expressional forms that are attested in other languages for the more or less explicit description of the perception relation.

(1)   a. Ein Kind überquert die Straße. Peter rührt sich nicht.
            (A child is crossing the street. Peter does not budge.)
        b. Ein Kind überquert die Straße. Peter erschrickt.
            (A child is crossing the street. Peter gets a fright.)
        c. Ein Kind überquert die Straße. Peter sieht zu.
            (A child is crossing the street. Peter is looking on.)

    d. Ein Kind überquert die Straße. Peter sieht das.
       (A child is crossing the street. Peter sees it.)
    e. Maria steht kurz vor der Lösung des Problems. Peter sieht das.
       (Maria is about to solve the problem. Peter sees it.)
    f. Peter sieht, daß Maria die Straße überquert.
      (Peter sees that Maria is crossing the street.)
    g. Peter sieht, daß Maria das Problem gelöst hat.
      (Peter sees that Maria has solved the problem.)
    h. Peter saw this to be the next logical step.
    i. Peter sieht, wie Maria die Straße überquert.
      (Peter sees Maria crossing the street.)
    j. Peter sieht Maria die Straße überqueren.
      (Peter sees Maria cross the street.)
    k. Peter saw Mary crossing the street.
    l. Pierre voie Marie qui traverse la rue.
      (Pierre sees Marie crossing the street.)
    m.Peter sieht in ihm den nächsten Präsidenten.
      (Peter sees in him the next president.)
    n. Peter sieht Marias langsames Verschwinden in der Dunkelheit.
      (Peter sees Maria's slow disappearance in the darkness.)
    o. Peter sieht seinen Freund.
      (Peter sees his friend.) (no habitual interpretation intended)
    p. Peter sieht einen Ausweg.
      (Peter sees a way out.)

Further research has to show whether the ordering of the examples that was chosen above and which documents the transition from a pragmatically complex aggegration to a syntactically coherent integration – the terms are Raible's (1992) – is confirmed by specimens from other language groups. First tentative forays into the spectrum of verbal strategies deployed in some Mayan languages, in Japanese and in Malagasy seem to show that a similarly organized continuum of expressional phenomena is at work in these languages as well.

    An analogous remark holds true of the parallelism between a spontaneous, epistemically neutral reading and a cognitive or conceptual reading of perception verbs, at least of those that stand for the 'higher' sense modalities like vision and audition. We have tried to highlight this parallelism by providing both examples for sensual experiences and cognitive insights. Peter may see a lion approaching and still remain absolutely serene because he mistook the approaching lion for a movement of the bushes nearby. Once he not only perceives the movement, once he understands it as the approach of a lion, once he sees that a lion is approaching him, this insight will have an immediate effect on his behaviour. Sensual experiences are accompanied by mental representations, but we do not entertain a propositional attitude towards them until we are consciously aware of the categories we apply in their classification.

Some of the adduced examples, though, can only be correlated with either the spontaneous experiential or the cognitive reading. The English infinitive with *to*, the French relative clause, the German copulative with *in*, the English *-ing*-form and the German naked infinitive belong to this group. This is not the appropriate place to uncover the reasons that are responsible for the restriction to one reading in the relevant cases. Let us put on record, nevertheless, that at the particular position on the continuum where the linguistic representation of the perceptual content loses its sentential status and assumes an appearance that partakes both of nominal and verbal features – the bare infinitive and the *-ing*-form – that at this designated position of the continuum the experientially spontaneous reading is the only available alternative.

2.3 The turning point

Most of the essential attributes of the turning point were already mentioned in the previous sections. There is, first, the prominent rôle played by the principle of iconicity at this position of the continuum and, second, the bridge function which is connected with the change from sentential complements to nominal arguments. It was already outlined above that the constructions – in English and other European languages at least – which mark this transition point between sentential and nominal forms exhibit a combination of event-related and actant-related features, a fact which is well known in the case of participles and infinitives and which is confirmed by experiments directed at uncovering associative links between lexical items. Since our main goal is the "natural" logic of perception reports the problems surrounding the fine structure of the perception dimension would detract us from our main line of argument. We shall, therefore, leave the detailed analysis of the factors which pertain to the turning point in its capacity as a joint between the indicative and the predicative parts of a dimension for another occasion.

When introducing the principle of iconicity we mentioned the concept of similarity. The example from the dimension of possession, in which the relation of appurtenance was connected with the relation of local nearness, points already to the risk of trying to compare anything with anything else. Since words do not normally resemble their denotations a certain tradition in philosophy holds it that the relation of similarity obtains between the external objects and the mental representations we have of them (Putnam 1981). The common aspect establishing a correspondence between parts of the world and their mental counterparts is to be found in their shared form, according to this tradition. Secondary qualities like colour, warmth and texture being excluded, for obvious reasons, from entering into a similarity relation one of whose members belongs to the realm of mental objects, the relevant aspects in virtue of which represented object and its (mental) representation correspond to each other have to be aspects of shared primary qualities like shape and length. Even primary qualities, however, have succumbed to a line of criticism that was started by Berkeley. He has shown convincingly that the cluster of arguments that tell against basing the relation of similarity between things and mental representations on shared secondary qualities are applicable in the case of primary qualities as well. If one considers, e.g., the impressions people form of the same object from different angles and varying distances the question whether one impression has the same length or is of the same shape as another impression does not seem to make any sense. There is, though, a different kind of question one may sensibly ask in these circumstances and which avails itself of a much more abstract notion of resemblance. This latter notion in turn is not predicated upon a common set of shared primary or secondary qualities but upon a second-order relation of structural similarity that holds between the networks of (first-order) relations embedding the worldly and the mental objects, respectively. In order to understand in more precise terms what such a higher-order relation consists of it is necessary to look at the algebraic concept of a mapping preserving all the operations and relations defined on a set. We will have occasion to return to the idea of a morphism preserving the structure of a complex of objects in the sections on mental models and on model-theoretic preservation theorems after we have gained a clearer picture of the network of relations which characterize the linguistic techniques at the turning point.

The debate about the right form of similarity theory was such a long-lived one because it mainly dealt with the reference of mental representations and treated the meaning of linguistic entities as a side issue. There has always been a general agreement that not all representational means can be brought under the umbrella of some similarity theory, natural language being one of the most recalcitrant candidates. Given this situation, the question whether there are any structural principles discernible that could sustain a higher-order connectedness between turning point-related verbal strategies and structural properties of mental models becomes even more pressing.

The principles which are relevant for an answer to this question have been the topic of intensive research conducted especially by students of situation theory (Barwise 1989). The overall picture that has emerged from this line of investigation is that of a coherent pattern of features that corroborates the assumption of a turning point from a syntactic and a semantic point of view.

Model-theoretic semantics adheres to a sharp distinction between logical and descriptive symbols. The meaning of the logical symbols is invariable, while the descriptive symbols change their interpretation from model to model. Montague Grammar retains this distinction by fixing just the denotation type for non-logical constants and letting the actual denotation change between different models. Perception verbs cannot be counted as logical symbols since it depends on the state of the world and on the position of sentient beings living in it what is perceptible under these circumstances. There are, however, as we will see in a moment, valid principles that are satisfied by perception reports in complete independence of the state of the world and its inhabitants. Model-theoretic semantics is in this respect confronted with a major problem that it tries to counter by the massive deployment of meaning postulates. The way out of this quandary is to isolate a set of constraints that are restrictive enough to set the perception relation apart from other binary relations of the same logical type.

Most of the following principles appear already in Barwise's pioneering study "Scenes and Other Situations" (1981, reprinted in Barwise 1989). They equate perception reports containing a naked infinitive or an *ing*-form as predicate with positive descriptions of non-stative situations. Let us elaborate this characterization.

Circumventing the problem posed by illusions, hallucinations and after-images, it is uncontroversial that *to see* – and similar remarks apply to the other sense modalities as well – belongs to the group of factive or implicative verbs whose distinguishing trait is that the perceptual content must be true if its attribution is true. The next near-tautology illustrates this claim:

(2)   *If* Peter sees Mary crossing the street *then* Mary is crossing the street.

This factivity of perception verbs is of a piece with the extensionality of (the description of) the perceptual content:

(3)   Peter sees Mary crossing the street.
         Mary is the dean of the school.
         Ergo: Peter sees the dean crossing the street.

Perception verbs do not create an opaque context as long as the content of a report, expressed with one of them as main verb, is itself expressed by means of a naked infinitive or *-ing*-form. Different descriptions of the same individual are therefore substitutable for each other.

As the following two examples seem to show

(4)   a. *Peter saw Mary own a house.
         b. *Peter saw Mary be tall.

states of affairs which are either not directly observable or which are stative and betray not the least bit of alteration are unsuited to become the object of a perception report. This observation is confirmed by the act that negated infinitives in perception reports have a very low degree of acceptability:

(5)   *Peter saw the ice not melt.

The connection with the unacceptability of stative events in perception reports is due to the effect of negation which transforms a process into a state, as shown in the last example.

If simple scenes and events are parts of the world, with an internal structure composed of properties and relations and their participants, one would expect that the principles underlying the construction of complex scenes and events distribute over the construction principles inherent in the formation of complex perception processes. If, e.g., an event consists of two component events, put conjunctively together, a perception of this complex event should be equivalent to the two perception processes that are directed towards the component events. Similar remarks hold true of the distribution of alternation and projection, i.e. existential quantification, as confirmed by the following examples:

(6)   a. Peter saw Mary arrive and John depart.
        b. Peter saw Mary arrive and Peter saw John depart.

(7)   a. Peter saw Mary arrive or John depart.
        b. Peter saw Mary arrive or Peter saw John depart.

(8)   a. Peter saw someone cross the street.
        b. There was someone Peter saw on the street.

In sharp contrast to the situation relating to the "positive" construction principles is the status of conditional perception reports:

(9)   *Peter saw Mary arrive if John depart.
        *Peter saw if John depart Mary arrive.
        *Peter saw John depart only if Mary arrive.

Apparently, it is impossible to form an acceptable perception complement by means of a conditional combination of two naked infinitives. There are several possible reasons for the ungrammaticality of (9). Let us suppose that antecedents of conditionals have to be analysed as sentential adverbs. Our example would then be rejected for the same reason that sentential adverbs generally are excluded from infinitival perception reports:

(10)   *Peter saw Mary probably arrive.

A different kind of explication is inspired by the observation that subordinate conjunctions require that sentences they introduce be inflected for tense. The types of complements at the turning point, being tenseless conditional events, are also excluded for this syntactic reason. Finally, there is a further explication that harks back to the presuppositions that have to be satisfied for something to be observable. The statement that Peter perceived a complex conditional event e splits into two sub-statements that he either perceived the non-occurrence of e' or the occurrence of e''. The first sub-statement comes under the case of negative events and we have already noted that this class of complex events is banned from the range of perceptible events for reasons that seem to be connected with the biological structure of our perceptual faculty.

For related reasons, the export of the universal quantifier is only allowed under appropriate circumstances:

(11)   a. Peter saw all the people cross the street.
        b. It holds of all the people that Peter saw them cross the street.

Events we see, hear or perceive in accordance with one of the other sense modalities constitute a tiny section of the world. Perception is intrinsically perspectival and it is just our immediate surroundings that are directly accessible to our senses. If the export of the quantificational phrase goes together with a change of the situational context where the universal quantifier is to be evaluated (11a) and (11b) are not equivalent any more. The perspectival limitation of a sensorily accessible event entails the concomitant limitation to a quantificational range that consists of participants in that very same event.

Let us summarize what we have observed of the cluster of principles that characterize the putative turning point of the perception dimension. In the interest of concision we restrict ourselves to the semantic side:

Perception reports containing a naked infinitive (or an -*ing*-form) relate to variable events. These events as facts of the world lack any modal or negative properties. The class of perceptible events is closed under finite products and arbitrary sums and does not contain complex items that are the result of an implication.

3 The geometry of perception

3.1 The mental foundations

When describing the general patterns that are discernible at the transition from sentential to nominal complements within the dimension of perception we have frequently passed from the formal to the material mode of speaking and vice versa. This alternation between different levels was intended as a preparation for the introduction of mental models. Towards the end of our brief discussion of similarity theory we noted that a resemblance between linguistic expressions and their meanings with respect to primary or secondary qualities is out of the question. The notion of similarity that is relevant here is that of a structure preserving relation between different systems. The concept of structure that underlies this abstract similarity relation grew out of the development of modern algebra in the beginning of the last century and has since become accepted as characterizing the nature, the aims and the organization of the whole of mathematics. Hilbert's axiomatic system for the foundations of geometry represents the first application of this concept of structure. The system constitutes an implicit definition of the groups of non-logical terms that are used in the formulation of its postulates. Once these terms receive an interpretation in such a way that all the postulates become true we are confronted with a structure in the relevant sense. Two such structures whose domains may be arbitrarily different count nevertheless as the same structure as long as there exists a biunique correspondence between the two domains under which one term can be truly predicated of a tuple of elements in one domain if and only if the tuple of their corresponding counterparts stands in the relation denoted by the term in the other domain. Under this approach, the concrete nature of a domain becomes completely irrelevant and the object of study – in the case of geometry, e.g. – is not the set of points and their relations considered as pebbles or numbers, but this second-order correspondence that abstracts from the interpretation in a structure and retains only its similarity class.

McGinn's (1989) account makes it abundantly clear that the members of the Cambridge school were aiming for this degree of abstraction. They did not, on the one side, succumb to the temptation to identify mental models with propositional content for which they were meant to provide a more tangible foundation. But on the other, the prominence given to the similarity of relational structures in their theory forestalls any confusion of mental models and miniature replicas of external objects together with their primary and secondary qualities.

Of utmost interest for our immediate concerns is the type of question the mental models provide an answer for. They form the nucleus of an empirical hypothesis which tries to derive the properties of the kind of representational system we are endowed with from the characteristic features of a quasi-mechanistic device. Mental models, according to McGinn, solve an engineering problem a psycholinguist confronts who investigates cognitive problem solving; they supply the psychotectonic framework to simulate a real process in our mind. In the same way a naval architect tests a model in a tank – McGinn's example – we perform dry runs with our cerebral copies:

Manipulating mental models thus constitutes the working machinery of cognitive problem solving. A thinking system, we might say, is a *simulation engine* [McGinn's emphasis] – a device that mimics, copies, replicates, duplicates, imitates, parallels reality. (McGinn 1989: 176)

According to this proposal, we have to imagine the process of problem solving as happening in three stages. During the first stage, triggered by perceptual input, a model is being generated. The external state of affairs is the cause for the internal simulation in the mind. At the next stage, this model is the object of a series of transformational processes whose outcome is critically evaluated. It is presupposed during this second stage that the manipulatory devices which transform the model correspond to real processes and that the results of applying these devices have their counterparts in reality. At the final stage, the practical knowledge gathered from the internal experiments is transferred to reality, its reliability being of the same sort as if it was acquired through real-world experiments.

In contemporary philosophy, it is not so much the idea of simulating the world by means of mental models as the idea of representing the world by means of a "sentence machine" that is held in favour. According to this hypothesis, we have a language of thought at our disposal, complete with a grammar and a lexicon, which enable us to produce mental sentences and texts. The trouble with this view, as we pointed out before, is the lack of any plausible candidate for an abstract resemblance relation between mental sentences and parts of the world. Sentences per se are not necessarily outside an account that stresses the importance of a manipulatory model, free for a certain class of structural transformations. We will have occasion to sketch such an account in the last section. Only this account does not take its point of departure from sentences as simulating models but from sentences as symbols describing states of affairs. Under this perspective sentences become objects of study in so far as they have logical structure along which truth conditions are spelled out. Rules manipulating this structure have to respect these semantic aspects and are totally different from transformations which rearrange a model simulating a part of the world.

Returning to models in their role as replicas simulating portions of the world it still behoves us to elucidate the internal structure of mental models. For obvious reasons it is impossible to perform any experiments on them and we are therefore reduced to a form of analogical reasoning.

3.2 Affirmative assertions and the logic of finite observations

We wish we had a transcendental argument which would establish the internal structure of mental models beyond reasonable doubt. The next best support we have to offer is a close analysis of what kind of constraints can be isolated for finite perceptions in the field of vision. The network of constraints holding in the domain of vision are then drawn upon to help us understand the empirical regularities that govern mental models.

Let us consider, following closely Vickers (1989), an assertion like

(12)   My baby has grey eyes.

Given the vagueness of colour terms we have to agree on a convention which tells us under which circumstances such an assertion shall count as definitely affirmed or as definitely refuted. Such definite affirmation or refutation, based on visual perception, should require only a finite amount of work. We therefore speak of them as of finite observations. Supposing that a convention has been agreed upon concerning the clear positive and negative instances we still have to ask ourselves how to handle the borderline cases, cases of blue-grey eyes, e.g. If we opt for the positive alternative we call statements under this stipulative interpretation strategy affirmative assertions. By definition, then, an *affirmative assertion* is true in circumstances where it can be definitely confirmed, this confirmation requiring only a finite amount of work.

An immediate consequence of this definition is the fact that affirmative assertions are not closed under negation. In order to confirm a negated statement about the eye colour of Vickers' child one has to confirm by means of a finite observation that the statement itself is definitely false. This, though, is impossible since it would entail a survey of all the borderline cases, a task which would not be completed after finitely many steps.

In sharp contrast with the operation of negation, affirmative assertions are closed under alternation. We are able to confirm an alternation $A \vee B$ by con-

firming either of its components (or both). From this follows that A ∨ B constitutes an affirmative assertion if both of its components do. Such an alternation
A ∨ B holds true just in case either A or B can be definitely confirmed. A similar remark applies to a finite sequence of alternatives. But even this restriction to
finite sequences can be lifted. We are in a position to confirm an arbitrary sequence A ∨ B ∨ C... of alternatives by just confirming one of them, and under
the assumption that all the component statements belong to the class of affirmative assertions this needs only a finite amount of work. The same line of reasoning covers existential quantification (∃x) A(x) as well. An existential quantification (∃x) A(x) is true just in case the alternation of all its instances
A(a) ∨ A(b) ∨ A(c) ∨ ... is. Thus, similarly to the case of arbitrary alternations,
we obtain the result that the operation of existential quantification does not
extend the class of affirmative assertions as long as all its instances are members
of this class.

In the same way we are able to confirm a conjunction A ∧ B by confirming
each of its conjuncts A and B separately. But if A and B are affirmative assertions then A ∧ B too is an affirmative assertion because this assertion is true if
both of its conjuncts are and, according to the definition of affirmative assertion,
this is equivalent with both of them being confirmable through a finite amount
of work. Again, this line of reasoning applies to finite sequences of conjuncts
without any change.

The restriction, however, to the finite case cannot be lifted for conjunctions.
In order to confirm an infinite conjunction A ∧ B ∧ C ∧... one has to confirm
each single component and this would generally necessitate an infinite amount
of work. For the same reason, universal statements (∀x) A(x) are not confirmable in the technical sense underlying our discussion since confirmation
would involve each of its instances.

Combining two affirmative assertions A and B into a conditional A→B pro-
duces a statement that is true if either A is false or B is true. When discussing
negated statements we were led to the conclusion that the (definite) falsity of an
affirmative assertion cannot be ascertained by means of a finite observation in
the general case. This proves our last result on the closure properties of affirmative assertions to the effect that the operation of implication properly extends the
class of affirmative assertions.

As in our discussion of the regularities characterizing the turning point of the
perception dimension we are again confronted with a limited set of construction
principles. The perceptible events and the class of affirmative assertions are both
closed under arbitrary alternations, finite conjunctions and existential quantification and they both reject negation, implication, infinite conjunctions and universal quantification. Adopting the formal mode of speaking we are free to
identify finite observations with affirmative assertions. A finite observation
would then amount to a claim to the effect that a perceptible event can be definitely checked for the properties upon which the focus of visual attention is
directed by investing only a finite amount of work.

There is a major distinction concerning our findings about the turning point and the class of affirmative assertions which has to be kept in mind. Adopting this time the material mode of speaking it would be a complete misunderstanding of the principles pertaining to the turning point if one interpreted them as absolute constraints on grammaticality. The examples that are starred are rejected for a variety of reasons, one of them relating to the structure of our perceptual apparatus. Most of the construction principles can be illustrated with other examples that become readily acceptable through the use of compensatory interpretation strategies. Take the case of negation. The following sentence is perfect if one interprets it as a deliberate action of Mary's towards the end of the race:

(13)   Peter saw Mary not win the race.

The situation is altogether different if one considers affirmative assertions and mental models. The class of affirmative assertions is sharply delineated once one has reached an agreement on what the clear cases are that definitely belong to the positive range of vague predicate terms. The same holds true of mental models in their capacity as psychotectonic entities destined to simulate real-world situations in engineering experiments. Being finite concrete structures it is out of the question to use them as a basis for negative or implicative situations. One could, of course, interpret a constituent of such a model as standing for negation or implication but such a way out would consist in a confusion of the modelling and the symbolic function of mental representations. Considered as finite simulation engines these structures can only be combined into more complex, but still finite patterns of the same kind. This combinatorial argument falls short of a transcendental deduction. It makes it very plausible, however, that mental models carry the same internal organisation as affirmative assertions and perceptible events.

4 Model-theoretic preservation

Up to this point we have collected evidence from linguistics, psychology and from the typology of finite observations and we have emphasised the relation of abstract, structure-preserving similarity that holds between these different types of data. Apart from some scattered remarks on perceptible events as the objective counterparts of perception verb complements and on mental models simulating parts of reality we have avoided an answer to our original question of how to combine a cognitive and an objective approach to semantics. If it is true that model-theoretic semantics starts from the assumption that representations, be they expressions of a natural language or of mentalese, stand for aspects of the real world, we have to make sure that the suggestions of the preceding sections are compatible with that very assumption. Otherwise our approach would remain entrenched within the cognitive-conceptual camp.

There is a recent attempt by a group of researchers in Amsterdam led by Michiel van Lambalgen (1998) in which a reconciliation between a psychological and a formal component of semantics is developed. They are mainly inspired by Marr's (1982) approach to 3D-vision for which they propose a model-theoretic account. Their main ingredient is an inverse system of finite models that is intended to capture Marr's insistence on the simultaneity of several descriptions of the same object or event. Reality, according to their approach corresponds to the inverse limit of such a system of finite models.

The Amsterdam approach does not seem to be entirely successful in its handling of this central tenet of Marr's postulate that every object or event gives rise to the simultaneous computation of a variety of 3D-models. Since these 3D-models are rendered by finite models that are partially ordered by a relation of refinement the sensible question to ask is which sentence forms survive on their way from coarse sections of reality to the fine-grained inverse limit. As it turns out the sentence forms that survive, i.e. that are preserved in the model-theoretic sense, are universally quantified implications of positive sentence forms. This is in flat contradiction to our result that implication is excluded from the construction principles under which observable events are closed.

The interpretation, however, of several views of the same object or event by means of a refining system of models is not forced on us, and a more congenial reading of Marr's intention appears to be possible. It would retain the suggestion of the Amsterdam group to picture 3D-models as finite structures but would substitute the weaker notion of a structure-preserving similarity for the stronger notion of a directed refining relation which underlies the idea of going to the limit. As long as one is inclined to think that an image of a human being showing every detail of bodily structure is more "real" than an image where, apart from the cylindrical trunk, hardly any articulation is discernible one will be tempted to postulate a refining order for 3D-models of one and the same person. But if one considers these images to be equally well anchored in reality with the more articulate ones serving a different range of purposes from the others, one will be led to see in these representations complementary renditions with different attributes.

Such a "democratic" standpoint has close ties to the concept of higher-order similarity, introduced in the section on mental models, as we will now explain. Formal languages that are used in linguistics to represent the level of analysis which acts as interface with the semantic domain are explicitly constructed and their syntax guarantees unique readability for all constituents built according to the stipulated rules. Examples are provided by Montague's disambiguated syntax and by the logical form of the generative tradition. This precisely specified syntax enables one to extend the interpretation of the non-logical or descriptive constituents by a unique homomorphism from the "algebra" of the syntax to the similar algebra of the interpretation.

Unless there exists one distinguished interpretation that one might designate as the standard or the intended interpretation other possible interpretations will have to be considered. These interpretations vary freely within the limits imposed by the structure of the non-logical vocabulary. The essence of this structural approach to meaning lies in the recognition that it is instructive to disregard the nature of the elements in a particular domain and to conceive of the descriptive operations and relations only as contributory to the truth or falsity of statements in which they occur.

It follows from this structural approach to semantics that transitions from one possible interpretation to another one should both respect the denotation types of the non-logical constants and preserve the structure of an interpretation, which means that an ordered sequence of elements of one domain standing in a certain relation corresponds, via the transition, to elements in the other domain also standing in the counterpart relation and that the result of applying an operation to a sequence of elements corresponds to the result of applying the counterpart operation to the corresponding argument elements in the new domain.

What we have tried to motivate in the last couple of paragraphs can easily be turned into a formal definition. Recall that we subscribe to the idea of using finite structures as abstract formalizations of parts of the world. Such a structure consists of a finite set A, called the domain of A, a set of elements of A, called constant elements, each of which is designated by a constant (symbol), for each natural number n, a (possibly empty) set of n-ary relations on A, each of which is named by a relation symbol and, finally, for each natural number n, a (possibly empty) set of n-ary operations on A, each named by a function symbol. Let us reserve a special term for the set of constant, relation and function symbols and call this set of linguistic elements a signature. Given a signature L and two structures A and B containing interpretations for all the elements in L, a structure- and truth-preserving mapping from A to B, called a homomorphism, is a function h satisfying the following conditions. For each constant element c in A, $h(c)=c'$, where c' indicates the denotation in B of the constant symbol in L that denotes c in A. Similar writing conventions are used for the next two conditions. For each n-ary relation R of A and all n-tuples a of A, if $R(a)$ then $R'(h(a))$. For each n-ary operation F of A and all n-tuples a of A, $h(F(a)) = F'(h(a))$.

We have noted above that there exists a unique homomorphism from an explicitly specified syntactic structure to each finite structure over the signature implicit in the syntactic specifications of the language employed for the semantic interface level. Accordingly, each sentence has a unique interpretation in each possible structure. With these technical preparations behind us, it will now be obvious that we cannot simply identify an arbitrary cluster of structures of this kind with the objective correlates of a family of 3D-models that were computed from inputs having their origin in the same object or event. If two 3D-models in a coherent group, describing an object from different perspectives, have a common part then the corresponding relation or operation in the two correlated finite structures should be interpreted in such a way that a transition from one of the structures to the other is truth preserving. Truth preservation, needless to say, is not a property connected with the unique interpretation a sentence has in each interpretation.

Is the class of syntactic structures that survives arbitrary truth preserving transitions in the sense specified above for homomorphisms better behaved than the class of syntactic structures that survive the inverse limit formation? The answer has long been given by Lyndon in his famous preservation theorem which says that the sentences preserved by homomorphisms are exactly the positive sentences. Lyndon's result is one of the few theorems which survive the transition from classical to finite model theory (cf. Ebbinghaus and Flum 1995). Notice, though, that in the infinite case attention has to be restricted to surjective homomorphisms. Recall that the positive sentences are built up using only conjunction, alternation, existential and universal quantification. Since we have restricted our attention to finite structures the universal quantifier can be dissolved into a finite conjunction. The remaining three operations of sentence formation are the recurrent ingredients we have encountered at the dimensional turning point and in our discussion of the affirmative assertions. We thus have finally found a model-theoretic confirmation for the intimate relationship between mental and linguistic representations of perception reports.

5 Conclusion

Perception verbs exhibit an extension of their meaning into the conceptual realm, an extension that seems to have its roots in our network of cognitive faculties and which is attested in every language that has been checked concerning this phenomenon. In our European "model" languages this reading of perception verbs is correlated with a finite sentential form of complements and is thus characteristically situated at the predicative pole of the dimensional continuum of perception. On its semantic side this construction displays all the features that are connected with propositional attitude reports and it partakes in the full set of problems surrounding this class.

Tackling these problems is quite beyond the limits of this paper. We shall therefore confine ourselves to sketching the bare outlines of a possible way out of these problems. The reader will recall our remark about 'sentence engines'. Since we can adopt attitudes to negated, modalized, tensed, conditional and universal propositions and not only to positive ones as in the case of spontaneous perception, the semanticist is confronted with the complete spectrum of construction principles that play a rôle in determining the meaning of a complex constituent. As has been known since Frege the behaviour of these construction principles in the context of attitude reports reacts even to the slightest alterations and shows a high sensitivity to the way such a report is put into language. Given this situation, it looks promising to enlist a body of knowledge that has been developed within the proof-theoretic approach to meaning. This type of semantical analysis suggests that every meaningful symbol must get its meaning from the conditions for asserting sentences in which it occurs and all inferences that are seen to be correct must be justifiable on the basis of the assertion conditions regulating the use of that symbol (Prawitz 1979). It was this kind of tectonics that we had in mind when referring to the metaphor of syntactic engines. Should it be possible to transform these last sketchy remarks into a well articulated theory, the conceptual and the sensory reading of expressions denoting perception processes would be affiliated with two cognitive engineering departments, the department for the psychotectonics of mental models and the department for sentence engins.

References

Abbott, B. (1997): Models, Truth and Semantics, *Linguistics and Philosophy* 20, 117–138.

Barwise, J. (1989): *The Situation in Logic*, Stanford: CSLI.

Chang, C. & J. Keisler (^{2}1977): *Model Theory*, Amsterdam: North Holland.

Ebbinghaus, H.-D. & J. Flum (1995): *Finite Model Theory*, Berlin: Springer

Hintikka, J. & al., eds., *Essays on Mathematical and Philosophical Logic*, Dordrecht: Reidel, 25–40.

Jackendoff, R. (1998): Why a Conceptualist View of Reference? A Reply to Abbott, *Linguistics and Philosophy* 21, 211–219.

Mc Ginn, C. (1989): *Mental Content*, Oxford: Blackwell.

Marr, D. (1982): *Vision*, New York: Freeman.

Montague, R. (1974): *Formal Philosophy. Selected Papers of Richard Montague Edited and with an Introduction by R.H. Thomason*, New Haven: Yale University Press.

Prawitz, D. (1979): Proofs and the Meaning and Completeness of the Logical Constants. In: J. Hintikka et al., eds., *Essays on Mathematical and Philosophical Logic*, Dordrecht: Reidel, 25–40.

Putnam, H. (1981): *Reason, Truth and History*, Cambridge: Cambridge University Press.

Raible, W. (1992): *Junktion*, Heidelberg: Winter.

Seiler, H. (1995): Cognitive Conceptual Structure and Linguistic Encoding: Language Universals and Typology in the UNITYP Framework. In: Shibatani, M. & Th. Bynon, eds., *Approaches to Language Typology*, Oxford: Clarendon, 273–325.

van der Does, J. & M. van Lambalgen (2000): A Logic of Vision, *Linguistics and Philosophy* 23, 1–92.

Vickers, St. (1989): *Topology via Logic*, Cambridge: Cambridge University Press.

Tübingen   Uwe Mönnich

Universität Tübingen, Seminar für Sprachwissenschaft, Kleine Wilhelmstraße 113, D-72074 Tübingen, uwe.moennich@uni-tuebingen.de